SLOW GROWTH
IN BRITAIN

SLOW GROWTH
IN BRITAIN
Causes and Consequences

edited by

WILFRED BECKERMAN

*[Proceedings of Section F (Economics)
of the British Association for the
Advancement of Science, Bath 1978]*

CLARENDON PRESS · OXFORD
1979

Oxford University Press, Walton Street, Oxford OX2 6DP

OXFORD LONDON GLASGOW
NEW YORK TORONTO MELBOURNE WELLINGTON
KUALA LUMPUR SINGAPORE JAKARTA HONG KONG TOKYO
DELHI BOMBAY CALCUTTA MADRAS KARACHI
NAIROBI DAR ES SALAAM CAPE TOWN

Published in the United States by
Oxford University Press, New York

© *W. Beckerman 1979*

British Library Cataloguing in Publication Data

British Association for the Advancement of
Science. *Meeting, Section F (Economics),*
Bath, 1978
Slow growth in Britain.
1. Great Britain – Economic conditions – 1945 –
I. Title   II. Beckerman, Wilfred
339.5′0941   HC256.5   79-40666
ISBN 0-19-828420-9
ISBN 0-19-828421-7 Pbk

Typeset by Hope Services, Abingdon
and printed in Great Britain by
Richard Clay (The Chaucer Press) Ltd
Bungay, Suffolk

PREFACE

The meeting of Section F (Economics) of the British Association for the Advancement of Science was devoted to the general theme of slow economic growth in Britain. This volume comprises all the papers that were submitted to this meeting. Apart from defining the theme and discussing with participants, in advance, the general manner in which their contributions could be fitted into the overall theme, I have not presumed to impose any editorial prerogatives on the participants as regards the substance of length of their papers. Hence, as will be obvious, some of the papers included in this volume contain much more material than their authors could have possibly presented orally at the meeting. But it seemed much more sensible to include this extra material rather than feel bound to restrict chapters to what was actually said at the meeting in the interests of uniformity of length or style.

The order in which the papers are given in this volume has no special significance—analytical, chronological, symbolic or mystical. It reflects, to a large extent, an arbitrary assertion of my own will given my decision—set out above—to abstain from trying to influence the contents of the contributions. This decision strained my self-denial to the utmost, so that I have compensated for it by imposing my preferences as regards the sequence of chapters.

The first chapter is my own—solely out of respect for precedents—and is partly addressed to the question of why one should worry about slow growth in Britain (my own answer being that it adds to poverty), but is mostly about the philosophical issue of how far theories of distributive justice, such as the Rawlsian theory, are of operational value for policy purposes and, if they are not, how far one should then replace concern with egalitarianism by simple humanitarian concern with poverty. This is followed by Richard Lecomber's contribution, which is addressed to a very similar question since it is mainly about the relationship between economic growth and social welfare.

The next two papers, by Andrew Dean and Jon Stern, examine in much more detail the impact of slow growth on the labour market, and their papers are particularly relevant to various aspects of the slow growth theme, such as how it affects welfare in general and poverty in particular, or how far the labour market operates in a way that would justify the sort of assumptions often made concerning the relationship between unemployment and inflation. The former of these issues is taken further in the next chapter, by Frank Field. The following chapter, by David Stout, examines another aspect of slow growth, namely its relationship to the level of investment.

In the next chapter, by Walter Eltis, we move into the field of the "causes" of slow growth, as Mr. Eltis' paper is an up-to-date and refined version of the thesis that—together with Bob Bacon—he has been propounding recently, namely that an excessive growth of the public sector has been largely responsible for Britain's slow rate of economic growth. In the following chapter, however, by Chris Allsopp, a more internationally-minded view is taken of the problem of slow growth in the modern world which, combined with an attempt to apply some basic growth theory, leads to very different conclusions. This is followed by Stanislaw Gomulka's paper, which comprises a more detailed analysis of the most popular hypotheses that are often proposed as explanations of Britain's slow growth, such as increasing managerial inefficiency or a low rate of technical progress. The longer-run and international context of the Gomulka paper provides a lead-in to Angus Maddison's paper which provides some of the latest results of his research into very long run trends in output and productivity in a number of countries and hence protects one from taking too short term and parochial view of the slow rate of growth that is currently being obtained in Britain.

The last two papers look more to the future. First, Michael Posner shows that energy shortages—which seem to colour over most peoples' visions of the future—are not likely, in fact, to constitute an effective brake on economic growth. But this is, of course, chiefly of interest insofar as growth is not limited on the demand side. And the next, and final, paper in the volume, by Wynne Godley, suggest that, unless there is a radical change in import policies, demand deficiency will become worse in the medium run so that supply constraints on growth will be irrelevant. But the most important point in Mr. Godley's paper is his particular proposed change in policies, namely a resort to import controls in order to reduce the overall import propensity of the British economy. This proposal, which has been associated with Mr. Godley and his Cambridge colleagues for some time, is set out here in what I believe to be the clearest and most persuasive form in which it has yet been disclosed.

If he is right, and I, for one, was largely persuaded, then perhaps there is some hope after all that Britain can be rescued from the prospect of continuous slow growth for the next decade or so. But this would require also convincing policy makers, and they may be a tougher bunch to convince than me—or just more obstinate.

Balliol College, Nov. 1978   WILFRED BECKERMAN

CONTENTS

DOES SLOW GROWTH MATTER?
EGALITARIANISM VERSUS HUMANITARIANISM

by Wilfred Beckerman
Balliol College, Oxford

1. The Prospects for Growth

It is perhaps appropriate that the theme of a meeting over which I have the honour to preside is the causes and consequences of slow growth in Britain. For, from time to time, I have worked on both these aspects of economic growth. In 1962 I published an article in which I advanced what became known as 'the export-led' growth hypothesis,[1] a hypothesis that, I was gratified to note, was rediscovered—albeit with some amendments—by Lord Kaldor in his Presidential Address to this same meeting in 1970.[2]

My 1962 article (and subsequent variants of it) was my only attempt to contribute to this side of the growth story. And, in any case, I was not attempting to provide anything as grand as a growth model of general applicability. I was merely trying to explain inter-country differences in growth rates over some specific period of time, namely the 1950s and early 1960s.

During the last few years, of course, the problem is not one of trying to explain large inter-country divergences in growth rates. They all seem to be going through a phase of relatively slow growth, at least by comparison with the earlier post-war years. Also, there is relatively little disagreement about the *immediate* causes of slow growth in the advanced countries as a whole.

These appear to include a reluctance by most governments to take the expansionary action that would be necessary to eliminate high unemployment. I do not want to enter here into the question of how far various governments may be justified in these policies—in any case,

---

[1] W. Beckerman, Projecting Europe's Growth, *Economic Journal* (Dec. 1962).
[2] N. Kaldor, Conflicts in National Economic Objectives, in N. Kaldor (ed.), *Conflicts in Policy Objectives*, (Oxford, 1971).

the judgement would vary considerably from country to country. In Britain, for example, it is arguable that a large part of the blame should be put on the shoulders of the institutions, notably the trade unions, but also including those that affect the quality of management, which are largely responsible for our poor record of productivity growth and innovation and for our inability to design a system of wage negotiation that will give us reasonable price stability.[3] These institutions are not easily changed by government action. Indeed, it would add point to one of the main themes I shall take up later, if the current slow growth, with its adverse impact on poverty, were largely the fault of the professed egalitarianism of the trade union movement. But leaving all this aside, the *immediate* reasons for governments' current policies seem to include:

(i) a fear of rekindling inflationary expectations that have not yet been squeezed out of the economy, following the special inflationary pressures of the 1973/75 period, on top of earlier gradual acceleration of inflation;

(ii) the problem of the OPEC surplus, which, as well as being deflationary, imposes a balances of payments constraint on many advanced countries; and

(iii) to recognise the vast scale of the intervention that would be needed now to offset what have become largely autonomous deflationary forces in the economy, and to act on this scale, would require far more imagination, daring, and political will than can be expected of any government, or, for that matter, almost any human institution.[4]

Whilst I no longer follow closely the debates in this area of economics, my impression is that neither as regards the longer-run factors specific to Britain, nor the more general factors that explain slower growth in all advanced countries over the last few years, is there any reason to expect any significant improvement in the near future. In short, I believe that Britain is condemned to slow growth for at least the next five to ten years, as is probably most of the world.

2. Does Slow Growth Matter?

This leads me to the other aspect of the growth problem, namely the effects of slow growth. This is an aspect of our general theme here in which I did become heavily involved at one time, namely in connection with the controversy in the early 1970s, partly around the doom-laden predictions of the Club of Rome and other groups, who took the view that continued economic growth was both undesirable and impossible.

[3] See a recent and powerful summary of this view of the responsibility of the trade unions in the letter by Lord Roberthall, *The Times*, 6th Sept. 1978.
[4] I am indebted to an official of the Bank of England for drawing my attention to this point which I am sure is extremely important if generally neglected in public discussion.

(I could never understand why, in that case, they seemed so alarmed and upset by the prospects before us. A situation in which what was undesirable was also impossible seemed to me to be ideal. By contrast, it is awful when what is undesirable is inevitable, or what is desirable is unattainable.)

In any case, my position in that controversy was that continued economic growth—over some relevant, if very long, time horizon—was possible and would not be brought to an end by exhaustion of raw materials, or asphyxiation from air pollution, or mass starvation and universal food riots, and so on.[5] Whether this made me an 'optimist' or not depends on how this term is defined. For I also believed that the human race would probably blow itself up long before it ran out of supplies of fissile uranium. On the other hand, I did not think that the end of the human race was necessarily a tragedy, largely because I found it difficult to attach any logical meaning to the notion that the resulting unborn generations would be worse off, in some sense, than if they had been born.[6] (For example, should one deplore the loss of welfare of those people who have not been born during the last few decades but who would have been born in the absence of the spread of contraception?)

Secondly, I believed that, on the whole, economic growth was desirable, and probably added to human welfare, particularly for the poorer sections of the society, and particularly in developing countries.

However, I never thought that continued economic growth would be good for everybody, especially for the better-off sections of advanced societies. In fact, I explicitly argued that much of the anti-growth movement was inspired by the better-off sections of society, since they were more likely to lose welfare as a result of the changes that economic growth inevitably entailed.

It follows from this position that, as far as *most* people in advanced societies are concerned, I do not think that the inevitable slow growth of the next decade will imply a significant loss of welfare. But I think that slow growth does matter, nevertheless. It matters because of its impact on poverty. Slow growth of the type currently being experienced in Britain and most other advanced countries means slow growth of demand for labour relative to the supply of it, so that unemployment will remain high and perhaps rise even further. In addition, governments believe that restraint on public expenditures is necessary to restore reasonable price stability, which is seen as essential if growth is eventually

---

[5]W. Beckerman, *In Defence of Economic Growth*, (London, 1974).
[6]For a criticism of this point of view see Brian Barry. 'Justice Between Generations' in P. M. S. Hacker and J. Raz (eds.) *Law, Morality and Society* (Oxford, 1977).

to be accelerated. Both these factors hit most those groups in society who are already poor or 'near-poor'. Thus slow growth will not merely hamper efforts to reduce poverty; it will add to it.

In saying that the most important harmful effect of slow growth will be its effect on *poverty* I am not talking about the effect of slow growth on *equality*. This is for two reasons:

(i) it is not possible to establish any firm general laws relating rates of economic growth to changes in inequality.

(ii) in my opinion further marginal changes in inequality are not very important compared to the persistence of, and even the likely increase in, poverty.

But I have said all that I have to say on the first of these two points already and do not intend to repeat it here.[7] It is the second point to which I wish to devote most of the remainder of this lecture. My argument on this point is in two parts. First, in spite of the officially pronounced objective of shielding the weakest sections of the community from the impact of the government's anti-inflationary policy and the resultant slow growth, it seems that poverty and "near-poverty" have increased in the last few years.[8] Secondly, in general discussion and debate, the objective of equality is given too much weight relative to the objective of reducing poverty. Put in other terms, the related object-ive of distributive justice is given too much weight compared with simple humanitarianism.[9] I shall argue, in fact, that the day has long gone by when the principles of distributive justice could provide a useful operational guide to policy, particularly social policy; and that much of the talk that one hears these days about equality is humbug anyway.

3. Slow Growth and Poverty: the Facts

As regards the relationship between growth rates and poverty, there has been too little comparative analysis to permit any general laws to be laid down. Fast growth has sometimes been accompanied by increases in poverty so that it is presumably conceivable that slow growth could be accompanied by reductions in poverty. But speculation on the basis of small and unrepresentative samples of historical observations is

[7]W. Beckerman, 'Some Reflections on "Redistribution with Growth", *World Development,* (Aug. 1977).

[8]The government's objective in this respect, could, of course, be interpreted as meaning only that it wishes to protect those who are already poor (notably the old, sick and unemployed) from any further erosion of their living standards, by means of the various tax cuts and improved social security benefits summarised in *Winning the Battle Against Inflation*, Cmnd. 7293, H.M.S.O., (July 1978).

[9]This is not to say that there are no countries in the world in which the basic principles of distributive justice are not relevant as guides to desirable changes, or that conditions that would make them relevant again in Britain and most other advanced countries could never return.

unnecessary since one can already see how the particular form of slow growth experienced in Britain during the last few years is adding to poverty.

First, official estimates show that the number of 'families' living below the SupplementaryBenefit Line, which will be adopted here as a 'poverty line', has risen by 26 per cent between 1973 and 1976, from 1.07 million 'inner families' to 1.35 million (out of a total of about 25 million families on the definition used in these data).[10] However, even this increase in poverty understates the full impact of the slack demand pressure on poverty in Britain, for four reasons:

(i) if poverty is measured in terms not of numbers of families (i.e. "head-count" terms), but in terms of "poverty gaps"—i.e. the amounts by which the incomes of the poor fall below the poverty line—the rise in poverty has been much greater than the rise in the numbers below the poverty line. According to my estimates the total post-benefit poverty gap rose from about £110 million in 1973 to about £330 million in 1976. Allowing for the rise in prices over this period means that the poverty gap rose by almost 80 per cent—composed of the 26 per cent rise in the number of poor and a 43 per cent rise in the poverty gap per poor family (at constant prices).[11]

(ii) the above estimates are in aggregative terms, and there seems to have been quite opposite movements in the position of those below and above pension age. The increase in total poverty is made up of a slight rise in poverty among those over pension age masking a much sharper rise in poverty amongst the rest of the population. As can be seen in the following table, in terms of numbers of families the relative position of 'non-pensioners' (i.e. families headed by persons below pension age) in poverty has deteriorated much more than the aggregative figures

[10] Results published annually in *Social Trends* (H.M.S.O., London). 'Inner families' approximate very closely to tax units. (See also notes to Table 1.1.).

[11] My estimates of poverty gaps in 1973 are contained in a study prepared for the Royal Commission on the Distribution of Income and Wealth, which refers mainly, however, to 1975. These estimates, which were prepared with the help of the Statistical Services of the Department of Health and Social Security, are explained in more detail in the 6th Report of the Commission, *Lower Incomes*, (London, 1978), and in a Working Paper of the I.L.O., *The Impact of Income Maintenance Programmes on Poverty in Britain*, WEP 2-23/WP 62 (Geneva, 1977). Further confirmation of the proposition that it is the poorest sections of society who have been most hit by the slack demand for labour is provided also by the contrast between the above estimates and those by Mr. P. S. Lansley (unpublished Reading University discussion paper) that show an increase in the equality of the overall income distribution over the last few years. Of course, the composition of the poor population does not stay the same over time, and members of certain groups of poor persons (notably younger people whose unemployment duration tends to be short, or younger lone mothers) may move out of poverty quite quickly to be replaced by other members of the same groups.

would suggest. For example, the number of pensioner families in poverty barely rose between 1973 and 1976, whereas the number of non-pensioner poor families rose by about 70 per cent.[12]

(iii) the above estimates only describe the situation up to 1976, and the subsequent prolonged weak labour market has no doubt led to a considerable worsening of the living conditions of the poor and the near-poor. As a result of the sharp increase in the duration of unemployment during the last two years, those already unemployed will gradually use up such slender savings or credit facilities that they may have had, as well as gradually wear out basic items of clothing and household equipment, and so on, at the same time as they exhaust their national insurance unemployment benefits and have to fall back on supplementary benefits at lower rates than those paid to pensioners and certain other

TABLE 1.1
Families in Poverty: 1973 and 1976

| | ('000 families) | | | |
| | Below Supplementary Benefit level | | Below Sup. Ben. level plus those in receipt of Sup. Ben. | |
	1973	1976	1973	1976
TOTAL	1,070	1,350	3,630	3,960
of which: Pensioners	690	700	2,530	2,360
Non-Pensioners	380	650	1,100	1,600

Notes: (a) 'Families' refer here to Supplementary Benefit units, which, since they exclude children aged 16 or over (except those in full time education) are much smaller than nuclear families and correspond closely to tax units.

(b) 'Pensioners' refers to families of which the head is over pension age, and similarly 'non-pensioners' refers to families of which the head is below pension age.

(c) The definition of the poverty adopted here corresponds to the poverty line that has been adopted for the purposes of these estimates and which is the Supplementary Benefit line.

(d) The above estimates are aggregates derived from more detailed estimates, in which the poverty line is adjusted for each family size according to the corresponding Supplementary Benefit scale rates.

Source: 1973 figures from *Social Trends*, No. 6, (1975), Table 5.31; 1976 figures supplied by D.H.S.S. and will appear in *Social Trends*, No. 9, (1978).

[12]Similarly, taking the poverty gap figures, the gap for persons below pension age quadrupled between 1973 and 1976, from £63 million to £256 million.

groups of long-term beneficiaries.[13]

(iv) the above results make no allowance for the changes in the relative prices of goods and services that carry a particularly heavy weight in the expenditure patterns of the poor. And some estimates suggest that the poor have been harder hit by price increases over the last few years than has the rest of the population, on account of the large relative weight in their expenditure on basic items such as food, fuel, and housing, the prices of which have risen more than the overall cost of living in recent years.[14]

The divergence between the change in poverty of 'pensioners' (shorthand here for families headed by persons over pension age) and 'non-pensioners' shown in the above estimates is consistent with the direction of change shown in official estimates of the total of families below the Supplementary Benefit line but not receiving benefit *plus* those receiving benefit. For example, the sum total of these two groups (which would correspond to one definition of post-benefit poverty) shows a rise of from 3.63 million families to 3.96 million between December 1973 and December 1976. But within this total there was a fall of 170,000 in pensioner families and a rise of 500,000 in non-pensioner families.[15]

Of course, the number of people over pension age who are in poverty is relatively little affected by prolonged high unemployment, although there is some impact, since many of these people normally work or seek work, but, given their age, they are particularly vulnerable to a fall in the demand for labour. Hence, other things being equal, one would have expected poverty amongst older people to have risen, if not as sharply as amongst the rest of the population. But any such effect seems to have been offset by other factors.[16]

As regards the non-pensioner population, poverty is not, of course, confined to those who become unemployed, and some increase in

---

[13]For a succint description of the effect of prolonged high unemployment on poverty see David Donnison, 'Against Discretion', *New Society*, 15th Sept. 1977.

[14]According to a special price index for the low-paid compiled by the Civil and Public Services Association and the Low Pay Unit (see *Income Data Report*, No. 283 (June 1978) and report in *The Times*, 2nd June 1978).

[15]*Social Trends*, No. 6 (1975), Table 5.31, and No. 8 (1977), Table 6.33.

[16]One of these seems to have been a switch by many pensioners from supplementary benefits to rent and rate rebates. The reasons why this may be advantageous for those whose supplementary pension entitlement would be small are set out clearly in the *National Welfare Benefits Handbook*, 3rd edition, Ruth Lister (ed.), Child Poverty Action Group, Poverty Pamphlet No. 13 (May 1974). See also 7th edition (Nov. 1977), for updating of the calculations. It appears that between October 1974 and January 1976, about 87,000 claimants came off supplementary benefits in order to switch to rent and rate rebates (*Hansard*, 25th Mar. 1976).

poverty amongst certain groups of non-pensioners, such as single-parent families, or the sick, could be due to factors that have nothing to do with slow growth. In fact, however, the changes in the size of these particular groups has made a negligible contribution to the rise in total non-pensioner poverty in the last few years.[17]

Thus, as one would expect, the 500,000 rise in the number of poor non-pensioner families (on the last definition of poverty given above—namely those on Supplementary Benefits plus those below the SB level and not receiving benefits) must be largely ascribed to the slack demand for labour. This will hit not only families of which the male head has become unemployed. Among non-pensioner families, about three times as many would be in poverty if the earnings of the wives[18] were excluded and these constitute another vulnerable group at times of slack demand.

Finally, if the poverty line is redefined to include also those who are less than 20 percent above the Supplementary Benefit line, which is a definition of the poverty line that many investigators would regard as being appropriate, the total number of poor families rose by 1,250,000 between the end of 1974 and 1976, of which 790,000 were non-pensioner families. Thus many of those who become unemployed may well draw national insurance benefits that keep them above the supplementary benefit line (at least for a year), but at an income that is not merely very low compared to their normal incomes and commitments, but is one that many people would regard as being appropriately defined as 'in poverty'.

Another aspect of the way that slow growth affects the weakest groups in society is the composition of the unemployed. For it seems that although the government may have shielded some of the weaker groups in society from the impact of the anti-inflationary slow-growth policy (notably old-age pensioners), the government has also shielded its chief supports among the non-pensioners, namely the employed members of strong trade unions. Thus the brunt of the sacrifice has been borne by those whose labour market position was already weakest,

[17]For example, the number of single-parent families seems to be increasing in recent years by about 35,000 per annum (*Population Trends* Sept. 1978). But even if the incidence of post-benefit poverty in this group stayed the same as my estimates for 1975 suggest (see fn. 11 above) this would only add about 3,000 families per annum to the total number of post-benefit non-pensioner families in poverty. Similarly, the long-run upward trend in persons off work for more than 13 weeks on account of sickness has been very slight—an upward trend for males having been largely offset by a downward trend for females.

[18] See Lynne Hamill (D.H.S.S.), *Wives as Sole and Joint Breadwinners* (forthcoming in Government Economic Service Working Paper series).

such as the young new entrants into the labour force, those nearing retirement age, female labour, unskilled workers, and ethnic minorities.

4. Inequality or Poverty: Which Matters?

As indicated above, I believe that it is the impact of slow growth on poverty, not on inequality, that matters, not merely because from a factual point of view, slow growth seems to have increased poverty but not inequality, but also because, in my opinion, poverty is far more important now, in principle, than marginal changes in inequality. I would advance three reasons for this view:

(i) I believe that very few people really care about inequality *per se*, or about distributive justice *per se*.

(ii) insofar as they are indifferent to further marginal changes in the degree of distributive justice in society they are, in my opinion, quite justified in being so, since, as I shall argue below, given the present situation with respect to inequality, further progress on the egalitarian front is far less important than further progress in reducing poverty. Or, to put it briefly, if inaccurately, within the sort of limits that are relevant today in Britain (and that, I expect, will remain relevant for some time), egalitarianism is less important than humanitarianism.

(iii) theories of distributive justice and such principles concerning equality as can be derived from them have to be general and abstract, and hence are severely limited for operational purposes. Hence, an attempt to reconcile, on the one hand, the increasing need on simple humanitarian grounds for more detailed policies to deal with persistent and increasing poverty in advanced countries with, on the other hand, the currently fashionable concern with egalitarianism which merely exposes the difficulty of reaching any satisfactory concensus concerning the principles of distributive justice, drives one into a state of intellectual schizophrenia. Of course, there is not necessarily a choice to be made, in all and any circumstances, between egalitarianism and humanitarianism; they are not mutually exclusive alternatives. However, the increasing complexity of policies needed to deal with poverty in Britain has led to some pressure to simplify and codify administrative procedures for dealing with poverty.[19] Such a move would presumably imply an attempt to identify some basic, logically coherent, principles of codification. But given that such an attempt would be doomed to failure, unless the principles that were established were of limited operational value, it would be better to continue to build on the present chaotic

[19]See, for example, the report *Social Assistance–A Review of the Supplementary Benefit scheme in Great Britain*, (July 1978). Of course, an even better alternative would be to abandon some of the assumptions adopted in this report, notably no increase in basic national insurance benefits.

system that serves, nevertheless, a humanitarian function, rather than shift into the vacumn of egalitarianism. Even chaos is sometimes better than nothing, as God decided—rightly in my opinion—after the first day of the Creation.

A more practical aspect of the conflict between concern with equality in general and poverty in particular is the extent to which scarce intellectual and statistical resources are devoted to the analysis of the former as compared to the latter. After all, who really cares if the position of the fifth decile has changed slightly relative to that of the fourth decile so that the Gini coefficient has fallen from 0.38 to 0.36?

In advancing these three arguments, I shall leave aside other arguments, such as the conflict between equality and efficiency, or the possibly more important, but ancient, argument—going back at least as far as de Toqueville—to the effect that greater equality may conflict with freedom, so that, in the end, it can lead to a reversion to a nastier and more immovable form of inequality. On the other hand, I would certainly not maintain that, in general, and in the absence of any limits on possible degrees of change, distributive justice is less important than the reduction in poverty. I am merely arguing that even if the existing inequality of income distribution is not enough to attain completely desirable levels of certain fundamental rights for everybody, notably effective rights to basic liberty, freedom of opportunity, and so on, the gain in social welfare that would be attained now by marginal improvements in the equality of income distribution is small compared to the gain that would be achieved by further reductions in poverty.

4.1. How Genuine is Egalitarianism?

The amount of humbug talked about equality these days is enough to turn anybody into an anti-egalitarian. For I suspect that very few people indeed are genuinely concerned with inequality *per se*, as distinct from the possible impact of equality on their own positions. That is to say, I do not believe that the vast majority of the population object to the existing degree of inequality of income distribution on the grounds that it offends their notions—however vague—of distributive justice.

Perhaps I can illustrate my distinction between peoples' attitudes to inequality *per se*, as distinct from peoples' attitudes to the impact of inequality on themselves, in the following way. Recently, the engineers attached to one particular type of cross-channel vessel threatened strike action because their pay was below that of engineers attached to some other type of vessel. They complained that this inequality was unjustified (i.e. they implicitly took the view that it was unjustified in terms of some relevant consideration, such as differences in skill required). And they may have been right. However, it should be noted that the higher-paid group of engineers were not threatening strike action on account of the injustice involved in their higher pay. Not only did they not demand a reduction in their pay, but they did not even make any visible show of support for an increase in the pay of the lower paid engineers. Now, of course, it may well be that, in this particular case, the higher paid engineers genuinely believed that no injustice was involved, and that there was some relevant differences that justified their higher pay. (If opinions as to the justice of the differential between all members of the two groups were entirely objective, this would, of course, be an astonishing coincidence. After all, what a fantastic fluke if all those who evaluated objectively the factors involved one particular way should happen to be in one group whereas all those who see things— quite objectively—the other way happened to be in the other group!)

But this is just one example. There are hundreds of such instances every year. They invariably take the form of some group complaining that it is unjustly paid *less* than it ought to be paid, usually by reference to some other group. If it was injustice *per se* that motivated people, how strange that there is never one case—compared with the hundreds of other cases—where some group complains that it is unjustly being paid too much!

Of course, one would not expect such groups to demand that the unjust excess of their pay be completely removed. After all, there is no reason why they should not trade off two objectives, namely their own income against their aversion to injustice. But they should be urging *some* cut in income, however small, in the interests of deriving more welfare from a reduction in the offending injustice. If they are not prepared to accept (let alone demand) *any* cut in their own incomes in the interests of greater distributive justice then, as economists, we must say that they attach no value to distributional justice *per se*. No doubt a few scattered individuals would accept a slight cut in their own incomes in the interests of greater distributional justice—I do not need to take an extreme position on this—but the clamour by such people for redress of the injustice of their own excessive incomes is really negligible compared with the clamour by those who complain of the injustice of their inadequate incomes.

In saying that the vast majority of the population do not really care about greater equality *per se*—i.e. in the interests of distributive justice— I by no means exclude some of the sections of the trade union movement who have often been most vociferous in their attacks on the injustices in the economic system (on which point they are no doubt right). For the same people often seem to believe firmly in the sanctity of differentials of pay, and hence of inequalities in society, as long as they reflect inequalities of skill and effort. For example, Mr. Hugh Scanlon, the ex-President of the A.U.E.W.., echoes a doctrine that goes back to Aristotle when he argues that 'those who obtain skilled or professional status as a result of training and study expect financial rewards for their achievements . . . There is an absolute need to restore differentials, not just for craftsmen, but also for middle management, the pro-fessionals—engineers, accountants, doctors and other sections of the community where there has been a loss of traditional relativities.' (*The Times*, September 17th, 1976).[20]

In short, my first reason for downgrading distributive justice and equality in general as an important social consideration is that the vast mass of the population really do not care a fig for it and all the talk about it is so much humbug that is brought into play to justify a claim for improvements in one's own relative position.

4.2. Poverty or Inequality: Which Matters Most?

My second reason for downgrading concern with further reductions in inequality, in the interests of greater distributive justice *per se*, is that insofar as people do not really care much about it they are probably right. That is to say, by contrast to indifference to poverty, indifference to marginal changes in the degree of distributive justice in British society today seems to be less morally reprehensible.

In the first place, even if the existing degree of inequality of income and wealth deviates from that which would be strictly required in the interests of some agreed set of principles of distributive justice, it is highly unlikely that many members of society are hurt by this deviation, in concrete terms, to the same extent as are those who are hurt by the existence of poverty. For hurting people is something relatively tangible, by comparison with distributive justice, which is an abstract concept that may not have much tangible counterpart, in the sense that some unjustified inequality is hurting more people (or hurting them more)

---

[20]Mr. Scanlon is advocating the old egalitarian precept that inequalities are justified insofar as they are related to relevant inequalities between the people in question, and that one such relevant inequality is inequality of contribution to society. This is perhaps one of the oldest of all such principles of distributive justice, having been advanced by Aristotle (who also, of course, first introduced the concept of 'distributive justice' as well as the idea of justice as fairness, which is so much in vogue these days) in maintaining that ' . . . a just act necessarily involves at least four terms: two persons for whom it is in fact just, and two shares in which its justice is exhibited. And there will be the same equality between the shares as between the persons, because the shares will be in the same ratio to one another as the persons; for if the persons are not equal, they will not have equal shares; and it is when equals have or are assigned unequal shares, or people who are not equal, equal shares, that quarrels and complaints break out. This is also clear from the principle of assignment according to merit. Everyone agrees that justice in distribution must be in accordance with merit in some sense, but they do not all mean the same kind of merit . . . What is just in this sense, then, is what is pro-portional, and what is unjust is what violates the proportion'. (Aristotle, *Ethics*, Penguin Classics edn. (Harmondsworth, 1976), pp. 4f.

than would its rectification. In other words, I am expressing a strong preference for the concrete as against the abstract concept (inequality) that can only be defined operationally, if at all, in relation to major differences in degrees of inequality.[21]

This is where poverty, as distinct from equality, enters the picture. For it is arguable that when people are below society's poverty line— i.e. society's accepted notion of what is the minimum access to resources that a person needs in order to satisfy certain conditions, such as life expectation, opportunities to enjoy some minimum participation in society as a normal human being, and so on—they are hurt in relatively concrete and tangible ways, many of which can be captured within some operational definition, which makes the concept of poverty meaningful. This stems from the fact that although men are unequal in innumerable respects they share a common humanity and, as such, they all share ' . . . the capacity to feel pain, both from immediate physical causes and from various situations represented in perception and in thought; and the capacity to feel affection for others, and the consequences of this, connected with the frustration of this affection, loss of its objects, etc.'[22]

Now, of course, this involves making a distinction between some

---

[21]Of course, it can immediately be argued that unjustified *inequality* also hurts people, namely the people who would be better off under a more just distribution. But this takes us back to the earlier distinction between inequality *per se* and the impact of inequality on people' incomes. It is true that some people would be made better off by a move from an unjust to a just distribution, so that, in a sense, they are "hurt" by the unjust distribution. But it is equally true that some people would be hurt in a move in the opposite direction, and nobody would claim that this constitutes a valid argument for a more unjust distribution!

The argument would presumable have to be put in terms of the distinction between hurting people for unjust reasons (when going from a just to an unjust distribution), which is 'bad', and hurting people for just reasons, when going from an unjust to a just distribution, which is acceptable. But this distinction obviously cannot help us decide what is a justified hurt and what is not. An argument for further distributive justice on the grounds that the hurt arising from, say, moving away from it, is less just than the hurt that arises from moving towards it, since the former is a just move and the other is not, would be a purely circular argument.

Thus, what one has to seek—if we accept the priority of the hurting principle— is the way in which inequality may hurt people in concrete terms, not in relation to the extent to which they would be better off with a different, and juster, distribution.

[22]Bernard Williams, 'The Idea of Equality', reprinted in J. Feinberg (ed.), *Moral Concepts*, Oxford Readings in Philosophy, (Oxford, 1969), p. 155. One might also say that failure to ensure that people enjoyed some social minimum standard of living, defined very widely, would involve a failure to give each person the minimum due to him in his Kantian transcendental capacity of a free, rational, moral, agent, which entitles him to the minimum of respect to which all such agents are entitled.

kinds of hurt and others in terms of the particular forms of deprivation to which people are subjected. It amounts to saying that the hurt suffered by a person deprived of adequate food, or clothing, or shelter, or special medical care and so on, is in a different class from that suffered by, say, somebody in the higher income range who, on account of a possible injustice in income distribution, is deprived of the yacht that he would otherwise have bought. I am making an assertion, that I expect most people would share, that, in the former case, the poor person is deprived of resources that everybody (or nearly everybody) in society would agree ought to be available to everybody else in society, whereas society as a whole would not agree that everybody has an inalienable right to a yacht. The grounds for the general agreement to the universal right to the former type of good are irrelevant for present purposes. They may be founded on intuitionism, or on humanitarianism, or on a form of utilitarian calculus, or on a redefinition of Rawls's 'primary goods' to include a specific list of vital needs, or on some other contract theory of justice.

The point is that this form of what is known in economics jargon as "specific egalitarianism", like many other "common sense" precepts of justice, can, as Rawls points out, be derived from a variety of underlying basic principles of distributive justice.[23] Hence, they can be adopted without too much soul-searching as to their validity in terms of one particular basic theory of justice or another. It is much more difficult to say the same about egalitarianism in general, since any attempt to apply general egalitarian principles to practical cases invariably encounters logical difficulties of distinguishing between one case and another. Egalitarianism seems to call for a more articulated, logical basis than does simple humanitarianism.

Of course, the 'no-hurting' precept advocated above does not, by itself, help one to resolve conflicts as to who should be hurt without bringing into play some underlying principles of distributive justice. This is why I refer to it here as a 'precept', rather than as a 'principle'. It is more like one of the 'common sense precepts' which, as John Rawls clearly shows do not really suffice, in many cases, to resolve questions of conflict of precepts or of the precise weights that should be given to conflicting precepts. To do this, as he argues, requires some full-scale, grand, set of basic principles of distributive justice. [24] But unfortunately, this is not

---

[23]John Rawls, *A Theory of Justice* (Oxford, 1972).

[24]Rawls argues that ' . . . as long as one remains at the level of common sense precepts, no reconciliation of these maxims (i.e. common sense maxims) of justice is possible . . . . . . it is essential to keep in mind the subordinate place of common sense norms. Doing this is sometimes difficult because they are familiar from everyday life and therefore they are likely to have a prominence in our thinking that their derivative status does not justify. None of these precepts can be plausibly raised to a first principle . . . . . . Common sense precepts are at the wrong level of generality. In order to find suitable first principles one must step behind them.' (Rawls, op. cit., pp. 304, and 307 f.).

available to us, which brings me to my third reason for ranking egalitarianism below poverty-reduction in the present state of society in Britain.

4.3. The Limited Operational Value of Egalitarianism

There are two aspects of this argument. First, there is barely any consensus concerning what is a 'just' distribution. Secondly, such partial consensus as does exist is of no operational value.

I usually begin my University lectures on income distribution by asking students how many of them believe that existing distribution of income is too unequal. And even in these relatively reactionary times (compared wth the late 1960s) a high proportion of them raise their hands. I then go on to ask them exactly what degree of inequality they would regard as optimum, to which there is usually very little response, as also to my next question, which is by what operational criteria they would define the optimum degree of inequality. By this means I have made the point that it is difficult—though not, perhaps, logically impossible—to hold firm views as to whether the existing (or any other) degree of inequality is too great or too small, if one has no idea of what is the optimum degree of inequality, or how one should define the criteria by which this optimum should be assessed.

All this provides a useful lead in to a discussion of the immense complexities of defining inequality in a way that lends itself to objective measurement or to the formulation of consistent principles that can provide a guide to policies to deal with inequality. The students soon recognise that the invention of the concept, or word, "equality", does not necessarily imply the existence of some independent "thing", having that name, whose autonomous characteristics can be identified if only one searches hard enough. My Oxford students then rapidly see the difficult choices involved in resolving conceptual issues such as how far to go in allowing for differences in peoples' needs, and the extent to which, for example, valid distinctions can be drawn between needs that are the "fault" of the persons concerned and those that are not; the allowance for the way that people differ with respect to their preferences between, say, income and leisure, or risk avoidance; the adjustment of data to allow for wealth as well as income; the relative importance of the distribution of lifetime incomes as against annual incomes; and so on.

It is easy to show that these issues, which are familiar issues in the economic and statistical analysis of equality, correspond to problems that the philosophers have discussed for at least two millenia, without, as far as I can see, having reached a point where they can provide us with any clear guide lines. This is, of course, hardly surprising and certainly not the fault of the philosophers. For there is no escape from the need to incorporate value judgements into any proposed solution, and any search for unchallengeable, axiomatic, value judgements in this area is likely to continue indefinitely.

As indicated above, it is well-known that Aristotle first put forward the notion that inequalities were justified insofar as they corresponded to certain relevant inequalities between the persons concerned. And, as he went on to say, what constitutes a relevant inequality is what people disagree about. Whilst they may disagree about what inequalities are relevant, however, it is true that there have been many adherents to the view that the problem of distributive justice is, as Robert Nozick has put it, the problem of filling in the blank in the sentence 'To each according to his . . . . . . '[25] That is to say, it is widely believed that it is just to treat people unequally provided they differ with respect to *some* relevant pattern of characteristics. This distributive principle involved is the 'historical patterned' principle (to use Nozick's terminology again) according to which people may qualify for unequal rewards by virtue of some previous, or existing, event or action or circumstance. For example, it is often thought that people have a valid claim to higher rewards if they have saved more, or worked harder, or retired later in life, or suffered some misfortune through no fault of their own (including, often, some physical handicap), and so on.

This illustrative list of 'relevant' characteristics includes examples of the two most popular candidates for justifying inequalities in treatment, namely differences in "needs" or "merits". In his well-known, lucid, survey of the idea of equality, Bernard Williams selects these two patterns for particular attention [26]. And there is little doubt that these two widely accepted criteria influence statistical measurement procedures and social policy in hundreds of ways; some big, some small. For example, the merit criterion probably influences the distinciton, for taxation purposes, between earned and unearned income, or the 'disregard' of small savings in the estimation of rights to Supplementary Benefits. Similarly, the 'needs' criterion lies behind child allowances, as well as the treatment of family size in the statistical analysis of income distribution, not to mention the operation of the whole system of 'exceptional needs payments' in the Supplementary Benefit programme.

Yet both of these criteria raise enormous conceptual difficulties. For example, apart from the fact that many people, including myself, find it very difficult—if not impossible—to pass moral judgements on people (as distinct from acts, perhaps?), the notion of treating people differently according to 'merit' raises all the basic philosophical

---

[25] Nozick, *Anarchy, State and Utopia,* (Oxford, 1974).
[26] Williams, *op. cit.*

problems of a free will versus determinism. At the less rarified level of familiar economic analysis, it raises all the difficulties associated with the concept of 'consumer sovereignty' and the assumptions behind this concept, such as that men are free moral agents, fully aware of the consequences of their choices, and motivated by preference patterns that are also unaffected by their environments. This set of dubious assumptions seems to be necessary if a valid distinction can be made between (i) differences in choices because people are faced with different choice sets and (ii) differences in choices when they are faced with the same choice sets, so that they can be said to be morally responsible for making inferior choices that may lead them, for example, to having less income or greater needs than their neighbours. I hardly need take up time here in expanding on the obvious and well-known difficulties to which such distinctions give rise.[27]

The same applies to the needs criterion, in spite of the argument advanced by Bernard Williams to the effect that 'it is a matter of logic that particular sorts of needs constitute a reason for receiving particular sorts of goods', whereas 'it is, however, in general a much more disputable question whether certain sorts of merit constitute a reason for receiving certain sorts of good'.[28] Professor Williams's argument is that, in the former case, the proper relevant ground for distributing certain goods, such as health care, is the need for it—i.e. the person's state of health. But this, of course, raises the usual problems about where to draw the line between those needs that are accepted as legitimate reasons for being assured access to the goods 'needed' and those that do not. One must put the question 'Needed for what?'[29] Presumably when we talk of a 'need' we mean that the good in question is a necessary condition for achieving some particular end-state (and if we do not mean that by 'need', what do we mean?). If this end-state is a certain level of welfare, or an increase in welfare, then what about my need for wine, women and song in order to increase my welfare? I suspect that my enjoyment of Opera, for example, is greater than that of many people who are financially better able to go to Covent Garden, so that as far as this principle is concerned access to Opera is not being distributed according to what Professor Williams would regard as the relevant criterion.[30]

Furthermore, neither the merit nor the 'need' criteria tells us what to

[27]See for example, Rawls, *op. cit.*, section 48, pp. 310 ff, 'Legitimate Expectations and Moral Desert', for a succinct analysis of the shortcomings of the merit criterion.
[28]Williams, *op. cit.*, p. 164.
[29]See an interesting discussion of this point and other related points in A. Weale, *Equality and Social Policy* (London, 1978).
[30]See, for example, a recent discussion of this general issue in Amartya Sen, *On Economic Inequality* (Oxford 1973).

do when they conflict, or when their application would involve very high costs. In the field of medical care, for example, there is the well-known problem of how much society should be prepared to spend on treatment for somebody whose particular condition could only be treated at astronomic costs (and hence at the cost of significant reductions in the resources available to other members of society). Again, therefore, one is tempted to conclude that such principles are really nothing more than 'common sense precepts', and that, as Rawls would argue, they are at a second level of generality and do not get us very far, so that we must step behind them to find some more basic, general, distributive principles.

Unfortunately, it seems that Rawls's own, important, and stimulating proposed set of basic principles are open to numerous objections. Not being a philosopher it would be impertinent and foolhardy of me to try to summarise these difficulties. But one of the main objections that has been raised to his theory happens to be central to my proposition here concerning the limited applicability of theories of distributive justice for purposes of practical social policy in general, and for the relief of poverty in particular.

To explain this objection it is necessary, for the benefit of the un-initiated, to sketch out the basic procedure adopted by Rawls, which is as follows. Valid principles of distributive justice are those that people would arrive at if they were completely impartial and unaffected by their own particular situations and interests. One device for deducing what principles would be arrived at in such a situation in Rawls's device of the 'original situation', which can be seen as a situation in which the parties to the agreement concerning the principles of justice to be applied subsequently do not know what their subsequent position will be when, as it were, the game starts. Nor do they know very much about what their tastes and preferences will be. They do, however, know enough to agree on two principles. First, they agree to ascribe priority to certain principles of liberty and equality, within limits, including basic rights to certain 'primary goods' which 'every rational man is presumed to want'.[31] These goods, which comprise notably certain basic 'rights and liberties, powers and opportunities, income and wealth', are, however, defined only in the most general and abstract terms.

A second principle of justice on which people will agree in the original position, behind what Rawls calls 'the veil of ignorance', is the 'difference principle' of equality. According to this principle, inequalities are only justified insofar as 'they work as part of a scheme which improves the expectations of the least advantaged members of

[31] Rawls, *op. cit.*, p. 75.

society.[32] Rawls goes on to explain that what he means by the least advantaged members of society is the representative member of the least advantaged, or 'worst off', group.

It would seem that these two features of the Rawlsian frame—the definition of primary goods in very general, abstract terms, and the concern with the average member of the worst-off group are, at best, unhelpful, and, at worst, inconsistent with the objectives I have proposed above.[33]

First, Rawls's concern with raising the position of the worst-off group, which he compares with unskilled workers, or with people whose incomes are less than half the median income, ignores the fact, as forcibly pointed out by Brian Barry, 'that in advanced industrial the problem of poverty cannot be tackled by raising the average income of all unskilled workers or increasing any other broadly-drawn average. It is now thought that the chief source of poverty are such things as having children, being sick or unemployed for a long period, being old or being disabled'.[34]

Secondly, the definition of primary goods in very summary and general terms means that no guidelines are provided for taking account of all the numerous detailed ways in which people may suffer exceptional deprivation or distress on account of exceptional needs or unfortunate circumstances. By contrast, a simple humanitarian approach would justify providing somebody with special care or additional income, and so on, not merely because he is worse off than the representative member of the least advantaged group in respect of his income or wealth, but because he has, say, special dietary needs, unavoidable excessive rent commitments compared to his income, etc. Rawlsian doctrine, however, could provide no criteria or guidelines for, say, all the various exceptional needs payments and additions provided for under the British system of Supplementary Benefits, ranging from special dietary needs to a new

[32]Rawls, *op. cit.*, p. 75.

[33]The resemblance between Rawls's concern with the 'worst-off' group and my proposal to give priority to poverty is superficial. Rawls's 'worst-off' group is not necessarily my poverty group. There will always be a worst-off group (in the absence of complete equality), whereas there is no logical reason why there must always be somebody below society's poverty line. Also, in Rawls, increases in equality that do not improve the position of the worst off are undesirable whereas I am fairly indifferent to them. That the rich may become unjustly richer ought not to worry anybody provided it does not constitute a threat to basic rights and liberties. To feel hurt because somebody else is poor, however, is morally desirable altruism (a sentiment that is excluded in Rawls's original position) whereas to feel hurt because somebody else is rich is usually morally undesirable envy.

[34]Brian Barry, *The Liberal Theory of Justice* (Oxford, 1973), p. 50.

pair of shoes for poor children.[35]

Now some critics of Rawls have argued that, although Rawls does propose the institution of a minimum income, he does not appear to be concerned with the way that income is spent, nor how far extra income or access to certain goods is necessary on account of special needs. It has also been argued that different assumptions about the psychologies of the actors in the 'original position' might have given rise to a much more articulated and detailed specification of 'primary goods' that could have included allowance for all sorts of detailed needs to which people are subject.[36]

This raises two points. First, is it true that Rawls does ignore the problem of special needs? Secondly, whether he does or not, can one construct a suitably general theory of distributive justice that would also provide practical guidance in individual cases by some appropriate tinkering with the list of 'primary goods' selected by impartial participants to the agreement? Now on the first point, it seems to me, with great respect, that his critics do not do justice to Rawls's discussion of the functions of what he says can be looked at as the 'transfer branch' of the 'background institutions' that a just society should have. For example, he states that 'the essential idea is that the workings of this branch takes needs into account and assigns them an appropriate weight with respect to other claims . . . . . . Competitive markets . . . set a weight on the conventional precepts associated with wages and earnings, whereas the transfer branch guarantees a certain level of well-being and honors the claims of need.'[37]

It is true that he does not spell out in detail what these various legitimate needs might be. But he is surely right not to do so, for it would be impossible for the detailed applications of this transfer function to be spelt out in advance in Rawls's original position or in any contract-negotiating position in which people were sufficiently

[35]Another difficulty arising out of the very general definition of 'primary goods' in Rawls is that it is not clear how much conflict is between the basic rights to some private property and the egalitarianism implied in Rawls's 'difference' principle. For discussion of this and related issues see *I.M.D. Little* "Distributive Justice and the New International Order" in Peter Oppenheimer (ed.), Proceedings of a conference in memory of Harry Johnson, September 1978, (forthcoming, Oriel Press, London, 1980).
[36]This argument is put briefly by Brian Barry, *op. cit.* (1973), p. 55–7, and in great detail, in connection with the important constitutional issue of whether people are entitled to minimum access to certain goods as part of their constitutional right to equal protection of life and liberty and so on, in Frank Michelman 'Constitutional Welfare Rights and A Theory of Justice', in N. Daniels (ed.), *Reading Rawls: Critical Studies of a Theory of Justice* (Oxford 1975) and 'Foreword: On Protecting the Poor Through the Fourteenth Amendment', in *Harvard Law Review* (1969), pp. 7–59.
[37]Rawls, *op. cit.*, p. 276.

ignorant of the detailed facts of life to be impartial and to take absoultely no account of their own particular interests. One of Rawls's critics, Professor Michelman, acknowledges that Rawls nowhere rejects the notion that society should provide some sort of guarantee against special forms of need and suggests that the reason why Rawls does not include it in a different 'hybrid' version of the difference principle is that it would not be suitably abstract. In fact, this is what Rawls himself does seem to be saying when he says that a definition of ' . . . the just distribution of goods and services on the basis of information about the preferences and claims of particular individuals . . . . . . introduces complexities that cannot be handled by principles of tolerable simplicity to which men might reasonably to be expected to agree'.[38]

But this is a separate issue which I hope to discuss elsewhere. For present purposes the conclusion is that principles of distributive justice that are sufficiently clear and simple to be candidates for agreement in a Rawlsian original position, or in any other contractual theory of justice, could not provide much help for dealing with the infinitely wide variety of concrete cases of special need and deprivation that are still widespread in modern societies and that may, perhaps, be a permanent feature of society long after minor unjustified differences in income distribution have ceased to matter to anybody except the very envious. In this connection, Rawlsian-type theories of justice are probably not unique in ' . . . having hardly anything to say about social policy (a significant low priority when one considers that for many working-class people in industrial societies 'fairness' is virtually entirely comprised in the provisions of the welfare state)'.[39] And if, before dealing with cases of special need or poverty amongst people who are poor not because they are in a 'worst-off' group but who, for some special reason, are worse off than the average member of such a group, one had to find some consistent set of distributive principles of the type that is sought in the context of egalitarian theory, one would finish up doing nothing, since such a set of principles does not seem to be at our disposal.

Meanwhile such cases exist and have to be dealt with. The answer is to adopt a simple-minded humanitarian approach, which does not presuppose any clear, coherent and logical set of first principles as would an approach via egalitarianism and the principles of distributive justice. For example, society should help a poor person irrespective of whether he was rich earlier and has simply failed to make prudent provision for old-age or a rainy day in the same way that one should

---

[38]*ibid.*, p. 304.
[39]Barry, *op. cit.* (1973), p. 57.

help a drowning person without first asking questions about whether he knowingly accepted the risks involved in swimming.

5. Conclusion

The upshot of all this is that I think slow growth does matter, at least when it takes the form that it does appear to take today, namely when it implies the persistence of high unemployment and increasing poverty. For the majority of the population I think it matters very little, but for the poor or the new-poor it is of the utmost importance. The fact that, over the longer run, poverty in this country has not fallen at all and, over the last few years, it has increased suggests that relief or prevention of poverty is not given its due place in the hierarchy of objectives. This might seem paradoxical in an age when there is so much talk about equality. But since most of the talk about equality is humbug anyway, perhaps this is not so paradoxical after all.

2

ECONOMIC GROWTH AND SOCIAL WELFARE

by Richard Lecomber

University of Bristol

1. Ask a Silly Question . . .

Does Economic Growth Promote Social Welfare?[1]

Economic growth is generally taken to be a major goal of economic policy. Politicians and other public figures stress the importance of growth,[2] while even economists write extravagantly, thus: 'Whatever a nation's goals—more help for the poor countries of the world, stronger defences, a larger public sector, a larger share of output for under-privileged persons at home—they can most easily be achieved by providing more resources through the growth of available output per head.'[3] and again 'Economic growth is the grand objective. It is the aim of economic policy as a whole.'[4]

---

[1] *Social welfare* is to be interpreted broadly and normatively. *Economic growth* is used precisely, to refer to the growth in constant-price Gross National Product (GNP). Population growth is not explicitly considered: implicitly it is taken as exogenously given so that growth in GNP per head is proportional to growth in GNP. Sometimes, growth is conceived more idealistically in terms of what one would like GNP to measure (social welfare). This usage is, however, misleading and therefore best avoided.

[2] Enthusiasm for growth stems partly from a tendency to equate it with reduced unemployment. In the short run GNP and employment are indeed strongly correlated, but in the longer term they can be decoupled by appropriate policies. Hence it is important to keep distinct the criticisms of overfull employment (dangers of inflation etc.) and criticisms of growth *per se*.

[3] M. Lipton, *Assessing Economic Performance* (London, 1968).

[4] R. Harrod, 1965. See also W. Beckerman, 'Why we need Economic Growth' *Lloyds Bank Review,* (Oct. 1971); 'The Desirability of Economic Growth' in N. Kaldor (ed.), *Conflicts in Policy Objectives*, (Oxford, 1971); and *In Defence of Economic Growth* (London, 1974). It should be stressed that in practice policy is not as obsessive as public statements appear to imply. Attention is given to such matters as redistribution, benefits for the unemployed, hours and conditions of work and pollution control despite conflicts with measured growth.

Recently, however, there has been a spirited reaction. Economic growth has come under increasing attack as a source of a wide variety of environmental and social ills, perhaps even endangering the survival of the human race.[5]

The resultant debate has been lively but confused.

One of the major sources of confusion has been the following: in order to appraise economic growth (or indeed anything else) it is essential to hold clearly in mind some *alternative*. Perhaps the obvious alternative is *no growth* ('Zero Economic Growth' or ZEG) and this is indeed advocated by some anti-growth writers. However, on examination, ZEG turns out to be an ambiguous and unhelpful prescription. GNP is a heterogeneous aggregate and there are an infinite variety of ways in which it could be frozen. One possibility would be an immediate freeze on all economic activity, but this is soon seen to be absurd. Among the numerous difficulties is the failure to expand certain vital activities (including some much stressed by the anti-growth school, such as the manufacture of pollution control equipment and insulation materials) and to cut back on others (for example car production and advertising). There would also be very serious transitional problems (as witnessed inadvertantly in recent years) including unemployment, inflation and an imbalance between consumption and investment. An alternative possibility would be to vary the structure of production in such a way that GNP remains constant, but it is difficult to see much value in such a purely statistical exercise.

The time scale could be expanded and ZEG seen as a long-term objective. This idea corresponds with the 'stationary state' as advocated by Daly and others; it is suggested that indefinite expansion is incompatible with the physical finiteness of the world, and that if stationarity is not adopted as a conscious objective it will be forced on us in a much more unpleasant form. These propositions have been questioned but the most relevant point here is that *eventual* stationarity provides almost no guidance to *current* policy. Which of many possible stationary states should be chosen? How soon should it be reached? Should the approach be monotonic, or might it be desirable for some activities to rise beyond their ultimate values before falling back?

For these and other reasons, ZEG has been vigorously attacked, especially by economists. Even if, and indeed perhaps especially if, one accepts the criticisms of the anti-growth school, it is essential to be discriminating, to tailor specific policies to meet specific problems. Thus

[5]See e.g. E. J. Mishan, The Economic Growth Debate, (London, 1977); D. H. Meadows et. al., *The Limits to Growth*, Earth Island (London, 1972); H. E. Daly, 'In Defence of Steady-State Economy', *American Journal of Agricultural Economics* (Dec. 1972); F. Hirsch, *Social Limits to Growth*, Twentieth Century Fund (Cambridge, Mass., 1976)

'The way to control pollution [or any other social problem] is to control pollution [or the other problem] not growth.'[6] The more thoughtful anti-growth writers recognise this. Thus Meadows[7] draws a distinction between goods production (which is to be frozen) and services (which can be allowed to expand)—a crude division, certainly, but one which concedes the essential point. Daly,[8] while viewing stationarity as the appropriate long-term objective, advocates short-term policies, many of which the pro-growth school would approve (e.g. externality taxes). Mishan,[9] though titling his book 'The Cost of Economic Growth' nowhere suggests a policy aimed specifically at slowing down growth.

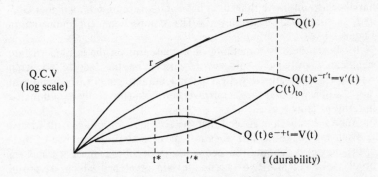

Countries A and B face the same range of alternatives, represented by the 'possibility frontier' $X_1 Y_1$. A chooses higher GNP (hence more growth from initial position Z) but a worse environment than B. C however moves to a more advantageous frontier $(X_2 Y_2)$ and is able to achieve higher GNP (and hence faster growth from the initial position) and a better environment than either A or B.

Fig. 2.1. Growth and the Trade-off between
GNP and Environmental Quality

[6]M. J. Roberts, 'On Reforming Economic Growth', *Daedalus* (Autumn, 1973).
[7]Meadows *et al*, op.cit.
[8]Daly, op.cit.
[9]E. J. Mishan, *The Costs of Economic Growth* (London, 1967).

Rather, he writes, 'to be tediously logical about it, there is an alternative to the post-war *growth rush* . . . . . . the simple alternative, that is, of *not rushing for growth.*' (ital. added)—a very different matter.

Rather similar difficulties arise in assessing historical experience. Has economic growth increased social welfare? Again, the question implies a comparison with some alternative historical development involving less or zero economic growth. But there are many possible such paths, some doubtless better, but others worse. One could enquire whether social welfare has increased most in countries experiencing the fastest economic growth. However, apart from the obvious difficulty of assessing social welfare, any answer is liable to be misleading. Country A may have grown faster than country B because it has unduly neglected its environment, and one may perhaps judge that country B has gained less in GNP but more in welfare. On the other hand country C may have been so inventive that it has been able to secure *both* a higher GNP *and* an improved environment. The comparisons are indicated in Figure 2.1.

In short, there is something of a consensus on the limited welfare significance of GNP. Anti-growth writers use the fact to condemn rapid growth, pro-growth writers to condemn zero growth. The important moral is however that these controversies should not really be conducted in terms of growth at all.

While it has been suggested that the attack of the anti-growth writers is often mis-focussed, this does not mean that the substance of their criticisms can be ignored. Consequently in Section 2, the criticisms are briefly reviewed and two taxonomies are developed which are useful in subsequent discussion. Section 3 focuses on a number of issues raised by the growth debates. Section 4 relates the debates to recent experience of involuntary slow growth. Finally, the conclusions are summarised in Section 5.

2. Problems Raised by the Anti-Growth School

The arguments that have been advanced against growth are many and varied. The aim here is to present a brief but systematic survey with minimal comment. First, observe that growth is rarely sought for its own sake but rather because it results in an increase in GNP. Accordingly, criticisms of growth may be divided into objections to high GNP and objections to the process of achieving a high GNP.

2.1. Objections to High GNP

Some of the most important ingredients of happiness (or whatever else is considered to constitute social welfare) are not marketed and are therefore excluded from GNP. A well known example is the quality of the physical environment. If higher GNP entails a degraded environment then it is not clear that the change is worthwhile (Figure 2.2). GNP is sometimes dubbed 'Gross National Pollution', but the term is not apt, as it suggests a unique relationship between GNP and pollution similiar

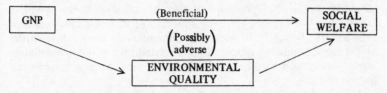

Fig. 2.2 GNP, Environmental Quality and Social Welfare

to that modelled in Limits to Growth.[10] In fact, pollution depends on the *structure* of economic activity and considerable reductions may be achieved by altering the mix of goods produced or the techniques of production. Nevertheless the attainment of any given level of environmental quality places a constraint on GNP, and in general the higher the level the more severe is the constraint.[11] Thus there is a trade-off between GNP and environmental quality, represented by the frontier illustrated in Figure 2.1 ($X_1 Y_1$ or $X_2 Y_2$).

The above analysis embraces not only pollution, but noise, congestion and visual effects. It embraces also possible *social* side-effects of affluence (substitue 'the quality of social relationships' for 'environmental quality' in Figures 2.1 and 2.2), for example the suggestion that affluence breeds idleness, boredom etc. manifesting themselves in violence, crime, vandalism and divorce and that the productive techniques required to maintain affluence involve worker alienation manifesting itself in instrumentalist attitudes to work and hence in industrial conflict, materialism and inflation. Other alleged symptoms of these problems include depression, mental illness and suicide.[12] Most of these phenomena appear to have increased and this is widely attributed to growth. The causal connection has not been adequately established (see below) but, for our immediate purposes this is not necessary; it is sufficient that these phenomena may be alleviated, at some expense in GNP, by foregoing particular productive techniques or by devoting resources to activities (e.g. probation services) which are underweighted in GNP.

Essentially, the analysis applies also to leisure (and to working conditions). While there is a market for labour (and hence implicitly for

[10]Meadows *et. al.*, op.cit.
[11]This statement assumes, realistically, that environmental quality impinges mainly on individuals. In as far as its impact is on productive activity (included in GNP), high environmental quality and GNP will be complementary.
[12]See e.g. Mishan, op.cit. (1967) for elaboration of these views.

leisure), leisure is not (though it easily could be) included in GNP.[13] Hence GNP may be increased by sacrificing leisure.

The *direct* connection between GNP and social welfare, as shown in Figure 2, has also been challenged. It has been suggested that happiness (or whatever) depends more on relative that on absolute income (The *Jones* effect) so that the effect on an increase, distributed *pro rata* is of little benefit. Hirsch[14], in particular, emphasises the competitive nature of the satisfactions of modern life. A related idea is the expansion of wants, partly as a result of advertising but also through more casual human contacts.

Finally, high GNP may jeopardise welfare in the longer term via resource depletion, persistent pollution and persistent degradation of social arrangements (e.g. increasing industrial conflict or propensities to crime which may be difficult or costly to reverse).[15]

2.2. Objections to the Process of Growth

It has been recognised that growth can be increased by current sacrifice—by diverting resources from consumption to investment (not only in plant and buildings but also in human skills and knowledge). Growth should never be maximised (for this would involve cutting consumption as much as poossible e.g. to subsistence) rather it should be optimised. Pro-growth writers go on to argue that the market mechanism is biased against investment and growth.[16]

However, these writings totally neglect other major current costs of growth—namely those associated with change.[17] Growth is promoted mainly by the adoption of more efficient (generally labour-saving) productive techniques. It is generally accepted that no *overall* shortage of jobs need result, as the greater efficiency yields higher incomes sufficient to finance the additional production. However, the process is likely to involve substantial shifts in the geographical and occupational mix of jobs and hence, given the very limited mobility of the work-force, to give rise to structural unemployment. The consequent loss of production is reflected in GNP, but the individual misery and other social side-effects of unemployment are not. Strictly, this problem is a *transitional* one, that is it would disappear in time (given no further

[13]W. D. Nordhaus and J. Tobin, 'Is Growth Obsolete', in National Bureau of Economic Research, *Economic Growth* (Columbia University Press, 1972)
[14]Hirsch, *op.cit.*
[15]See e.g. Mishan, op. cit. (1967), and Hirsch, *op. cit.*
[16]See J. Tobin, 'Economic Growth as an Objective of Policy', *American Econimic Review: Papers and Proceedings* (May, 1964); E. S. Phelps, *Fiscal Neutrality Towards Economic Growth*, (New York, 1970), and for a critical review, J. R. C. Lecomber, *The Growth Objective*, International Institute of Social Economics (Humberside, 1975).
[17]See Mishan, *op.cit.* (1967).

change) as the workforce adapted itself to the new structure of jobs. But the adjustment period is often long (witness old mining areas or the inner cities) and, since change is a continuing process, the problems may persist indefinitely and even increase over time.

Frequently, these structural shifts involve population migrations, e.g. from the country to the town or from the depressed regions to the South East. The benefits of these shifts (higher output) are reflected in GNP, but the costs are not; these costs may include epidemics, unsettled communities, and infrastructure needs.

Growth also involves changes in familiar physical environments, and in skill requirements, institutions, social habits and values. Some of these changes may be perceived as acute social distress by those unwillingly affected. The poor and the elderly are often the greatest sufferers, because they are both least adaptable and least able to resist the pressure for change. The process may also create a generation gap, as the skills and values of the old become increasingly obsolete and the respect of the young increasingly difficult to maintain. If the old continue to maintain positions of power, a crisis of authority is liable to result. If, on the other hand, control passes to the young, the loss of role of the older generation becomes more acute. It has also been suggested that rapid change creates a pervasive sense of impermanence which is destructive of contentment.

Discharges into the environment give rise to similar adaptation problems. Ecosystems can adapt to small changes, but not so easily to large ones. Large increases in the number and quantities of new chemicals released into the environment have not only increased the risk of damage but made it much more difficult to monitor all the effects in time to prevent such damage.[18]

Frequently, changes require new laws and institutions to cope with new problems e.g. congestion, pollution. It takes time to create new institutions and even longer to adapt to their use. Thus it may be difficult for a society experiencing rapid growth to match economic change with the necessary social and institutional change.

Finally, rapid growth increases the vulnerability of society. The future becomes very uncertain, making planning difficult. Society becomes reliant on technical change (e.g. to overcome resource depletion and environmental degradation),[19] any faltering of which could spell disaster. Moreover, people accustomed to rising material living standards are very resistant to any diminution in the rate of increase, as recent U.K. experience illustrates.

---

[18]See Massachusetts Institute of Technology, *Man's Impact on the Global Environment: Assessment and Recommendations for Action*, M.I.T. Press, 1970.
[19]Note however that such problems arise even at the current level (and structure) of activity and may indeed be insoluble without further technical advance.

2.3. The Basic Problems

Various as the problems are, they can all be traced to one (or more) of the following basic causes—a taxonomy which proves useful in assessing remedies:

(i) Problems associated with the failure of the market mechanism to reflect consumer preferences (externalities). Many of the costs of growth (e.g. pollution, congestion, noise, want-expansion effects of advertising, envy, and many of the wider social ramifications of change) are not adequately considered by decision makers, because they fall largely on others. We may include here externalities created by government taxes or expenditure (e.g. unemployment benefit, support of 'lame ducks'). In principle, these externalities may be corrected by regulations or fiscal arrangements which force decision makers to take into account the full social costs of their action. Such correction would tend to reduce GNP.[20] In practice, however the appropriate remedy may conflict with other objectives (notably distribution) or involve high or even prohibitive enforcement costs.

(ii) Maldistribution of income. It is recognised that neither market mechanisms nor aggregate statistics such as GNP take account of distribution. Growth can conflict with distribution (e.g. costs of change tend to fall on the poor and elderly).

(iii) Bad decisions, due to ignorance or other causes. At best, the prices used in constructing GNP reflect people's preferences as expressed in the market. If these are based on misinformation or on values judged (by the commentator) to be immoral or foolish or otherwise inappropriate, then (in the eyes of the commentator) GNP will be distorted, and its growth not necessarily desirable. Many of the criticisms of growth imply such adverse judgements of people's market behaviour.[21]

(iv) Neglect of future generations. This is a major criticism of growth. Strictly, such neglect can be analysed in terms of the three previous categories, but such analysis is complex and it is more convenient to present it under a separate head.

(v) Market values not reflected in GNP. The previous four categories of problem are all associated with the inability of the market to promote social welfare; their solution entails intervention to override or modify the market outcome. However in some cases the problem is rather that GNP fails to pick up market values. The outstanding examples (apart from inaccurate statistics are leisure and the work environment. Labour markets will tend to reflect worker evaluations of these (albeit imperfectly)

---

[20]See Meadows *et al.* op.cit.
[21]See especially Mishan, *op.cit.* (1967).

but neither is reflected in GNP. Similarly, capital markets reflect (again imperfectly) relative evaluations of present and future consumption. In such cases, no intervention is required. The point is rather that governments obsessed with growth statistics may be tempted to intervene (e.g. to encourage long hours and high saving), to the detriment of social welfare.

2.4. The Pro-Growth Reaction

Some of the specific arguments catelogued above are in principle accepted by the pro-growth school, particularly those clearly associated with externalities. The need to make individual decision makers bear the full marginal costs of their actions is accepted, but this conventional type of modification to the market system is mostly viewed as straightforward and having little if any effect on growth ('The pollution problem is a simple matter of correcting a minor resource misallocation by means of pollution charges'[22]). Moreover, many of the anti-growth arguments are disputed as empirically unproven while those based on the rejection of the individual preferences are rejected as elitist and undemocratic ('satisfying human preferences is what our kind of society and economy is all about'[23]). It is suggested that growth, by allowing the poor to become richer without the rich becoming poorer, facilitates greater equality of incomes.

These arguments are taken up in the next section.

3. Selected Issues

3.1. Difficulties with the Discriminatory Approach

The case for discrimination—as opposed to across-the-board measures like ZEG—is irresistible. Nevertheless the kind of fine tuning which pro-growth writers tend to advocate, that is carefully gearing policies towards particular activities to estimates of the externalities involved, may be seriously inadequate in practice. Problems stem from the probable range, importance and pervasiveness of externalities and from costs and difficulties of control. Firstly there is a danger that attention will be confined to the most immediate and tangible externalities; effects which are difficult to trace or measure may be neglected. In some contexts (especially environmental ones) there is a systematic tendency for such neglected effects to be adverse, so that ommission can impart a substantial bias. A particular danger arises from the tendency to neglect cumulative or 'systems' effects. For example in the transport field, car journeys contribute to the decline of public transport, the deterioration of inner

[22]W. Beckerman, 'Economists, Scientists and Environmental Catastrophe', *Oxford Economic Papers* (Nov. 1972).
[23]Tobin, op.cit.

cities and the expansion of the suburban fringe, the decline of local facilities and hence of community spirit.[24] These trends make it increasingly difficult to do without a car and thus society is pushed almost irresistably from a position in which no family owns a car to one in which every family (who can) owns at least one. The few unfortunates who, through poverty or other causes, are debarred from car ownership are severely disadvantaged. It is very difficult to evaluate the comparative merits of the two societies — and it would certainly be wrong to dwell exclusively on the disadvantages of the car-owning one. What is clear is that simply internalising the immediate external costs associated with particular journeys does little to guide society to the right outcome.

Externality analysis would also need to be extended far beyond its normal range of application (to pollution and congestion phenomena). For example the effects of advertising and of the size and structure of industrial plants allegedly involve important external effects. Moreover, some externalities, notably relative income effects, are of a very general and pervasive nature, requiring very general solutions.

Also, controlling externalities is often difficult and expensive. Again, motoring provides a useful illustration. Congestion—the most obvious external cost—varies widely with time and place according to road conditions, from zero on empty roads to several pounds a mile in conditions of heavy traffic. A charge which reflects such variations at all accurately is ruled out by the costs of monitoring, administration and compliance. A feasible scheme inevitably involves a crude price structure, implying that some journeys are overpriced, perhaps by a factor of ten, while others are underpriced by a similar margin. Certain externalities, for example littering in the countryside and various aspects of social behaviour (e.g. politeness), are prohibitively difficult to police and are best left to the individual conscience reinforced by informal pressures. A corollary is the importance of maintaining a society in which informal pressures and altruism can thrive.

One implication of enforcement costs is that it will often be beneficial to concentrate on a relatively small number of instruments. Suppose one activity, say motoring, has a wide variety of adverse side effects. In principle, ignoring enforcement costs, it is optimal to operate separately on each, pollution controls to tackle pollution, congestion pricing to tackle congestion, oil taxes to tackle depletion etc. But, when enforcement costs are taken into account, it could well be preferable to impose a general deterrent on car use.

---

[24]For elaborations of these points, see Mishan, *op.cit.* (1967), and S. Glaister, 'Transport Pricing Policies and Efficient Urban Growth', *Journal of Public Economics* (Jan.–Feb. 1976).

Interestingly, Zero Economic Growth is the *reductio ad absurdum* of this line of argument. While ZEG is manifestly too crude, the sweeping absolutist criticisms of the pro-growth writers are not altogether appropriate.

3.2. Change

One manifestation of growth is change and indeed many of the arguments against growth (especially Mishan's)[25] are basically arguments against change. As we saw (p. 28) they range widely. However, it is important to realise that these arguments cut many ways. For it is not only growth that involves change; curbing resource depletion and environmental degradation likewise requires the adoption of new technologies, involving dangers of structural unemployment, obsolescent skills and even unforeseen environmental impacts. Again, while the stationary state is one of no change, the process of attaining it involves very radical change. Currently (and despite the stagnation of the 1970s) the economy is geared to growth in very many inter-locking ways (e.g. the size of the investment sector and expectations of regular rises in living standards) and halting this growth (change) involves a change in direction. Certainly, the advantages of 'less change' provide no case for hasty and indiscriminate abandonment of growth or its attendant mechanisms.

It is unhelpful to suggest general principles: 'no change' or 'minimal change' would certainly be as inappropriate as 'no growth' as a guiding principle. Change is a complex multi-dimensional concept and in practical cases it is rarely obvious what a 'minimal change' policy would be. In any case, not all aspects of change are equally harmful at all or indeed harmful at all. Generally, changes that are embraced willingly may be presumed desirable. It is the unwanted side-effects falling on others that cause harm. Very different is the position of the man who voluntarily leaves his job to take another created by new technology from that of one made redundant. Likewise the problems associated with new housing estates are generally greatest where the occupants have been compulsorily rehoused.[26] Notwithstanding, even those embracing change willingly may suffer from unforeseen effects, witness the high incidence of T.B. among nineteenth century migrants to the cities[27] and the greater incidence of child problems in families which have recently moved house.[28] Even where changes are judged to be harmful *per se*, this must be weighed against the benefits (whether in terms of higher GNP or of resource conservation) which the changes are designed to achieve.

[25]Mishan, *op.cit.* (1967).
[26]Fried's paper in M. B. Kantor (ed.), *Mobility and Mental Health* (Illinois, 1965).
[27]R. Dubos, *Man Adapting* (Yale University Press, 1971).
[28]M. B. Kantor, *op.cit.*

The purpose of this discussion has been rather to emphasise the tendency to neglect the problems of change. Thus, although strenuous efforts are made to alleviate structural unemployment (for example retraining schemes, regional employment subsidies and even financial support for 'lame ducks') little attempt is made to influence the key causal factor, the direction of innovation and its impact on the job structure. In considering innovation, attention seems to be focussed almost exclusively on the manifest benefits (a reduction in production costs) while the social side-effects are virtually ignored, to be tackled if at all by a variety of supplementary measures. In most cases these are expensive and only moderately effective, in view of which society might have been better off had some innovations been suppressed.

Little is known about the impact which change may have (via industrial relations, structural unemployment, changing physical environment, break-up of established communities etc.) on social behaviour, especially crime, vandalism, truancy, mental illness etc., and little attempt seems to be being made to discover more (see section 3.6 below).

3.3. Is Tackling Externalities Enough?

The pro-growth school accept the need to tackle externalities. However, much of the anti-growth case is directed at the inability of decision makers to act in their own best interests. Thus their actions, it is alleged, do not reflect their true preferences. These allegations are anathema to orthodox economists, for whom the assumption that behaviour reveals preferences is the corner-stone of their creed.

It is difficult, even as an approximation, to maintain that people do act in their own best interests. Ignorance, addiction and the influence of apparently irrelevant features of advertisements are clearly important factors. 'Irrationality' is indeed recognised by governments in legislation on drugs, prostitutes, seat belts and crash helmets, product standards, building regulations etc. as well as in the duties on cigarettes and beer (which cannot be adequately defended on distributional or externality grounds).[29]

It is true that, for such actions to be justified, it is necessary not only that individuals do not know their own best interests but also that government knows them better. It is also important to recognise that intervention may involve a disutility arising from the feeling of coercion as well as costs of enforcement and dangers associated with abuse of power. But these are all factors to be weighed up and decided case by case. A general appeal to a manifestly nonsensical assumption is unhelpful.

---

[29]Such actions are indeed attacked by extreme advocates of individual freedom, for example Enoch Powell and Milton Friedman.

In extreme cases individual behaviour is constrained, and in my view rightly, on paternalistic grounds. Some anti-growth men would suggest that the potential dangers from resource depletion, environmental degradation and collapse of the social structure are so great as to constitute the outstanding 'extreme' case for paternalistic intervention.

However, the overriding problem is that, despite such precedents, the scope for government action to protect individuals from their own folly is severely limited by democratic checks, especially when the folly is widespread. Folly in the market place is generally matched by equal folly in the ballot box. Folly is, in any case, a matter of opinion. Who is to say that the pleasures of smoking do not outweigh the future suffering and early death from lung cancer (especially if discounted at a conventional 10% p.a.!). Thus anti-growth writers and others who wish to legislate against 'folly' are often accused of being elitist and opponents of democracy. But here it should be borne in mind that anti-growth writings may be directed not at the government but at the population at large.[30] (This isn't always made clear, and economists accustomed to regard preferences as given are apt to jump to unwarranted conclusions!). This may be didactic but it is scarcely undemocratic.

3.4. Responsibility to Future Generations

Our responsibilities to future generations are more widely conceded but raise very similar problems. In fact it is by no means obvious that we do neglect these responsibilities. Each generation accumulates physical capital and knowledge and indeed by conventional yardsticks (such as GNP) such accumulations have been so substantial as to leave each generation much better off than its predecessors. It is possible to argue that such accumulations are insufficient, although in the context of continuously rising conventional living standards such an argument is not especially convincing. Alternatively, it may be suggested that the resource base is eroded and the physical and social environment allowed to deteriorate so that sooner or later the quality of life and perhaps also material consumption must begin to fall. These problems may arise from externalities (especially environmental externalities and fiscal deterrents to saving, viz. taxes on unearned income, capital gains, bequests and other capital transfers) but anti-growth writers often suggest also 'facile optimism', myopia and generational selfishness. Again the critic would do well to address his strictures to the population at large, without whose support, any government is virtually powerless.

It is worth noting that aid raises rather similar issues. Often, in the interests of growth, countries are niggardly in the aid they give to poorer

[30]This point is indeed appreciated by some of the opponents of growth, see e.g. several papers D. H. Meadows (ed.), *Alternatives to Growth I: A Search for Sustainable Futures* (Cambridge, Mass., 1977).

countries or to their own disadvantaged majorities. Generosity, to the poor and to our descendants, must come from the people.

3.5. The Distributional Issue

The relationship between growth and distribution is not clear. Certainly, rising GNP makes it easier to equalise incomes but equalisation, by damaging incentives and directing purchasing power to those with a low marginal propensity to save, is likely to damage growth.[31] However, it is useful to discuss the issue in more general terms. Firstly, there is a pervasive conflict between efficiency and distribution. In general, efficiency is promoted by penalising or rewarding each decision maker according to the marginal effects of his actions on others. The market mechanism is an approximation to such a system of rewards and penalties; a government pursuing efficiency will attempt to adjust these incentives by fiscal or other means. But if the outcome is *efficient*, it is not necessarily *fair*. In particular, those with poor endowments of relevant skills and/or wealth will receive low returns, possibly not even sufficient on which to subsist. The answer to this is of course redistribution, typically comprising grants to the poor financed by taxes from the rich. Unfortunately, however, such taxes and subsidies interfere with the efficiency conditions, providing a variety of disincentives (not only to work, but to train, to accept responsibility and to save) as well as incentives to tax avoidance and evasion. Additionally, substantial costs are involved in tax collection and in complying with the demands of the system. In general, the higher the tax rates the stronger the mis-allocations and the greater the compliance costs. This gives rise to the well-known conflict between efficiency and distribution.

The issue is independent (though the *magnitude* of the conflict may not be) of the precise nature of the efficiency objectives. Thus conservation, like growth, will conflict with distribution to a greater or less extent and compromises must be sought.

One partial escape from the conflict is to encourage small-scale activity (small firms, small settlements etc.) where, within the group, formal incentives can be supplemented or replaced by informal pressures and motives of altruism.[32] This is indeed often recommended by anti-growth writers.[33] A supplementary measure is the reduction of mobility, for the mechanisms discussed require some stability of group

---

[31]The redirection of purchasing power gives more weight to the (present-oriented) preferences of the poor. The slowing of growth is to this extent appropriate. By contrast, the damage to incentives represents a clear loss of economic efficiency.
[32]M. Olson, Jr., *The Logic of Collective Action* (Cambridge, Mass., 1965).
[33]e.g. E. F. Schumacher, *Small is Beautiful* (London, 1973); Daly, op.cit.; E. Goldsmith, *Blueprint for survival*, (Harmondsworth, 1976--reprinted from *Ecologist*, 1972).

membership.[34] The social and distributional advantages are however likely to be at the expense of economies of scale, so that there is again some conflict with material affluence, although arguably this could be offset by the satisfaction of life in a small community.

Change (and not only in the quest of growth) has important distributional consequences. The poor are particularly vulnerable to the adverse impacts of change—thus the old suffer most from the loss of familiar landmarks and changes in social *mores*, the unskilled are most prone to structural unemployment and poor areas are generally chosen for new urban roads (in order to minimise cost). Change also heightens awareness of inequality. Thus, in a more static society (as before the Industrial Revolution), positions are more likely to be accepted as unalterable. Whether this is desirable is debatable: which is better—an unequal society in which all are happy in their inequality, or a more equal one in which the inequalities which remain are deeply resented and aggressively contested?

3.6. *The Evidence*

Thus far, the allegations of the anti-growth school have been recorded without comment. In fact one of the most striking features of the Growth Debate is the lack of evidence; positions (on both sides) have been supported largely on the basis of the most casual empiricism.

A distinction should be made between areas where better evidence would be valuable and ones where it would not. For example, the historical question of the effect of economic growth on social welfare is not only academic but unanswerable unless the alternative to economic growth can be clearly specified (see Section 1). This has never been attempted and would indeed be somewhat difficult. Futuristic questions about ultimate resource depletion and environmental degradation are unanswerable for a different reason, namely the inherent uncertainty surrounding the key factor of technical progress. Extrapolation of past experience either à Meadows or à Nordhaus[35] is unilluminating and carefully prepared inventories of ultimate resource stocks are of limited value. This is not to say that the interests of the distant future should be ignored, rather that their interests are not significantly furthered by elaborate exercises in model-building or data gathering. The problem is one of decision-making under extreme and largely irremediable uncertainity.

Turning to more promising areas for research, evidence is already being sought on the impact of economic activities on the physical environment (and hence on people), if with insufficient vigour. The

[34]A. O. Hirschman, *Exist, Voice and Loyalty* (Cambridge, Mass., 1971).
[35]Meadows *et al*, op.cit., and W. D. Nordhaus, 'World Dynamics: Measurement Without Data', *Economic Journal* (Dec. 1973).

major lacuna concerns the impact of economic activity on social attitudes and behaviour. The more extreme manifestations, e.g. crime, vandalism, industrial strife, mental illness, family break-up, terrorism, are perhaps particularly important, but the determinants of friendliness, social concern etc. also merit investigation. After all, in a society in which the basic necessities of life are met, the quality of personal relationships (not only with friends but with workmates and casual acquaintances) is surely a more important ingredient both of happiness and richness of life than material possessions or even the quality of the physical environment.

The determinants of these phenomena have been studied, but from a rather restricted viewpoint in which the present framework of society, its aspirations and broad economic policies are taken as given. In the short run this is only realistic, but it does leave almost totally unanswered the questions raised by the anti-growth school. Indeed some of the findings of social science may, in a wider context, be totally misleading. For example it is generally accepted, on the basis of cross-section evidence, that poverty is a major cause of crime; but, through time, as societies get richer, crime increases.[36] Among possible explanations are the following: (i) crime depends on perceptions of deprivation which depend on relative poverty. Over time, any narrowing of inequality has been outweighed by heightened perception of inequalities that remain. (ii) the secular increase in crime is due to such concommitants of growth as competitiveness and mobility (generating rootlessness). No great weight should be placed on these particular hypotheses which have the flimsiest empirical basis. The point is rather that these or rival hypotheses to explain such key phenomena as crime are vitally important and should be vigorously investigated. It is deeply depressing that, a full decade after the publication of *The Costs of Economic Growth*, so little should have been done in examining the real issues.

4. Recent Slow Growth

The British economy (like many others) has experienced unusually slow growth over the last few years. It is worth considering what light this experience can shed on the issues raised in this paper.

In general, one may say that the experience has not been pleasant. Not only have living standards risen very slowly if at all, but the economy has experienced heavy unemployment, inflation and industrial strife and important social services have had to be cut back. At first sight these facts seem to bear out the views of the pro-growth school. But it is important to recognise that recent slow growth was both sudden and unplanned.

---

[36]Similar arguments apply to a wide variety of social problems, which are both concentrated among the poor and increasing over time.

Consider the causes. To a minor extent, slow growth may have stemmed from a diversion of resources from 'productive' purposes to social services, pollution control, etc., arguably a desirable and deliberate attempt to trade GNP for unmeasured components of social welfare. The merits of such shifts may be disputed but clearly the impact on growth is not a relevant criterion. The main factor involved, however, was a tightening of the constraints facing the economy. Some of these were external, notably the sharp rises in the prices of oil and other raw materials, which have necessitated a diversion of resources to exports. Additionally, the short-run trade-off between inflation and unemployment deteriorated and, moreover, the government was converted to the need to consider the longer-term impact on inflation of its employment policies. For both these reasons, the amount of slack in the economy was allowed to increase.

Now, whatever social objectives are adopted, a tightening of constraints may be expected to hinder their attainment and thus reduce social welfare to below what it would otherwise have been. Such an outcome is admittedly not certain for, if social choice mechanisms are sufficiently defective, then the imposition of additional constraints could conceivably improve social choices. (In that externalities associated with new technologies often prove difficult to control, this possibility is not altogether fanciful).

Of course, individual groups (e.g. environmentalists) are likely to judge social choices in terms of their own values and preferences. Using their (possibly atypical) criteria, it is rather more likely that additional constraints improve social choices. Even so, in practice, such groups are likely to view enforced slow growth with mixed feelings. There is on the one hand a gain from reduced road building (for example), but on the other a loss from reduced expenditure on pollution control. From this viewpoint, the effects are arbitrary and indiscriminate, somewhat as considered in the context of ZEG in Section 1. This is certainly not the kind of slow growth that the environmentalist or anti-growthman has in mind.

Another important consideration is the relative suddenness of the onset of slow growth and the various factors which brought it about. It has, for example, been difficult to adapt to the sharp changes in relative prices and one result has been structural unemployment. People accustomed to steadily rising living standards, have strongly resisted static ones and this resistance, besides directly indicating a welfare loss, has provoked industrial strife and aggravated inflation. This is not strictly a problem of slow growth but rather one of decelerating growth.

One implication of this line of thought is that it is unwise to promote rising living standards if there is a serious possibility that such a trend cannot be maintained. This point is indeed emphasised by resource pessimists, who call for a far-sighted and gradual adaption to the cessation of growth which they see as inevitable. More immediately, it seems probable that, as North Sea oil flows diminish in the 1980's, growth will again slow down; this too is a problem which should be anticipated.

The 1970's have greatly added to the variety of available data for assessing the implications of slow growth. But this superficial examination has indicated the care required in interpretation if misleading conclusions are to be avoided.

5. Conclusions

(i)   GNP and its growth are crude and irrelevant aggregates and unsuitable as focuses for policy. Neither indiscriminate growth nor indiscriminate halting of growth are likely to be beneficial (Section 1).

(ii) Even if for 'GNP' we substitute some more complete measure of welfare and for 'economic growth' the growth in this wider measure (call this 'progress'), it must be recognised that 'progress' involves considerable costs. The principle of these are

    (a) current sacrifice, including the costs of *change*

    (b) effects on the distant future via resource depletion and progressive environmental deterioration.

(Sections 2.2., 3.2.).

(iii) The need to control externalities is generally agreed. However insufficient recognition is generally given to the range, importance and pervasiveness of externalities and to various difficulties of control. As a result current policies may be seriously inadequate. (Section 3.1.).

(iv) Much of the anti-growth case is directed against the inappropriateness of individual preferences, especially through ignorance and generational selfishness. There is rather little that a democratically-based government can (or should?) do to correct such preferences. Such criticisms must therefore be directed primarily at the people rather than the government. (Sections 3.3., 3.4.).

(v)   Many of the anti-growth arguments are based on disputed assertions concerning cause and effect, notably on the relationship between economic activity and a wide range of social phenomena. Virtually no research has been done to investigate these vital questions. Vigorous investigation should be mounted as a matter of urgency. (Section 3.6.).

3

THE LABOUR MARKET
IN A SLOW GROWING ECONOMY

by Andrew Dean*

Organisation for Economic Co-operation and Development, Paris.

1. Introduction

The most obvious and tragic feature of the labour market in the last
five years of slow growth is the intolerably high level of unemployment
from which we now suffer. This chapter suggests, although not all
economists would agree with this, that by far the most important reason
for the present high level of unemployment is that growth has been so
low. That growth has indeed been remarkably low in the last five years
is not controversial; whatever reservations one might have about the
measurement of GDP and its usefulness as an indicator of welfare one
can hardly dispute that the United Kingdom, like many other countries,
has experienced a far lower growth rate, and for a more sustained period,
than at any other time in the post-war period. Latest figures show that
the level of GDP was almost exactly the same in 1977 as it had been in
1973; during the intervening period there had been two years of negative
growth (1974 and 1975). In fact the latest Blue Book on National
Income and Expenditure, which has recently been published, uses
1975 prices as compared to the 1970 prices hitherto used for cal-
culating such estimates and this change has the fortuitous effect
of apparently boosting the growth rate by about half per cent per year
in those years since North Sea oil has become important.[1] Nevertheless,
even such a revaluation will not disguise the fact that we have recently
experienced a period of slow growth which has been unprecedented in
the post-war period. The experience this year (1978) is slightly different;

*The author is grateful to colleagues at the National Institute for comments and
discussion on this topic but presents these views in a personal capacity.
[1]For an explanation of why this change in the measured growth occurs when the
national accounts are revalued see A. J. H. Dean, 'North Sea Oil and the Growth
Rate', *National Institute Economic Review* (Feb. 1978).

most economic forecasters seem agreed that growth this year may be around three per cent. But the outlook beyond this year is for a period of lower growth once again, although not at such low rates as in the 1973-77 period.

Although I have mentioned that revaluation to 1975 prices will, because of the large change in the relative price of oil and the development of domestic oil production on a large scale during the period, have the fortuitous effect of increasing the apparent growth rate of GDP by about half per cent a year for some years, the employment consequences of this increase are minimal. The total numbers of workers involved in North Sea oil production probably amount to no more than about 50,000, or one fifth of one per cent of the workforce. The major employment gain which arises from North Sea oil occurs indirectly through the improvement to the balance of payments; this permits the economy to grow at a faster rate. The calculation is not a simple one, however, because the gain on the balance of payments which accrues from the development of North Sea oil production also leads to a higher-than-otherwise exchange rate, which is detrimental to exporting and import-competing industries. On balance the effect of North Sea oil on employment is much smaller than commonly supposed and in no way leads us to salvation from the present high levels of unemployment.

In choosing the theme of this conference as the economic and social consequences of slow growth I have assumed that the President has had it in mind that growth will indeed be lower than the pre-recession average. This paper will, however, look backwards and forwards; at the experience over the 1973-77 period as well as the prospects for the next ten or twenty years. The paper starts by looking at the current unemployment situation and at the nature of the present unemployment. It then looks at the prospects for unemployment, at Government policy on employment, and at the consequences of continued slow growth.

2. The Current Unemployment Situation

Unemployment in the United Kingdom, excluding school leavers and seasonally adjusted, is currently standing at just under 1.4 million; including school leavers and without seasonal adjustment it is over 1.6 million. The highest previous peak it had reached in the post-war period had been just over 900,000 in the winter of 1972, and before that just under 600,000 in the winter of 1963. Unemployment has now been over the magical one million mark for 36 consecutive months. Of course compared with the 1930s, when unemployment was above 20 per cent of insured workers for over two years, the recent figures of six per cent unemployed may seem mild. But in the context of the post-war period they are unusually high. In the 1950s and 1960s full employment, or at least very low unemployment, was the accepted norm, not only in

Britain but in other industrialised countries. The way in which this situation was so quickly and drastically changed is shown in Figure 3.1.

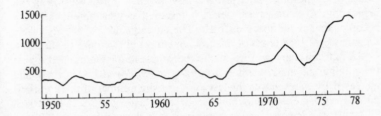

Fig. 3.1. Unemployment excluding school-leavers 1950–1978

At one time a figure of half a million unemployed was enough to make headline news; now more than a million unemployed is accepted rather calmly, albeit reluctantly. One reason for this bland acceptance of the situaion is undoubtedly that a Labour Government is in office; it is surely inconceivable that there would not have been a far more vocal protest against Government policy had the Conservatives been in power. The existence of unemployment and social security benefits, which are now generous compared to what was available in the past, may also have muted the protests. A further reason is that there is a widespread feeling that events are really beyond our control. Ever since the 1973 oil crisis and the ensuing world recession there has been much talk that a country like Britain, acting alone, cannot, because of balance of payments constraints, attempt a one country economic recovery. The existence of very large OPEC surpluses has deflated the world economy. It is only if correspondingly large deficits are accepted elsewhere that the world economy can be prompted to move again, and one country such as Britain, with a fragile balance of payments, cannot move ahead unilaterally. That, at least, is what one might call the international Keynesian position and it is one that was broadly accepted at the recent Bonn summit meeting. Even more pessimistic however is the monetarist view which denies that reductions in unemployment can be achieved by demand management policies; according to that view any fiscal or monetary stimulus is eventually reflected in higher inflation and no output or employment gain. The ultimate in pessimism is provided by one of the monetary journalists who has recently claimed 'that neither of these opposite courses (increased or reduced budget deficits and monetary targets)—nor the middle one actually adopted at the summit—will be very successful in eliminating the so-called cyclical element in unemployment'.[2]

Even given this new pessimism, the lack of reaction to present levels of unemployment, a fact which has been specifically noted in a special House of Commons report just recently issued,[3] is both surprising and depressing. As soon as a problem is regarded as inevitable its solution becomes that much more difficult. The consequences of a fairly placid acceptance of high levels of unemployment require require spelling out.

An extraordinary feature of the recent rise in unemployment is that the number of male workers *becoming unemployed* has not actually increased by much. Over the last ten years the number of male workers moving onto the unemployment register has averaged 2.9 million each year with the largest number being just over three million in 1975 and the smallest number 2.6 million in 1973. For women, as Table 3.1. indicates, the position has been slightly different, with a decline in the inflow from just over to just under one million between 1967 and 1973 and then a rapid rise to 1.7 million in 1977. The main explanation for the increase in the *stock* of unemployed, from not much more than half a million in 1973 to more than 1.3 million in 1977, does not lie with the increase in the *flows* of unemployed persons but with the *average duration* of unemployment. It is this feature of the present unemployment which is so unacceptable. That view is based on the value judgement that a situation where half a million workers become unemployed each week but remain unemployed for only two weeks each is preferable to 50,000 becoming unemployed each week for twenty weeks each. Both result in an unemployed stock of one million persons but the former results in only temporary inconvenience whilst the latter is likely to cause genuine hardships. Of course repeated spells of even short-duration unemployment are also likely to result in great hardship.

The increase in the duration of unemployment during the present recession has really been rather startling. The estimated average duration of spells of unemployment ending during the year has increased for men from nine weeks in 1973 to seventeen weeks in 1977, for women from five weeks to eleven weeks (see Table 3.1.). These are very substantial increases, and since they are only averages indicate that some spells of unemployment must be becoming extremely long. This is reflected in the fact that at the most recent count, in April, there were 332,000 unemployed persons in Great Britain who had been out of work for over a year, 270,000 males and 62,000 females, representing just under a

[2]Samuel Brittan, 'A New Approach to Unemployment', *Financial Times*, Aug. 10 1978.
[3]House of Commons Expenditure Committee Thirteenth Report, Session 1977–78, *People and Work, Prospects for Jobs and Training* (London, 1978).

quarter of the total number of unemployed. A further 284,000 had been unemployed for between twenty-six and fifty-two weeks, so that a total of over 600,000 persons had been out of work for over half a year. In contrast, in the 1950s and 1960s it was very rare for those unemployed for more than six months to exceed 100,000 and *total* unemployment exceeded 600,000 in only two of the twenty years. Furthermore, as unemployment rises, there is a tendency for the long term unemployed to become a larger and larger proportion of the total. Thus by April 1978 forty-four per cent of the unemployed had been out of work for at least half a year, compared to around twenty-five per cent in the 1950s.

TABLE 3.1.
Stocks and Flows of Unemployment in Britain

Year	Annual average unemployment, excluding school leavers, (thousands).		Annual inflow to unemployment, (millions).		Estimated average duration of spells of unemployment ending in year (weeks).	
	Male	Female	Male	Female	Male	Female
1967	413	96	3.0	1.1	7.1	4.4
1968	453	85	3.0	1.0	7.7	4.2
1969	453	78	3.0	1.0	7.7	4.2
1970	485	82	3.0	1.0	8.4	4.5
1971	625	112	3.0	1.0	11.6	6.0
1972	686	130	2.7	0.9	12.1	6.5
1973	488	93	2.6	0.9	9.1	4.9
1974	490	91	2.8	1.0	9.6	4.9
1975	722	169	3.1	1.3	14.1	7.8
1976	941	282	2.9	1.5	16.5	10.5
1977	976	347	2.9	1.7	17.1	11.2

Source: *Cambridge Economic Policy Review*, (Mar. 1978); based on data in *Department of Employment Gazettes*. Figures refer to Great Britain.

So effectively the incidence of unemployment becomes concentrated on particular individuals as the level of unemployment rises. Furthermore, so long as unemployment remains high or continues to grow, the numbers of long-term unemployed increase still further. Judged by past recessions this trend to long term unemployment even continues for some time after the total of unemployed has peaked. It is clear that long term unemployment is itself a handicap to getting a job. Whether it is motivation which disappears, whether employment offices tend to overlook the 'old lags' or whether employers tend to discriminate against the long term unemployed, is not clear; but it is depressingly true that the longer a person stays unemployed the more difficult it is for him to find a job. Recent research by Nickell has shown that the conditional probability of obtaining work declines rapidly after six months and falls to very low levels thereafter.[4] Additional evidence is also provided by surveys of the characteristics of the unemployed which show that the proportion of jobless who are considered to have a good chance of finding work declines with the duration of unemployment. This is not surprising, given that good candidates will get jobs more quickly and never reach the longer duration categories, but that is hardly reassuring for the long term unemployed. Insofar as this development creates a group of 'unemployables' it also has very serious consequences beyond the present recession. It is therefore especially important to ensure that much attention is devoted to this group; an acceptance of their situation will only mean that we are committed to high levels of unemployment for long periods ahead.

We have concentrated so far on the long-term unemployed, but one should not forget that recession has an unequal impact on unemployment in other ways. Coloured workers are known to suffer disproportionately during recessions. Between 1974 and 1977, when total unemployment increased by 120 per cent, unemployment amongst coloured workers increased by 350 per cent. Young people have also been hit disproportionately hard; on this subject the facts are well known and well documented so do not need repeating here.[5] One should perhaps add, however, that, firstly, high rates of youth unemployment have been a particular feature of this recession and have been common to all the industrialised nations, and, secondly, that unemployment of young people is thought to be particularly harmful in destroying the 'work ethic'. It is only natural, when there is high unemployment, for employers to prefer mature, possibly trained men to inexperienced youngsters in recruiting new workers. This will continue to be the case so long as slow growth and high unemployment continues.

[4]S. Nickell, 'Estimating the Probability of Leaving Unemployment' LSE mimeo (1977), forthcoming, *Econometrica*.
[5]See, for example, the Holland Report, *Young People and Work*, Manpower Services Commission (1977), or Table 110 of any recent issue of the *Department of Employment Gazette*.

An illustration of the greater susceptibility of young workers to unemployment when the number of workless increases is given in a recent Department of Employment study.[6] This study of unemployment among young workers shows that youth unemployment moves in step with the overall level of unemployment but is subject to larger variations. Thus a one per cent increase in unemployment among male workers has been accompanied in the past by a 1.7 per cent increase in unemployment among young males. For females a one per cent rise in unemployment has been accompanied by a three per cent rise among the young. One hopes that such movements are reversible and that a future decline in overall unemployment will lead to a more than proportionate decline in youth unemployment. It is a belief in such an effect which prompts some people to recommend as a solution to youth unemployment not just special measures (such as the Youth Opportunities Programme) but a general increase in demand.

Whether such a stimulus to demand would reduce unemployment will depend to a large extent on the nature of the present unemployment, a problem which we now explore. This is an urgent question because the social consequences for the relatively disadvantaged groups mentioned above will if anything become more acute if the present levels of high unemployment are not reversed.

3. The Nature of the Present Unemployment

There is some confusion as to the proximate causes of the present unemployment. It has become common to categorise unemployment in three ways frictional, structural and cyclical. The former two, together with the now rather unimportant seasonal component of unemployment, had been discussed at the beginning of the century by people such as Pigou and Beveridge. Cyclical, or demand deficient, unemployment was something which was invented by Keynes in the 1930s. In the period from then until the 1970s increases in unemployment were regarded as being cyclical in origin and thus susceptible to treatment by raising the level of aggregate demand. This changed the whole tenor of the debate about unemployment. Nevertheless, there is still much disagreement about the nature of the present unemployment and the extent to which it is possible to classify it into separate types. In this section we therefore look at these various classifications and discuss whether it is relevant and useful to divide up unemployment in this way. We start by mentioning seasonal unemployment, then introduce frictional and structural unemployment, and lastly look at cyclical unemployment.

Seasonal unemployment, which was first mentioned by economists as a winter phenomenon, reflecting lower activity in agriculture con-

6*Department of Employment Gazette* (Aug. 1978).

struction etc. in the winter months, is really self-explanatory. At the time that Beveridge was first writing about unemployment at the turn of the century this type of unemployment was more serious than today when the vagaries of the weather affect the total level of economic activity far less. Furthermore, although seasonal fluctuations are still quite marked they are now connected most importantly with man-made causes such as regular holiday periods.

The most important group of seasonally unemployed workers today is not out-of-work crop pickers or building labourers during the winter months, but unemployed school leavers and students. Because, until recent years at least, these groups were felt to be only a temporary problem, soon passing off the unemployment register, they are often excluded from the unemployment figures. In the last year there have been as many as 250,000 unemployed school leavers (July 1978) and 145,000 adult students (September 1977) on the register. The majority of these pass off the register very rapidly. Nevertheless, although the number of adult students registered for vacation employment subsides very rapidly as term restarts the numbers of school leavers remaining on the register has in recent years tailed off far less slowly.[7] In the summer of 1977, for instance, there were at one stage 253,000 unemployed school leavers on the unemployment register. At Christmas, including a few new leavers, there were 60,000, and even in March there were still 40,000 on the register. This is a very recent phenomenon, and one which clearly has a close connection with the state of the labour market generally. As recently as the school-leaving year 1973 (when total unemployment was below half a million) there had been as few as 23,000 school leavers in the summer peak (August 1973) and as few as 2,000 left on the register by December. Unemployment amongst school leavers had until recently always been seasonal but never been substantial in the post-war period. Now this type of unemployment is substantial, though still remaining seasonal. One must seriously consider whether the total of unemployment excluding school leavers is the best way to measure the impact of unemployment.

Frictional unemployment is also a type of unemployment which was discussed by economists such as Beveridge at the turn of the century. It is that unemployment which results from workers moving between jobs, but the distinction between it and *structural* unemployment is by no means clear. The latter is said to arise when there is a mismatch of jobs between different skills, occupations and regions due to a change in the structure of industry. Beveridge, in his 1944 Report,[8] tried to draw a

[7]For an examination of this problem see the report of the working party chaired by G. Holland, op.cit., or A. J. H. Dean, 'Unemployment among School Leavers; an Analysis of the Problem', *National Institute Economic Review* (Nov. 1976).
[8]W. H. Beveridge, 'Full Employment in a Free Society' (London, 1944).

precise distinction between the two as follows:

> "Frictional unemployment is unemployment caused by the individuals who make up the labour supply not being completely interchangeable and mobile units so that, though there is an unsatisfied demand for labour, the unemployed workers are not of the right sort or in the right place to meet that demand."

whereas,
> "Structural unemployment means the unemployment arising in particular industries through a change in demand so great that it may be regarded as affecting the main economic structure of a country."

This distinction is not clear however. If there is unsatisfied demand then that structural unemployment just described is effectively a type of frictional employment. On the other hand, if there is no unsatisfied demand then that unemployment is part of what became known, following Keynes, as demand deficient or cyclical unemployment, which we now consider.

Cyclical unemployment is that unemployment which is associated with a lack of effective demand, or demand deficiency. This type of unemployment had been suggested by Keynes in the 'General Theory' in 1936. It would probably be fair to suggest that most of the discussion of unemployment in the next twenty years was concentrated on Keynes' concept of the deficiency of effective demand, partly to the exclusion of the previous concepts. This was despite the importance which people like Beveridge still attached to the non-demand deficient explanations of unemployment. In the 1944 Report he ascribed the 1930s depression to two factors, not just one; firstly, "the drastic reduction of overseas demand . . . which led to chronic structural unemployment during almost the whole period between the two wars" and secondly, "the cyclical depression which followed 1929 and . . . was more severe than most previous depressions".[9] I do not know whether the ordering of these two factors had any significance at all but it is clear that there was less emphasis on demand deficiency than was general in the 1950s and 1960s.

For much of the post-war period it was believed that Keynes had solved the problem of unemployment. Demand management policies could be pursued which would adjust the level of demand in the economy so as to produce levels of full employment or near full-employment.

It was only in the 1960s that the problem of reconciling full employment with a low rate of inflation reawakened interest in the two related issues of what the previous or other causes of unemployment were, and

[9]Beveridge, op.cit., para. 26.

what that level of 'full' employment actually is. This problem was appreciated by the British Government in the mid-1970s. In a notorious speech to the Labour Party Conference in September 1976, the Prime Minister, James Callaghan, spelt out what he saw to be the realities of the post-war economy:

> 'We used to think that you could just spend your way out of a recession and increase employment by cutting taxes and boosting Government spending. I tell you in all candour that that option no longer exists and insofar as it ever did exist, it worked by injecting inflation into the economy. And each time that happened the average level of unemployment has risen. Higher inflation followed by higher un-employment. That is the history of the last twenty years.'

This way of looking at things led to a redefinition of structural unemployment as 'that amount of unemployment which cannot be removed by monetary and fiscal policy without creating substantial continuing inflation.'[10] This became known by the monetarists as the natural rate of unemployment.

We see from the above that the concepts of different types of un-employment are not well defined. In particular, there is some confusion over whether structural and frictional unemployment can be separated or whether one is just a special case of the other.[11] In fact it becomes clear that when we attempt measurement it is not easy to separate the two, so we here treat them as the same category of structural employ-ment.

There has been much talk in recent years, perhaps because of the depth of the recession and more recently because of the development of microprocessors etc., of a further category of unemployment, namely technological unemployment. The argument is that modern industrial processes, which are very capital intensive and highly labour productive, require fewer and fewer workers than their predecessors. Furthermore, the advance of such machinery cannot be prevented because the most productive companies or countries are likely to be the most competitive and hence the most viable in the long term. However, technological unemployment can be subsumed under one of our previous categories. If the result of technological changes is to reduce aggregate demand

---

[10]B. R. Bergmann & D. E. Kaun, *Structural Unemployment in the United States* (Washington, 1966).

[11]One author has also pointed out that such classifications are commonly made on two bases, according to, firstly causes, where structural unemployment is a part of a frictional unemployment and, secondly, cures, where the opposite is true; see A. P. Thirlwall, 'Types of unemployment; with special reference to non-demand deficient unemployment in Great Britain', *Scottish Journal of Political Economy* (Feb. 1969).

then the resulting unemployment can be categorised as being demand-deficient. If, on the other hand, the general level of demand remains high, but jobs in one particular industry are lost through technological improvements whilst jobs in other industries or skills remain, then that is an example of structural unemployment. The evidence for a sharp rise in technological unemployment is actually rather negative. If such unemployment were a fact then one would expect to see signs of it in increased productivity, whereas the level of productivity in 1978 is much the same as in 1973, even in engineering where one might have expected large advances.[12]

One problem that arises from equating demand deficient unemployment with cyclical unemployment is that it implies that there is no cyclical element in structural unemployment. However, when there is an overall shortage of demand this worsens the job prospects for those workers who are suffering from structural unemployment. Thus structural unemployment is likely to be reduced as demand increases. Furthermore, as shortages of workers of the right type develop during the economic cycle employers are more likely to train or retrain workers and hence reduce some of the structural unemployment.

Although it may be difficult to distinguish between different types of unemployment it is nevertheless very important from the policy point of view. If the main cause of unemployment is found to be due to demand deficiency then the cure is likely to be found in appropriate monetary and fiscal policies.[13] If, on the other hand, the unemployment is diagnosed as being structural in character then any attempt to increase aggregate demand would have serious inflationary consequences. The solution to structural unemployment is via manpower policies; encouraging labour mobility and increasing training and retraining possibilities. In order to devise the correct unemployment policies one therefore wishes to know two things:

(i) What the minimal level of unemployment is which can be aimed at without producing inflationary consequences—this may be defined as the Keynesian 'full employment' rate or as the 'natural' rate of unemployment, depending on the school of thought;

(ii) How the level of unemployment is split between demand deficient and structural factors.

[12]This factor is also mentioned by the Cambridge Economic Policy Group in their *Economic Policy Review* (Mar. 1978).
[13]There has of course been much recent debate, re-echoing that concerning the 'Treasury view' in the inter-war period, as to whether an *effective* boost to demand is possible, given the possible 'crowding out' of any Government monetary or fiscal action. Although this debate is not yet resolved there does seem to be some agreement that there is scope for action when unemployment is above the full employment or natural rate.

From time to time the National Institute has examined these problems of measurement, the two most recent analyses being in the November 1973 and February 1977 issues of the *Review*. At the time of the first exercise, in 1973, the level of unemployment was around 500,000, or 2.2 per cent of all employees, and the concern then was to establish whether the economy, in the immediate period ahead, was likely to 'overheat' and whether the optimal level of unemployment had been reached. The Institute concluded that the 'immediate' target should be between 300–400,000, i.e. one and a quarter per cent to one and three quarter per cent of the labour force. They thought that ' . . . macro-economic management has an important role to play in bringing down the general level of unemployment, but as that level falls the relative significance of sectoral policies addressed to different regions, industries or occupations, and to retraining and deployment of labour become increasingly important'.[14] As it happens the total of unemployed excluding students and school leavers reached its low point of 402,000 in Great Britain in December 1973 and has been rising, almost without interruption, ever since.

By the time of the second National Institute exercise, conducted in the winter of 1976–77, the issue of the exact magnitude of full employment may have seemed rather unimportant, for by then unemployment had reached 1.3 million, where it is today (after peaking at close to 1.4 million at the end of 1977). Despite the size of the then unemployment and despite the economic commentators who claimed that the 'natural' rate of unemployment was now about one million, the Institute, having surveyed the evidence, concluded that the level of full employment probably meant no more than 450–550,000 (two to two and a half per cent) unemployed.[15] It seemed difficult to explain the move from two per cent unemployment in 1973 to almost six per cent in 1977 as being anything but mainly due to depressed demand.

Various factors of a structural nature were considered but none seemed likely to have increased by a significant amount. The effect of the Redundancy Payments Act in December 1965 has often been suggested as a reason for higher unemployment levels because of longer periods of job search, but the average number of payments made has only amounted to about 20,000 a month and those payments have represented only about three months of the average earner's previous net pay.[16] Earnings-

[14]*National Institute Economic Review* (Nov. 1973), p. 33.
[15]*National Institute Economic Review* (Feb. 1977), p. 51.
[16]See the Department of Employment's Working Party report, summarised in the *Department of Employment Gazette* (Oct. 1976), which estimated a maximum effect of 20,000 on the level of unemployment, and also two other studies; 'Effects of the Redundancy Payments Act', Office of Population Censuses and Surveys (1971), and D. Mackay and G. Reid, 'Redundancy, Unemployment and Manpower Policy', *Economic Journal* (Dec. 1972).

related benefits, which were introduced in October 1966, have been mentioned as a major reason for the rise in structural unemployment;[17] but until the present recession the largest number of recipients at any one time was 166,000 in May 1972. Given that many of those would have been unemployed anyway it is difficult to believe that more than about 50,000 would be added to unemployment in a peak year as a result of such benefits. The evidence on other factors such as increased registration rates, increasing maldistribution of labour, and the growth of union monopoly power is hard to quantify. One factor, the pace of structural change (in industrial terms) has been examined by Turvey, who concluded that ' . . . statistics for a number of countries (including the United Kingdom) fail to show that industrial structural change has been more rapid in recent years than it was in the 1960s. Hence one possible major cause of increasing structural unemployment was not operative'.[18]

Recent work at the OECD has used different methods, examining labour demand and supply separately and deducing figures for cyclical and other types of unemployment by rather indirect but ingenious methods.[19] Their examination covers only the years 1974 to 1976 but the estimates which they produce for the United Kingdom (they also cover eight other major countries) are rather interesting. Cyclical unemployment of only 0.1 per cent of the labour force is estimated for 1974, the remainder of the 2.2 per cent actual unemployment rate being accounted for by frictional unemployment (2.0 per cent) and capital-shortage unemployment (0.1 per cent). By 1976, when the actual unemployment rate had increased to 5.0 per cent, cyclical unemployment had grown to 1.7 per cent, frictional unemployment had risen marginally to 2.4 per cent whilst capital-shortage unemployment had increased to 0.9 per cent. These figures must be treated with some caution, as the OECD themselves warn, because of the 'operational difficulties of obtaining accurate results with this approach', but the results are interesting. For they suggest that what is needed is a dual approach to the problem; demand management policies which will directly affect the cyclical component and have secondary affects on the frictional and capital shortage components, and manpower policies, which will act more directly on the latter two. In the short run the target level of unemployment must be the actual rate less the cyclical element (i.e. just over three per cent in

[17]See for instance Z. A. Maki and O. Spindler, 'The Effect of Unemployment Compensation on the Rate of Unemployment in Great Britain', *Oxford Economic Papers* (Nov. 1975).
[18]R. Turvey, 'Structural Change and Structural Unemployment', *International Labour Review* (Sept.-Oct. 1977).
[19]O.E.C.D., *A Medium-term Strategy for Employment and Manpower Policies* (Paris, 1978).

1976) but in the longer run it is possible both to expand capacity by encouraging investment and to reduce frictional unemployment by adequate manpower policies, so that the full employment level of unemployment can be reduced.

The estimates presented so far have been in terms of the Keynesian concept of full employment. Although monetarists reject demand management policies as a cure to high levels of unemployment there are some areas in which they are in agreement with the Keynesian analysis. The Keynesian full employment level of unemployment turns out to depend on the same structural factors which determine the natural rate of unemployment.[20] Also the estimates of the magnitude of the natural rate of unemployment are, surprisingly, not substantially greater than Keynesian estimates of the full employment rate, although the natural rate is thought to have increased rapidly in the last few years.

Estimates of the 'natural' rate of unemployment or of the minimal non-inflationary unemployment rate are widely available. They usually emerge as a byproduct of work on wage equations. The important fact is that such estimates vary through time. Thus Laidler[21] in 1975 thought the natural rate might be a 'little less than two per cent', Parkin, Sumner and Ward[22] in 1974 arrived at a figure of 1.7 per cent for the period 1956-71, Saunders[23] in 1973 estimated a variable natural rate of 2.1 per cent in 1963 and 1.9 per cent in 1970, and Gray, Parkin and Sumner[24] estimated a natural rate of 1.8 per cent for 1952-67 and 3.7 per cent for 1968-74. A more recent paper by Batchelor and Sheriff[25] attempts to decompose the level of unemployment into trend and cyclical components. From this analysis they are able to derive an unemployment rate consistent with fully anticipated inflation which is around one per cent in the early 1950s and rises to between three and four and a half per cent in 1977, depending on the specification of the equation used.

[20]For an interesting discussion of this idea see J. A. Trevithick, 'Inflation, the Natural Unemployment Rate and the Theory of Economic Policy', *Scottish Journal of Political Economy* (Feb. 1976).

[21]D. E. W. Laidler, 'The End of Demand Management', appended to M. Friedman, *Unemployment versus Inflation* (London, 1975).

[22] M. Parkin, M. Sumner and R. Ward, 'The Effects of Excess Demand, Generalised Expectations and Wage Price Controls on Wage Inflation in the U.K.', in K. Brunner & A. H. Meltzer (eds.) *The Economics of Price and Wage Controls* (Amsterdam, 1976).

[23]P. G. Saunders, 'The Expectations Hypothesis and the Natural Rate of Unemployment', Stirling University Discussion Paper No. 21 (1973).

[24] M. Gray, M. Parkin and M. Sumner, 'Inflation in the United Kingdom; Causes and Transmission Mechanisms', University of Manchester Discussion Paper 7518 (1975).

[25]R. A. Batchelor and T. D. Sheriff, 'Unemployment and Unanticipated Inflation in Post-War Britain', Centre for Banking and International Finance, City University, Discussion Paper No. 4 (Feb. 1978).

The interesting feature of these estimates of the natural rate of unemployment is that they all lie substantially below the present level of unemployment of around six per cent. This would seem to imply that it should be possible for unemployment to come down without undesirable inflationary consequences. Yet it is the apparent fear of renewed inflation and of the country's fragile balance of payments situation, as expressed in Mr. Callaghan's speech to the Labour Party Conference in 1976, which has prevented the Government from pursuing any widescale reflationary policies.

4. The Government's Economic Policy

The solutions which the present Government has been offering to the problems of high unemployment, given that it has felt constrained against any general reflationary action, have been twofold; first, a series of special measures, including employment subsidies, increased provision for training, and special youth programmes, and second, the industrial strategy.

The special measures are correctly regarded as palliatives. They were introduced as such at an early stage in the recession with the express hope that they would cushion the impact of unemployment until the coming world (and British) upturn. That upturn was a long time coming and so each of the schemes was either extended or replaced by a rather grander successor, so that by mid-1978 as many as 300,000 workers were being supported by these schemes and enormous sums of money had been committed. The advantage of many of the schemes was felt to be their low net cost once allowance had been made for paying less unemployment benefits and recouping money in additional taxes. But the net saving or creation of jobs has been highly uncertain, given that it is difficult to calculate either the displacement effect of such schemes or what the effect on jobs would have been if the expenditure on special measures had instead been put into either tax cuts or increased public expenditure.

In the short run the net effect of these schemes has been beneficial as regard jobs. In the longer run however the success of these schemes is far from clear. No permanent jobs have been created and some jobs in declining industries, especially textiles where the temporary employment subsidy has been heavily used, have been temporarily reprieved. Much of the retraining which has taken place has probably been unnecessary, given the low level of labour demand and the forecasts of continuing high unemployment. Furthermore, the labour market, in so far as it works, may have been unnecessarily distorted. Ultimately one must ask whether all the expenditure on special schemes actually means that additional jobs have been created. The question is a difficult one and the answer is not clear, but the present Government's claims that they have kept unemployment down by 300,000 are crude and undoubtedly far overstate the case.

The other arm of employment policy has been the industrial strategy. This was also devised at the start of the recession. It has always been intended as a means of boosting Britain's employment prospects through an improved net trade position brought about by increased competitiveness. It was soon realised, however, that increased competitiveness in manufacturing, to which the strategy was geared, would not necessarily lead to an increase in the number of jobs in manufacturing. The hoped-for rise in manufacturing productivity, which would enable the country to compete more effectively with other countries, might lead to a net loss of jobs. This would occur if the rise in productivity was greater than the increased output which it would generate. There were two problems, therefore; firstly that the increased productivity must logically precede the payoff in terms of output, thus generating a short-term reduction in employment, and secondly that the employment gain in manufacturing might never materialise.

The realisation of the latter problem led to a change in the presentation of the strategy. In a speech in Glasgow earlier this year the Chancellor pointed out that the gain to employment would most likely be generated not in the manufacturing sector itself but outside. The improved net trade performance of the manufacturing sector would enable the Government to reflate to an extent which would generate between 500,000 and one million jobs, mostly in non-manufacturing. This prospect has been challenged however by research work sponsored by the Manpower Services Commission at the Manpower Research Group at Warwick University.[26] They point out that ' . . . the government's industrial strategy will not suffice to increase domestic output *and* employment because, in so far as it is successful at all, its main impact is likely to be the encouragement of higher investment and productivity rather than the discovery of hitherto unexploited possibilities for increasing "non-price competiveness". We estimate that . . . the resulting boost to domestic production for export will be significantly less than is necessary to offset the employment effect of higher productivity. Moreover . . . the rest of the economy could only absorb one half of the loss in manu-facturing employment.'[27] That is indeed a gloomy account of the employment prospects of the industrial strategy but it is certainly a more realistic assessment than the Chancellor's.

Nevertheless the industrial strategy does at least aim at confronting the problem of competitiveness which lies behind the problem of Britain's

[26]R. M. Lindley (ed.), *Britain's Medium-Term Employment Prospects*, Manpower Research Group, (Warwick, 1978).
[27]Ibid. op. cit., p. 108.

low growth rate. The problem of how to accelerate the rate of growth without coming up against the balance of payments constraint is one that has exercised economists throughout the post-war period. It is one that has been receiving renewed attention and interest in the last year with the realisation that the development of North Sea oil is still leaving the country with an extremely 'fragile' balance of payments position. That particular topic is one that is being tackled by other speakers at this conference but it is perhaps worth mentioning some work by the Department of Employment on the association between trade performance and employment growth. A recent study of theirs which looked at the industrial performance of eighty-two separate sectors concluded that; 'There was a strong association between the growth of exports and higher rates of output, employment and productivity growth. This suggests that industries whose productivity is increasing fastest are able to remain internationally competitive and enjoy higher rates of export growth, which, in turn, raises growth rates of output and employment. Faster growing output then stimulates further growth of productivity, and so a virtuous circle is established.'[28] Unfortunately, and importantly for this conference, the converse argument is true and there is also a vicious circle of low output, employment and productivity growth.

5. The Prospects for Employment and Unemployment

It will not be difficult for anyone to guess at this stage that I am rather pessimistic about the future level of unemployment in this country. This pessimism comes both from the demand and supply side. On the demand side I have been asked to consider the consequences of slow growth, but I am anyway persuaded that the immediate prospects are not rosy. The latest National Institute *Review* indicates that growth is likely to fall off in 1979 following the rapid advance this year.[29] Taken with the large expected rise in the labour force, which is discussed below, this leads to a sharp projected rise in unemployment to 1.5 million (in Great Britain, excluding school leavers) by the end of 1979. Although there is expected to be a current account surplus of £2 billion by then, that would soon disappear in the event of further reflation, so that unemployment would still seem likely to remain high. In Table 3.2 I have summarised the view of other forecasting bodies on the prospects for unemployment. None of the forecasts presented there give any prospect of reducing unemployment below the present level apart from the

[28]R. Wragg and J. Robertson, 'Britain's Industrial Performance since the War', *Department of Employment Gazette* (May 1978).
[29]*National Institute Economic Review* (Aug. 1978).

Cambridge Economic Policy Group's import controls variant.[30] That particular forecast is regarded by some as rather unlikely, given the assumptions and trade elasticities which have been used to generate it.

TABLE 3.2.
Unemployment Projections, 1977–1990

		1977	1978	1979	1980	1981	1982	1985	1990
NIESR[a]		1.4	1.3	1.5	-	-	-	-	-
LBS[b]		1.323	1.329	1.379	1.427	1.447	-	-	-
CEPG[c]	(A)	-	1.460	1.656	1.809	-	-	2.930	4.623
	(B)	-	1.414	1.516	1.521	-	-	1.477	1.370
	(C)	-	1.393	1.381	1.321	-	-	0.973	0.497
MRG[d]		(1.332)[e]	-	-	-	-	2.259	-	-

(a) *National Institute Economic Review*, no. 85 (Aug. 1978); 4th quarter, rounded to nearest million, Great Britain, excluding school leavers, seasonally adjusted.
(b) London Business School, *Economic Outlook* vol. 2, no. 9 (June 1978). Wholly unemployed, Great Britain, annual average.
(c) Cambridge Economic Policy Group, *Economic Policy Review*, no. 4 (Mar. 1978); (A) orthodox policies, (B) devaluation strategy, (C) import controls strategy.
(d) Manpower Research Group, Warwick University, *Britain's Medium-Term Employment Prospects*, ed. Robert Lindley (Aug. 1978).
(e) 1976 figure.

Furthermore I do not see how the development of a new mercantilism could in any way benefit a nation such as Britain which must necessarily depend on trade for meeting many of her needs. It is also not clear how import controls can contribute to solving the problem of low industrial efficiency. To return to the main point, however, it is clear that on present policies we can expect little increase in employment in the next few years as the result of a large stimulus from demand.

This pessimism on the demand side is then compounded on the supply side. Not so long ago, when the American economist Edward Denison was investigating why growth rates in different countries differed, any

[30]The import controls argument has been presented to this conference by Wynne Godley (See Chapter 12). An alternative to his view is that presented by the National Institute, namely slow devaluation (to increase competitiveness), incomes policy (to cope with inflation and ensure that devaluation is effective) and a stimulus to demand to promote growth, reduce unemployment and to revive investment.

additions to the labour supply were regarded as a positive advantage in increasing a nations's productive potential. In present circumstances, however, the projected increase in the labour supply is regarded as a handicap, as another person to be added to the unemployment register. This is as a result of the present recession coinciding with an abnormally large growth in the labour force. This growth is due partly to a continuing increase in the female participation rate and partly to a large rise in the number of school leavers each year up to the mid-1980s. The peak annual increase in the labour force is expected to be some 264,000 in 1983, but an increase of an average 200,000 per annum is expected in the seven years from now to 1985; by 1991 there are expected to be a further two million in the working population.[31] If this projected growth in the labour force is to occur, then it is clear that a massive expansion of employment opportunities is necessary if the current unacceptably high levels of unemployment are to be reduced. Such an expansion is highly unlikely to take place if slow growth persists.

At this point therefore we should perhaps return to the theme of this paper—the labour market in a slow growing economy. I will first say something about the labour market as such and I will then return to the consequences of slow growth.

I do not want to talk narrowly about how the labour market is likely to change as a consequence of slow growth. My feeling is that there would be little change in the actual mechanics of the labour market, that methods of hiring and firing will remain much the same, that the collective bargaining scene will remain the jungle that it unfortunately is, and that government intervention in the labour market, which is considerable, will continue. In fact the term labour market is one that I have some difficulty with. I frequently use the term myself since it is widely understood to define an area of labour matters where a price (wages or earnings) and a quantity (employment and hours) are the central factors. But I am far from believing that the labour market as such operates as the perfect market described in the text books. Economic theory suggests that labour is paid the value of its marginal product and that employment is determined by a market clearing process in the same way as a goods market. However there are many reasons why the labour market in practice does not operate in a fully competitive fashion. It would be idle to deny that there is not a certain amount of imperfect competition, if not monopoly, amongst the buyers and sellers of labour (the employers and employees). A large part of the labour market is also characterised by output which is not directly marketed, especially in the public sector. Governments are also heavily involved in

---

[31]'Labour Force Projections; Further Estimates', *Department of Employment Gazette* (Apr. 1978).

the labour market through various pieces of employment legislation (including Wages Councils) and from time to time (and rather frequently in recent years) through incomes policies.[32] Traditional comparisons of pay between different groups, which tend to be cited in collective bargaining, also lead to distortions in market rates of pay. Professor Hayek recently summed up the situation as follows: 'The effect of the present system of wage determination in Britain is no less than that the country no longer has an internal price structure which guides the economical use of her resources'.[33] Thus discussion of the 'labour market' does not imply that the market ever operates in a competitive fashion although economists must admit that in the long run there are of course strong economic forces which will be important in determining the employment and pay in different industries and occupations.

However I do not expect the labour market as such to change in any startling way as a result of slow growth. On the other hand, as outlined earlier in the paper, the consequences of slow growth for the participants in the labour market are not encouraging. It is clear that a persistence of slow growth will mean that unemployment will remain high or become even higher. The numbers of those with long durations of un-employment would then increase, with particular groups, especially the young, the old, the educationally disadvantaged and certain ethnic groups, suffering disproportionately worse and enduring much higher than average levels of unemployment. Whilst there are clear economic losses involved in high unemployment it is the social consequences which are worse. It is worth repeating Beveridge's view that ' . . . the greatest evil of unemployment is not physical but moral, not the want which it may bring but the hatred and fear which it breeds'.[34]

There has been much discussion in recent years that, given persisting unemployment, we should consider various schemes of worksharing such as shorter hours or earlier retirement. The problem with these ideas is that they all have a cost. If workers were prepared to accept a cut in wages to match the loss in work input then the schemes could be used to reduce unemployment. If that does not happen then unit costs must be increased and that would mean both a loss of markets and an increase in living costs. A recent House of Commons inquiry on this subject reported that ' . . . despite the superficial appeal of this idea we must conclude that the combination of shorter hours, reduced unemployment

---

[32]For a discussion of the determination of relative rates of pay and the effects of incomes policies see A. J. H. Dean, 'Incomes Policies and Differentials', *National Institute Economic Review*, (Aug. 1978).

[33]F. A. Hayek, 'The Exploitation of Workers by Workers', *The Listener*, 17 Aug. 1978.

[34]Beveridge, op. cit.

and no increase in living costs can only be achieved simultaneously if there is also growth in the economy'.[35]

That brings us back once again to the central theme of slow growth. As far as the labour market consequences are concerned, the conclusion must be the simple one that slow growth of the sort we have recently been experiencing is likely to foster high unemployment and to impose unacceptable strains and misery on society. In this respect, therefore, this paper is in complete agreement with Beckerman's well known position in defence of economic growth,[36] even though that position was heavily qualified in his talk to this conference.

[35]House of Commons, op. cit., para. 356.
[36] Wilfred Beckerman, *In Defence of Economic Growth* (London, 1974).

4

WHO BEARS THE BURDEN OF UNEMPLOYMENT?

by Jon Stern*

Department of Health and Social Security

1. Alternative Measures of Unemployment Incidence

The conventional answer to the question in the title is to analyse the unemployment stock i.e. all those registered as unemployed at a given date. One reason for so doing is that it is a simple concept. In addition, the unemployment stock is reported monthly in the Department of Employment Gazette which also regularly publishes analyses of the stock such as the January and July age and duration analyses. Thus, it is quite common to see arguments like 'the young suffer disproportionately from unemployment' on the reasoning that in January 1978, 18.5 per cent of the unemployed were under 20[1] while only 7.8 per cent of the estimated labour force for 1978 was under 20.[2]

I want to argue in this paper that the issue of the relative incidence of unemployment is more complex and that there are alternative measures of the distribution of unemployment. Moreover, the differences between the measures is not just of academic interest but also of significant policy relevance. As an example, although the under 20s made up 18.5 per cent of the unemployment register in January 1978, only 5.9 per cent of them were unemployed for over 12 months as against 22.5 percent of the register as a whole.[3] Thus, if we judge the relative burden of unemployment by the incidence of the longest unemployment spells, then the under 20s do not appear to suffer disproportionately.

A more formal way of considering this issue is to distinguish between completed and uncompleted unemployment spells. The unemployment

*The views expressed in this paper are those of the author alone and do not necessarily reflect the views of the Department of Health and Social Security nor of any of its officers. I would, however, like to acknowledge the assistance of Heather Joshi, Nick Morris and Ruth Hancock in the writing of this paper and a general intellectual debt to Steve Nickell, Sue Owen and Clive Smee.
[1]*Department of Employment Gazette* (Feb. 1978) p. 205.
[2]*Department of Employment Gazette* (Apr. 1978) p. 427.
[3]*Department of Employment Gazette* (Feb. 1978).

register is a count of the unemployment stock at a given date, i.e. those people who having become unemployed at some date in the past are still unemployed on the day when the register is counted. As such it is a count of uncompleted unemployment spells. But the size of the stock is determined by the size of inflow into unemployment and the outflow from unemployment. Assuming these are equal and the unemployment rate is steady, we have a stationary unemployment register. From this, one can estimate the average duration of a completed spell using the following identity:

Number unemployed at one moment = Number becoming unemployed
   (The unemployment stock)   each week (the inflow)
                                       multiplied by Average duration
                                       of completed spell in weeks.

In January 1978, there were 1,484,700 unemployed and the weekly inflow to unemployment was about 80,000. Thus, using the identity above, the average length of a completed unemployment spell was 18½ weeks. However, the average uncompleted spell was 31 weeks in January 1978.[4] It can be shown that the fact that the average uncompleted spell length is greater than the average completed spell length implies that the probability of finding a job falls with unemployment duration.[5]

How should we interpret these statistics? The average completed spell is the average length of spell for all those who become unemployed at a given date. Thus, it is analogous in concept to the expected length of life of a new-born baby. When unemployment inflows and outflows are equal, the average length of a completed spell is equal to the expected length of unemployment spell for someone entering unemployment. Using the identity shown above, unemployment will rise either if unemployment inflows rise and completed durations remain constant or if inflows remain constant and completed durations lengthen (the latter implies a fall in unemployment outflows) or, of course, if both increase. In January 1974, there were 597,700 unemployed and the weekly inflow was about 70,000. From this, we can calculate that the average completed spell length was 8½ weeks. Thus, unemployment durations have more than doubled between January 1974 and January 1978 while inflows have risen by less than 15 per cent. This shows clearly that over this period unemployment has risen primarily because of an increase in unemployment durations rather than from increased inflows. Inflows were relatively stable over the cycle as increases in the number of redundancies

---

[4]The estimate of the average length of uncompleted spells was calculated on the assumption that spells lasting over 12 months had an average length of 78 weeks.
[5]For a formal demonstration of this proposition see S. Salant, 'Job Search, A

as unemployment levels rise were offset by the decline in voluntary separations.

I have tried to explain the meaning of the concept of the average completed spell and show its use. I have also showed its analogy in population theory. In considering the meaning of average uncompleted spells (which I have not yet done) and of the distribution of completed spells and changes in that distribution, it might be helpful if I were to take the population analogy further, not least because demographic modelling techniques have been used with some success in considering unemployment and its incidence.

In population models, the distinction is drawn between the average age of any population and the average life expectation. Only if death rates were constant by age and if, in total, births equalled deaths would the average age of those living equal the average life expectation at birth. However, even for populations where births equal deaths in sum, the death rate varies by age. For males in the U.K., the age specific death rate is highest for new born babies then falls to a low plateau until the age of 40, from which point it rises steadily.[6] The unemployment register shows that, for the unemployed, continuation rates rise continuously. This means that for each successive 3 month duration group, the lower is the probability that its members will leave unemployment in the following 3 months. Thus, the demographic concepts of the average age of population and the life expectation at birth are precisely mirrored for the unemployed in the measures of the average unemployment duration of those unemployed and the expectation of unemployment duration for those entering unemployment.[7]

A typical population transition for Third World countries is a sustained decline in the infant mortality rate. Clearly, this will significantly raise the life expectancy at birth and, by increasing the proportion of surviving children, will reduce the average age of the population. Such a change could well leave the life expectancy at age 50 completely unchanged, although in time the decline in the infant mortality rate will increase the numbers surviving into old age. Similarly, a fall in the proportion of the unemployed who leave unemployment with short spells will lead to a rise in the number unemployed for very long periods even if the probability of remaining unemployed for those already unemployed for such long periods remains unchanged. Thus, whereas the proportion of men unemployed under 3 months who were still unemployed 3 months later (i.e. unemployed 3-6 months) has varied over the range of 30-50 per cent during the period October 1973 to April 1978, the proportion

Theory of Sorts', *Quarterly Journal of Economics* (Feb. 1977).
[6] *Annual Abstract of Statistics 1976*: English Life Table No. 13, p. 51.
[7] I am grateful to Sir Bryan Hopkin for pointing out a confusion in my original argument.

of those men unemployed over 9 months who were still unemployed 3 months later (i.e. over 12 months) has remained in the range of 78-85 per cent.[8] But, whereas there were only 129,200 men unemployed over 12 months in October 1973, by April 1978 the number had reached 270,400.

Having tried to set out and to explain some of the inter-relationships between unemployment flows, durations of completed spells, and the unemployment register, I propose to describe the composition of each measure of unemployment incidence and where possible discuss the determinants of the distributions. To complete the picture of unemployment incidence, I propose to integrate this with an analysis of recurrent unemployment and its effects on the total length of time spent unemployed. When this has been done, we can consider the burden of unemployment in the sense of the incomes of the unemployed when in work and how family incomes are affected by unemployment and unemployment duration.

The discussion of the composition of unemployment by the various measures will, I regret, have to be largely confined to the male unemployed. This is because a large proportion of unemployed married women do not register as unemployed as they are ineligible for benefit. As a result, the statistics for female unemployment are very difficult to interpret.

2. Unemployment Flows

Our knowledge of the characteristics of the unemployment flows is small. The main feature is that they are very large both in absolute terms and relative to the unemployment stock. Thus, since 1971, the total unemployment inflow (males and females) has remained within the range of 278,000-389,000 per month.[9] The range of variation for the male inflow is considerably smaller. Over the same period it has remained between 206,000-264,000 per month. (Female inflows were around 130,000 per month in 1977-78. It is unclear how far this is because of an increased propensity to register as unemployed and/or how far it is a result of the changing composition of total female unemployment (registered and unregistered).)

Unemployment outflows are very similiar in magnitude to inflows. Unless the level of unemployment is changing rapidly as in late 1973 or in 1975-76, outflows are usually less than 10-20,000 different from inflows.

The main feature that we do know of the unemployment inflow is that it is primarily made up of young people. Thus, if we take un-

[8]*Department of Employment Gazette* (June 1978).
[9]*Department of Employment Gazette* (Apr. 1978) p. 479.

employment duration of under one week as a proxy for the inflow, in January 1978, 21.8 per cent of the male inflow was under 20 and a further 20.5 per cent was aged 20-25. Conversely, only 14 per cent of the male inflow was aged over 50.[10] These are typical results. For instance, Cripps and Tarling[11] find that in 1966, 30 per cent of the male labour force aged 18-24 flowed into unemployment as against 10 per cent of the over 50's. However, the high rate of inflow of young people into unemployment does not mean they have a correspondingly high unemployment rate. The age-specific unemployment rate for young men is currently higher than any other age-group. However, because on average they have significantly shorter durations than older men, the age-specific unemployment rate relative to the average unemployment rate is not nearly as high as their relative inflows. This is shown in the Table below:

	January 1978			Males					
Age Group	All Ages	16–17	18–19	20–24	25–29	30–39	40–49	50–59	60+
Age specific unemployment rate index (stock)	1.0	1.8	1.4	1.4	1.0	0.9	0.7	0.7	1.3
Age specific unemployment inflow index	1.0	3.3	2.0	1.7	1.1	0.9	0.6	0.5	0.6

Source: *Department of Employment Gazette* (Feb. 1978) p. 205
(May 1978) p. 585

It can easily be demonstrated using the identity on p. 63 that the stock index when divided by the inflow index yields an index of average completed spell lengths.[12] This is shown for January 1978 in Table below, using the information above.

	January 1978			Males					
Age Group	All Ages	16–17	18–19	20–24	25–29	30–39	40–49	50–59	60+
Age specific average completed spell duration index[13]	1.0	0.5	0.7	0.8	0.9	1.0	1.1	1.5	2.4

[10]*Department of Employment Gazette* (Feb. 1978) p. 205.
Note that the male under 1 week duration group is not a particularly satisfactory proxy in that the total for January 1978 was 37,500 against a weekly inflow of about 55,000. This shows a considerable proportion leaving the register with durations under a week.
[11]T. F. Cripps and R. Tarling, 'An Analysis of the Duration of Male Unemployment in Britain 1932-73', *Economic Journal* (June 1974).
[12]This is only strictly true for a stationary register. The male register had almost equal inflows and outflows in the months up to January 1978.

(Given the imperfections of the inflow measure, these results should be taken as orders of magnitude.)

Thus, the 25–39 age group is average on flow, stock and average completed spell duration incidence; the younger age groups are progressively more heavily represented in the flow and stock incidence and less on the average duration incidence; the 40–59 age group is underrepresented in the stock and flow, have longer average durations; and the over 60s are heavily over-represented in the average completed spell duration index and are thus over-represented in the stock although under-represented in the flow.

Our knowledge of the characteristics of the unemployment outflow is even smaller than of the inflow. We know its size. In addition, given the inflow, any age-specific outflow index must be the inverse of the completed spell duration index, for a stationary register.[14] Thus, the younger unemployed make up a much larger proportion of the outflow than of the stock of unemployed.

There is some limited information on the destination of the unemployment outflow. The 1976 Characteristics of the Unemployed Survey showed the percentage of the original stock sample of the unemployed who left unemployment between June 1976 and January 1977. Of those identified, 87 per cent left unemployment for employment. However, of men aged 55 and over only 66 per cent went into employment and

---

[13]For any age group i, the unemployment stock $S_i = F_i \times d_i$ where F_i is the inflow and d_i is the completed duration for group i. Thus the unemployment stock index for any age group can be written as $\dfrac{F_i \times d_i}{L_i} \div \dfrac{F \times d}{L}$. Similiarly, the unemployment flow index can be written as $\dfrac{F_i}{L_i} \div \dfrac{F}{L}$ (The unemployment flow index is very similiar to but not identical to the unemployment inflow *rate* index which can be written as $\dfrac{F_i}{L_i - S_i} \div \dfrac{F}{L - S}$) Dividing the stock index by the flow index gives us $\dfrac{d_i}{d}$ — an index of relative durations.

[14]Using the previous notation, for any age group i, the probability of being in the outflow of a stationary register is equal to $\dfrac{F_i}{F_i \times d_i} = \dfrac{1}{d_i}$ Similarly, the average probability of leaving the register is $\dfrac{1}{d}$. Thus the age specific outflow index is $\dfrac{1}{d_i} \div \dfrac{1}{d} = \dfrac{d}{d_i}$. This is the inverse of the duration index.

only 48 per cent of those men who had been unemployed for more than 12 months. The rest presumably became sick, retired, or died.

3. The Distribution of Completed Spell Duration

The examination of the determinants of completed spell durations and their variation can best be done with data on a cohort of people becoming unemployed at a given date. With such data we know how long each man is unemployed and can relate his unemployment duration to his personal characteristics and the pressure of demand in the labour market. This data does not currently exist for the U.K., but the D.H.S.S. are carrying out a study that will produce it.

In the absence of proper cohort data, investigation of completed spell durations has been carried out either (a) on a time-series of the register observed at regular intervals broken down by duration band or (b) on survey data using the duration split of a sample of the unemployment stock. Both of these methods use complicated mathematical techniques to transform a set of observed uncompleted spells into a distribution of (unobserved) completed spells.

The first method takes quarterly observations of the unemployment register broken down by duration band to show continuation rates. Demographic techniques can then be used to fit a 'survival curve' which shows the distribution of completed spells. From these studies, it is clear that in the late 1960s the median completed duration for a newly unemployed man was about 2 weeks.[15] In other words, half those men who became unemployed had left unemployment in about a fortnight. Only about 15 per cent of spells lasted over 13 weeks, but spell lengths in excess of 13 weeks accounted for over half the man-weeks of unemployment. Thus, the distributions are highly skewed with long tails in the high duration bands. These studies also show that the *aggregate* probability of leaving the register declines with duration.

However, Cripps and Tarling[16] have shown that the pattern observed is quite consistent with different groups among the unemployed having different probabilities of leaving the register, but all individuals having an unchanged probability of leaving unemployment irrespective of how long they are unemployed. In this way there is a 'sorting' process by which those people less attractive to employers (e.g. the old, the sick) will fail to leave the register and end up as the majority of the long-term unemployed. Any specific effect on individuals of longer durations reducing the probability of re-employment because of labelling or

---

[15]Cripps and Tarling, op. cit., p. 306. R. Weeden, 'Duration of Unemployment and Labour Turnover' University of Reading (1974), p. 10. *Department of Employment Gazette* (Feb. 1973), p. 114.

[16]Cripps andTarling, op. cit.

demoralisation, would be in addition to this 'sorting' process but cannot be analysed with aggregate data.

The synthetic analyses of aggregate duration data can be supplemented for the period 1971-72. D.H.S.S. carried out a pilot exercise on the collection of unemployment benefit statistics which gathered direct evidence on the duration of unemployment spells and on spell repetition for all spells ending for the period June 1971-June 1972. This period had the highest level of post-war unemployment until 1975, with male unemployment averaging 715,000—about two-thirds of the current level. There were doubts expressed as to the reliability of the sample, but as it is the only direct observation of the distribution of completed spell lengths, and the results tally with the synthetic distributions calculated by mathematical interpolation, the results from the study will be treated as reliable. Some of the main results are presented in the table below.

TABLE 4.1.
Duration of Completed Unemployment Spell Lengths
for Male Spells Ending in the Year June 1971-June 1972.
Percentages of Unemployed Leaving the Register
within the Stated Period.

Period	Age Per Cent							
	All Ages	Under 18	18–19	20–29	30–39	40–49	50–59	60+
0– 4 days	27.7	19.4	18.0	20.8	27.4	38.1	32.5	35.4
0– 4 weeks	59.2	59.5	58.9	57.3	58.3	64.0	62.5	53.8
4–13 weeks	21.2	28.2	26.6	24.2	22.9	18.0	16.8	13.2
0–13 weeks	80.4	87.7	85.5	81.6	81.0	82.0	79.2	67.0
13–26 weeks	10.5	8.7	9.7	11.3	11.1	9.8	9.7	10.1
26–39 weeks	4.5	3.0	3.0	4.3	3.3	4.5	5.7	6.3
39–52 weeks	1.3	0.4	1.1	1.5	1.7	1.6	2.5	5.2
Over 52 weeks	2.7	0.2	0.8	1.3	1.9	2.3	2.9	11.6
Median unemployment spell length/weeks	2.6	2.6	3.0	2.9	2.8	1.3	1.4	2.6

The table confirms that most of the men who become unemployed leave the register quickly. Over one-quarter of all spells lasted less than 4 days, 60 per cent less than 4 weeks and 80 per cent less than 13 weeks. Only 8.5 per cent of spells lasted more than 6 months and only 2.7 per cent more than a year. In this period under 1 per cent of unemployment spells of the under 20s lasted more than 12 months as against 12 per cent of spells of men over 60. However, half the over 60s left the register in under 3 weeks. The main reason why so many of the over 60s had such long spells was that far fewer of them were able to leave the register in the 1–3 month period. Thus, unless old men left the register within a

a few weeks of becoming unemployed, they were liable to remain unemployed for long periods—much longer than younger men. Cripps and
Tarling (1974) find a similar pattern for 1966 and suggest that it reflects
old people accepting re-employment in inferior jobs.

To distinguish between the effects of individual characteristics relative
to the effect of lengthening durations per se on the incidence of long
unemployment spells requires an analysis of data on individuals. This
has been done using complicated maximum likelihood techniques by
Lancaster[17] using data collected by Daniel[18] and by Nickell (1977 (a)
and (b))[19] using data from the 1972 General Household Survey. Nickell
(1977 (a)) clearly establishes that the *conditional* probability of leaving
the register *for an individual man* declines sharply the longer he is
unemployed for spells lasting more than 6 months. (This is consistent
with a continuously declining absolute probability of leaving the register.
Table 4.1 above shows absolute probabilities.) He also finds the following
characteristics are associated with longer spells:

   (i)   low labour demand
  (ii)   lack of skill
 (iii)   increased age
 (iv)   being unmarried
  (v)   if married, increase in the number of children
 (vi)   ill-health
(vii)   not having a car
(viii)   entering unemployment voluntarily
 (ix)   having a manual worker as father
  (x)   increases in the ratio of income when unemployed compared to
       income when in work. For the U.K., in terms of personal charac-
       teristics, by far the most important single determinant of the
       probability of becoming unemployed for very long periods is
       age. (See Metcalf and Nickell (1977) for a full discussion of age
       and its effects on unemployment durations.)[20]

The effect of benefits on lengthening unemployment durations is
found by Nickell only to be present for the first 6 months of unemployment (Nickell 1977(b).) He estimates that the elasticity of unemployment

---

[17] T. Lancaster, 'The Duration of Unemployment', Hull University (1977).
[18] W. W. Daniel 'A National Survey of the Unemployed', P.E.P. Broadsheet No. 546
(1974).
[19] S. J. Nickell, (a) 'Estimating the Probability of Leaving Unemployment', L.S.E.
Centre for Labour Economics Discussion Paper No. 7 (1977); and (b) 'The Effect
of Unemployment and Related Benefits on the Duration of Unemployment',
L.S.E. Centre for Labour Economics, Discussion Paper No. 8 (1977).
[20] D. Metcalf and S. J. Nickell, 'The Plain Man's Guide to the Out of Work: The
Nature and Composition of Unemployment in Britain', L.S.E. Centre for Labour
Economics Discussion Paper No. 6 (1977).

durations with respect to benefits is about 0.6. This is very similar to the result obtained by Lancaster and to the results from cross-section studies done in the U.S.A. e.g. Ehrenberg and Oaxaca (1976).[21] Assuming that the level of unemployment benefits has no effect on unemployment inflows, this estimate of the benefit effect on unemployment durations implies that the introduction of the Earnings Related Supplement and the raising of Supplementary Benefit rates in 1966 increased the level of unemployment by about 40–50,000. The Department of Employment estimated the effect to be not more than 50,000.[22]

In summary, the completed spell data shows great concentration of unemployment incidence. Table 4.1 shows that in 1971–72, the 60 per cent of the unemployment spells that lasted 4 weeks or less accounted for only about one-tenth of all the weeks of unemployment experienced, while the 8.5 per cent of all spells lasting over 6 months accounted for about one-half of all unemployment weeks and the 2.7 per cent of unemployment spells lasting over one year accounted for about one-quarter of all unemployment weeks.[23] The synthetic techniques produce very similar results. In terms of personal characteristics, long unemployment spells are particularly associated with increased age, lack of skill and, among younger men, with larger numbers of children. These are themes to which I will return in the next section.

4. The Composition of the Register

In previous sections, I have tried to explain how unemployment flows and durations interact to determine the composition of the register. The characteristics of the people on the register are relatively easy to observe and have been extensively surveyed e.g. in the 1973 and 1976 Department of Employment's Characteristics of the Unemployed Surveys and in Daniel (1974). The results are clear-cut and relatively well known. Thus, by age, the young and the old are over-represented compared to the working population; by occupation, the unskilled are enormously over-represented compared to men in employment (see Metcalf and Nickell,[24] Table 6); by family status, single men and men with large families are over-represented among the unemployed. (See Smee and Stern[25]

[21]Ehrenberg, R. and Oaxaca, R. 'Unemployment Insurance, Duration of Unemployment and Subsequent Wage Gain', *American Economic Review* Vol. 66, No. 5 (1976).

[22]*Department of Employment Gazette* (Oct. 1976).

[23]These figures are calculated on the assumption that spells lasting over 12 months had an average length of 78 weeks. Even if they had an average length of 60 weeks, those spells lasting over 12 months would still account for one-fifth of the unemployment weeks.

[24]Metcalf and Nickell, op. cit.

[25]C. H. Smee and J. Stern, 'The Unemployed in a Period of High Unemployment: Some Notes on Characteristics and Benefit Status', D.H.S.S. (1976).

Tables 4 and 5). Of course, these factors will interact for many men.

It is often asserted or assumed that the groups who are most over-represented among the unemployed 'suffer worse' when unemployment is high than when it is low. If this statement is interpreted to mean that their share of the register is higher at unemployment peaks, then it can be shown to be false. As unemployment increases, there is no doubt that the characteristics of the unemployed increasingly tend toward those of the employed. This is shown in Table 4.2.

TABLE 4.2.
*Composition of the Unemployment Register
at Unemployment Peaks and Troughs*

	Age Composition of the Male Unemployed (%)			
	Under 20	20–50	50–60	Over 60
January 1972[x]	10.9	58.7	14.5	15.8
July 1973[o]	9.6	51.7	16.5	22.1
January 1978[x]	13.3	60.5	13.3	12.9

% Unskilled

(% of the Male Unemployed registered at ESD offices for jobs as General Labourers)

June 1973[o]	49.4
Dec 1977[x]	40.6

	Family Composition of Unemployed in receipt of Benefit (%)				
	No Dependents[1]	Married without children	Married with 1–2 children	Married with 3 children	Married with 4 or more children
November 1973[ol]	45.3	20.8	19.2	6.4	8.3
November 1975[xl]	53.8	12.8	20.8	6.4	6.3

[x] Unemployment peak   [ol] Low unemployment
[o] Unemployment trough   [xl] High unemployment
[1] Includes childless couples with working wives

Source: *Department of Employment Gazette*, Tables 110, 199.
Department of Health and Social Security, Unemployment Benefit Statistics. Supplementary Benefit Annual Statistical Enquiry.

The table clearly shows how as we consider higher unemployment levels we find a higher percentage of the male register aged 20-50 and a sharp fall in the percentage aged over 60.

The change in family composition (for which unfortunately data is not available for true unemployment peaks and troughs) reflects the change in the age composition of the unemployed with a sharp fall in the percentage of men claiming benefit for a dependent wife only. Many of these men will be the older unemployed. The table also shows a small increase in the percentage with small families (1-2 children) between November 1973 and November 1975 and a fall in the percentage with large families (4 or more children). A very similar pattern is observed if we compare the Census results for 1966 and 1971—respectively trough and peak unemployment years.

The role of the factors considered above in determining the composition of the register can be further explored if we consider the characteristics of the unemployed by duration bands of the register. As unemployment rises or falls so the share of the register accounted for by those men unemployed 3-12 months rises and falls. The share of the 3-12 month group fell from 35.7 per cent of the male register in January 1972 to 27.1 per cent in July 1973 before rising again to 34.3 per cent in July 1977. The share of those unemployed over 12 months rises as unemployment levels fall unless the low level of unemployment is sustained for some period (because this group finds it hardest to find work when the demand for labour recovers). Conversely, the share of the over 12 month group falls as unemployment rises but rises if unemployment remains at a high level. Thus, the share of the over 12 month unemployed was only 16.7 per cent at the unemployment peak of January 1972 but rose to 29.2 per cent in July 1973 before falling to 19.6 per cent in July 1976. The seasonally adjusted unemployment rate for males (excluding school leavers) was 5.3 per cent in July 1976 and only rose slightly to 5.5 per cent in January 1977 and 5.9 per cent in January 1978. However, over this period, the share of those men unemployed over 12 months rose from 19.6 per cent in July 1976 to 23.4 per cent in January 1977 and 25.5 per cent in January 1978.

As the share of the long term unemployed has risen, so the age composition of the long term unemployed has grown to resemble that of the register as a whole. This is particularly true in this recession when there has been a very sharp rise in the proportion of men aged 20-29 and to a lesser extent of men aged 30-39 among those unemployed over 12 months. In January 1972, 34.1 per cent of men unemployed over 12 months were aged over 60 and only 9 per cent aged 20-29 and 11.6 per cent aged 30-39. (These groups respectively made up 15.8 per cent, 26.0 per cent, and 17.2 per cent of the total male register.) However, by July 1976, the share of the over 60s among the long term unemployed was down to 25.8 per cent, the share of the 20–29s up to 19.7 per cent and the 30–39s to 15.6 per cent. By January 1978, the share of the over 60s among the long-term unemployed had fallen a little further to 22.3 per cent (their share of the total register was 12.9 per cent) while the share of the 20–29s and 30–39s was 20.0 per cent and 17.2 per cent respectively (as against shares of the total register of 29.3 per cent and 18 per cent).[26] Thus, while the young are still under-represented among the long term unemployed compared to the register as a whole, the difference is far less than it has been since the Second World War. The age composition of the register by duration band is quite similar to that of the 1930s (see Beveridge's 1937 article on unemployment in *Economica*, Vol. IV). (This recession has also seen a very sharp increase in the level of registered female unemployment and long term female unemployment. In January 1978 there were 61,400 women registered as unemployed for more than 12 months, of whom almost half were under 30.)

The family composition of the long term unemployed has directly reflected the change in the age distribution. Thus, whereas in November 1973, 34.3 per cent of men unemployed over 12 months and receiving benefit had children, by November 1975, this had risen to 37.7 per cent and the proportion of men with small families (1 or 2 children) had risen from 16.9 per cent to 19.5 per cent. Between November 1975 and November 1976, the number of men unemployed and on Supplementary Benefit for over 12 months (a rather smaller group than those unemployed for 12 months) rose by 71 per cent. But the group with the largest increase over this period was men with 1 or 2 children (81 per cent) and the group with the smallest increase was men with 4 or more children (53 per cent).

The reasons for the over-representation of large families among the unemployed—the 1971 Census shows unskilled men with 4 or more children having an unemployment rate of over 20 per cent—and even more among the long term unemployed are unclear. Dependency additions to unemployment benefits are an obvious candidate particularly for low paid unskilled men. However, Nickell (1977 (a)) found that increases in the number of children was a clearly significant variable in increasing the length of unemployment spell after having controlled for skill levels, unemployment benefits, earnings in work, local labour demand and ill-health. His expectation was 'that the larger the number of dependents an individual possesses, the greater are the family's basic needs and this may exert pressure to return to work'.[27] This a priori

---

[26]The source for these age and duration breakdowns is the semi-annual age and duration analysis published in the *Department of Employment Gazette*.
[27]S. J. Nickell, 1977(a) op. cit.

expectation was clearly controverted by his results. It may be that the unskilled unemployed with large families are a group who tend to suffer multiple social deprivations, many of which were not variables available in his data set.

No data is collected regularly on the skill composition of the unemployed by duration. However, the 1973 Characteristics of the Unemployed Survey showed that 38.4 per cent of those classified as General Labourers were unemployed over 12 months as against 30.9 per cent of the total sample.[28] By 1976, the position of the unskilled had deteriorated in that the 1976 Characteristics Survey showed 31 per cent of General Labourers unemployed over 12 months as against 22.4 per cent of the total sample.[29]

In general, economic theory would lead one to expect the unskilled to have shorter unemployment durations as they can work in a wider range of jobs than men with specific skills. In the U.S.A., the unskilled do appear to have shorter durations. The reasons why they do not in the U.K. are unclear. Among the explanations that have been suggested are the decline in the number of jobs for the unskilled (particularly to the extent that this has been concentrated in particular areas), the rise in relative wages of the unskilled compared to the skilled, and the lack of geographic mobility of the unskilled. (For a fuller discussion, see Metcalf and Nickell,[30] and Nickell (1978).)[31] However, it is not surprising that the share of the unskilled among the long-term unemployed should rise when unemployment rises in that more skilled workers can displace less skilled workers in less skilled jobs.

In broad terms, the structure of the unemployment stock and of men unemployed over 12 months is what one would predict from our knowledge of flows, completed spell durations and their determinants. This is not wholly true. There is the particular problem of explaining the concentration of large families among the long term unemployed. In addition, although there are possible explanations, it is not clear why the unskilled should be over-represented among the long-term unemployed. However, at first sight, the age composition of the long-term unemployed may appear inconsistent with the age distribution of completed spells discussed in the previous section. I will try to reconcile the two in the next section on unemployment spell repetition.

---

[28]*Department of Employment Gazette* (May 1974), p. 387.

[29]*Department of Employment Gazette* (Sept. 1977), p. 972.

[30]Metcalf and Nickell, op. cit.

[31]S. J. Nickell, 'Unemployment and Policy Issues', L.S.E. Centre for Labour Economics, Discussion Paper No. 32 (1978).

5. Unemployment Recurrence

The fragmentary information available shows that a considerable proportion of the 4 million unemployment spells experienced each year are experienced by the same people i.e. far fewer than 4 million people experience unemployment each year. Thus, the 1973 Characteristics of the Unemployed Survey reports that of their male unemployment stock sample, almost 30 per cent had experienced another spell of unemployment within the previous 12 months. The 1976 Characteristics Survey found that of those men with unemployment durations of less than 3 months, 40 per cent had been unemployed within the previous 12 months. The 1976 Survey also gave an age breakdown which showed that of those men with 3 or more spells in the previous year, 38.5 per cent were aged 18-24.

As the young are far more likely to have multiple spells than the old, given that they also tend to have short spells, it is necessary to have cohort data to obtain a true picture of spell recurrence and its contribution to unemployment flows. Fortunately, the 1971-72 D.H.S.S. pilot statistical exercise collected data on spell repetition. This showed that 66 per cent of all unemployed men in the sample had one spell only in the year June 1971-June 1972, but that 14 per cent of claimants had had 3 or more spells, and 1.7 per cent had experienced 10 or more spells in the previous year! The role of repeated unemployment in the inflow is shown by the fact that the 66 per cent of male claimants with 1 spell accounted for only 35 per cent of all spells whereas the 14 per cent of men with 3 or more spells accounted for 43 per cent of all spells (and the 1.7 per cent with 10 or more spells for 9 per cent of all spells). Almost half (47 per cent) of those men with 3 or more spells were under 30. Conversely, only 21 per cent of the over 60s had more than one spell in the year.

Unfortunately, the D.H.S.S. pilot study does not allow spell recurrence to be cross-tabulated with spell duration. However, a technique has been developed by Kaitz[32] and Disney[33] that enables the total number of weeks spent in unemployment to be decomposed partially into spell and duration incidence. The fullest investigation of such data for the U.K. is by Owen.[34] Her results for 1971-72 confirm that the younger unemployed have frequent but shorter spells of unemployment. In addition, she finds that when the period considered is extended to

[32]H. Kaitz, 'Analysing the Length of Spells of Unemployment', *Monthly Labour Review* (Nov. 1970).
[33]R. Disney, 'The Distribution of Unemployment and Sickness Amongst the U.K. Population', Reading University Discussion Paper No. 87 (1976).
[34]S. Owen, 'The Inequality of Male Unemployment and Sickness', University College of Cardiff (1978).

the 4 years 1970-74, spell repetition becomes even more important in determining the concentration of unemployment. In other words, many of the men with repeated spells in one year had repeated spells in subsequent years.

If we consider spell repetition within any year and how far it is concentrated on young men we may have a clue as to why the current recession has resulted in so many men in their 20s having unemployment spells over 12 months. The age specific inflow index on page 66 above shows a higher than average likelihood of men in their 20s entering unemployment—particularly for the 20-24 age group. In 1971-72, the absolute probability that any single spell would last over 12 months was only 0.013 (1.3 per cent). It is unlikely to be greater than 0.05 (5 per cent) currently. However, this 5 per cent chance of being unemployed over 12 months is an average and applied over all spells. It may well not be independent of spell repetition. If employers are more reluctant to hire the recurrent unemployed and screen them out when they apply for jobs, then the probability of being unemployed over 12 months in the current spell could well be rather lower for the person in his first spell than for the person in his third spell.[35] Thus, the probability of being unemployed for long periods would be a positive function of the number of spells experienced. This would particularly affect men under 30 who experience most spell repetition. There are other possible exacerbating reasons why young men with recurrent spells may be more prone to long periods of unemployment, such as employers' use of 'last-in, first-out' procedures when reducing their labour force and the possible inability of the young recurrent unemployed to find anything other than temporary employment when the demand for labour is low.

The reasoning above is highly speculative. The data available does not allow us to test any of the reasons I have put forward. They may, however, provide some inkling into a way by which we can explain why so many men in their 20s are currently experiencing such long periods of unemployment when completed spell duration data for the 1971-72 period would lead one to predict otherwise.

6. Unemployment Concentration

The National Insurance cohort data examined by Owen (1978) gives a direct measure of unemployment concentration. Her results on a sample of 39,000 men show that the incidence of unemployment is highly

---

[35]For recurrent unemployment to have contributed significantly to longterm unemployment among young men in recent years, it would have to be the case that employers had applied such a screening test to a greater extent in the current recession.

concentrated.[36] Thus, in 1971-72, 9 per cent of the male labour force experienced all the weeks of unemployment, 3.5 per cent experienced three-quarters of all unemployment weeks, and 2 per cent experienced half the unemployment weeks.

These results are the direct consequence of the interaction of two very highly skewed distributions—(a) the distribution of completed spells and (b) the distribution of spell repetition. We showed earlier on (a) that 8.5 per cent of all male unemployment spells accounted for half of all unemployment weeks and 2.7 per cent of spells accounted for about one-quarter of all unemployment weeks. On (b) we showed that in 1971-72, 14 per cent of claimants—of whom almost half were under 30—accounted for 43 per cent of all spells.

The interaction of the distributions is not, however, a random one. Older workers make up a small proportion of the flow and have very little recurrent unemployment. Thus, their unemployment concentration is almost entirely determined by spell concentration. As a result, Owen (1978) finds that of men aged 50-59, 6 per cent experienced all the unemployment weeks and 3 per cent experienced three-quarters of the unemployment weeks in 1971-72. The high inflow rate of young people will increase the proportion experiencing any unemployment and large portions of it—but less so the more spell repetition exists. For men aged 20-24, Owen found that 14 per cent of them accounted for all the weeks of unemployment but 6 per cent of them accounted for three-quarters of the weeks. It is this last figure, in particular, that shows the effect of spell repetition.

Owen's results also show considerable unemployment repetition across years. Thus, of those men in her sample who experienced unemployment, only 54 per cent were unemployed in one year only, while 28 per cent were unemployed in 2 years, 12 per cent in 3 years, and 6 per cent in all of the years examined. This pattern was unaffected by age. Moreover, whereas those men who were only unemployed in 1971 had an average of 11 weeks of unemployment, those who were unemployed in all 4 years had an average of 22 weeks of unemployment in 1971. This result gives support to the hypothesis that spell length and spell repetition are not independent.

The effect of spell repetition on unemployment incidence is shown at its starkest in the figures for the concentration of unemployment for 1970-74. If unemployment were randomly distributed between years then one would expect that 36 per cent (4 × 9%) of the male labour

[36]Her sample was of men with at least 8 weeks out of paid employment in one of the four years 1970-74. As such, men with very short spells of unemployment are under-represented. This implies that the percentage of the labour force experiencing all the weeks of unemployment is slightly under-stated. For a full discussion, see S. Owen, op. cit.

force would account for all the weeks of unemployment and 8 per cent (4 × 2%) for half of all unemployment weeks. In fact, 19 per cent of the labour force experienced all the weeks of unemployment and only 3 per cent accounted for half the unemployment weeks over the 4 year period.

7. The Effect on Family Incomes of Unemployment

Thus far, I have discussed the relative incidence of unemployment. I now propose to discuss the burden of unemployment in the sense of the effect of unemployment and unemployment durations on family income. This area is far more difficult because of the paucity of data and any results quoted are much less firmly established than the unemployment incidence results.

The fullest analysis of the effect of unemployment on income is in Chapter 6 of Layard, Piachaud, and Stewart[37] which is based on the 1972 General Household Survey. Layard et al examined household income relative to Supplementary Benefit income for the unemployed and total net income out of work relative to total net income when in work. This latter is usually termed the 'replacement ratio'. Although their data is now 6 years old, there is no reason to expect significant differences on either of their measures from benefit changes although they may be affected to some extent by the change in the composition of the unemployed (the most notable of which is the sharp increase in the proportion of the long-term unemployed accounted for by the 20–40 age group), an increase in the proportion of multi-earner households and, perhaps to a lesser extent, from a decline in the value of tax thresholds relative to earnings. A greater difficulty arises from the fact that the benefits ascribed both in and out of work are calculated on a 'quasi-hypothetical' basis by imputation from reported earnings and employment, assuming 100 per cent take-up of benefits. In spite of these caveats, their results are very persuasive and are consistent both with prior expectations and with our knowledge of the characteristics of the unemployed.

Layard et al show that only 7 per cent of the unemployed households have replacement ratios in terms of weekly income of 1.0 or over (i.e. are better off out of work than in work). They also show that households with an unemployed man lose on average 25 per cent of their net weekly income whereas those not unemployed would lose 31 per cent on average. Since replacement ratios fall as earnings rise, this suggests that the unemployed have low earnings when in work.

The most clearcut result of the work by the Layard team is that

[37]P. R. G. Layard, D. Piachaud and M. Stewart *The Causes of Poverty* (H.M.S.O., 1978).

relating incomes when unemployed to unemployment durations. In 1972, 32 per cent of the households with an unemployed man had household incomes of 120 per cent or below the short-term Supplementary Benefit rate. However, under 30 per cent of households with a member unemployed under 6 months had net weekly incomes at or below 120 per cent of Supplementary Benefit as against almost 50 per cent of those unemployed 6–12 months and 80 per cent of those unemployed over 12 months.[38] Although the benefit imputation may lead to some over-estimation of income in the first six months of unemployment (because, in fact, only about 40 per cent of men unemployed 2–28 weeks receive any Earnings Related Supplement), the Layard team results show clearly the plight of the long-term unemployed in terms of poverty. Whereas 80 per cent of the long-term unemployed households had incomes at or below 120 per cent of short-term Supplementary Benefit levels, under 10 per cent of those in work had incomes so low.

The results quoted above can be substantiated to some extent by evidence from the 1976 Family Expenditure Survey. Let me examine this on the basis of the economic activity status of the first two adults in the household. For households in which one of the first two adults was unemployed but for less than 52 weeks, 43 per cent of such households were in the lowest income decile when adjusted for family size.[39] For households where one of the first two adults was unemployed over 52 weeks, 53 per cent of the households were in the bottom equivalent income decile. However, for households where neither of the first two adults were out of work but another adult was receiving Unemployment Benefit (e.g. households with unemployed adult children, multi-adult shared flats etc.) only 15 per cent were in the bottom decile of equivalent income. These results (particularly the last) are subject to the problems resulting from small sample size and thus should be considered as orders of magnitude rather than as firm estimates. However, a virtually identical pattern of relativities between the income figures by duration results if we consider unemployment for less than or more than 52 weeks among FES household heads, with 63 per cent of households with the head unemployed over 52 weeks in the lowest equivalent income decile. For households where any member was unemployed for less than a year, 35 per cent were in the lowest equivalent income decile.

The incidence of severe poverty among the long-term unemployed is shown on other indicators by a study of unemployed men on Supplementary Benefit in 1974. The men in that sample who were unemployed over 12 months (who were predominantly middle-aged or older) reported

[38]Layard, Piachaud and Stewart, op. cit., Tables 6.11 and 6.14.
[39]This is on the basis of current net income adjusted by D.H.S.S. equivalence scales.

severe financial hardship, Thus, only 16 per cent reported the possession of any savings at all and about half reported having borrowed money, most usually to buy food. Nearly all of the long-term unemployed claimed to have had to economise on both essentials and leisure activities, and over half did not possess the Supplementary Benefit clothing standard (a change of clothing, two pairs of shoes, and an overcoat).

One particular issue concerning the long-term unemployed men is that they are particularly unlikely to have a working wife if they are receiving benefit.[40] In Smee and Stern (1976) attention was drawn to the fact that, according to the 1971 Census, the unemployed were much less likely to have an economically active wife. Further work has shown that the absence of a working wife is primarily associated with being unemployed and on Supplementary Benefit. Thus in May 1977 about 40 per cent of unemployed men with children receiving National Insurance benefits without Supplementary Benefit appear to have a working wife (i.e. the wives had an activity rate similar to that of wives of employed men with children) as against about 10 per cent of men receiving National Insurance benefit with Supplementary Benefits. Similarly, in November 1975, only 11 per cent of married unemployed men on Supplementary Benefit without National Insurance benefit had a working wife, whether or not they had children. These results and the role of Supplementary Benefits are confirmed in a recent micro study of North Tyneside by Turner and Dickinson (1978).[41]

The importance of working wives in the context of the incomes of the unemployed is that the 1972 and 1974 FES indicate (albeit with small sample numbers) that, for unemployed males, the average household income where wives are working is nearly double that of households where the wife does not work.[42] Again a sizeable income differential between the two groups is reported by Turner and Dickinson. The point to observe in this context is that the overwhelming majority of long-term unemployed men receive Supplementary Benefit without any National Insurance benefits. Thus, they are pre-eminently unlikely to have a working wife which greatly reduces the ability of the family to increase its income by its own efforts. The absence of a working wife is less common for the shorter term unemployed.

[40]In May 1977, 83.2 per cent of men unemployed over 12 months were receiving benefit as against 89.1 per cent of men unemployed under 12 months.
[41]S. Turner and F. Dickinson, 'In and Out of Work: A Study of Unemployment, Low Pay and Income Maintenance Services', North Tyneside CDP, The Home Office (1978), Ch. 15.
[42]Some of the long-term unemployed not receiving benefit will have a working wife whose earnings are sufficient to keep the family's income above the Supplementary Benefit level. For a full discussion of the contribution of wives' earnings to family income and their importance in preventing family poverty, see L. Hamill, 'Wives as Sole and Joint Breadwinners', D.H.S.S. (1976).

The reasons why the long-term unemployed are so unlikely to have a working wife are complex. Turner and Dickinson point to the role of the Supplementary Benefit disregard rule by which the family's income is reduced £ for £ (i.e. 100 per cent tax rate) after the first £4 of her earnings. However, this is not the only factor at work. Other effects, both from the demand and supply sides are important e.g. the level of labour demand in the same area for husbands and wives, and assortative mating which might mean that men with severe unemployment problems have wives with less marketable skills than other men.[43]

This section has shown that the vast majority of the families of unemployed men do have a significant income loss while they are unemployed, but that the incidence of poverty among the unemployed is heavily concentrated among those unemployed for more than 12 months. An interesting and significant factor involved in this is the incidence of working wives.

8. Policy Implications

One of the two main themes of this paper has been that unemployment is very concentrated in its incidence—much more so than the unemployment register of uncompleted spells would suggest. This concentration arises (a) from the small proportion of very long spells among all completed unemployment spells and (b) spell repetition leading to a small number of the unemployed experiencing a large proportion of all spells.

Until the current recession middle-aged and older men have accounted for almost all the long-term unemployed. However, since 1975 the share of prime age males among the long-term employed has risen sharply so that almost 40 per cent of men unemployed over 12 months in January 1978 were aged 20-40. But, even in January 1978, males under 20 accounted for less than 4 per cent of the long-term male unemployed as against 13 per cent of the male register. Although older men now make up a much smaller proportion of the long-term unemployed, the over 60s in particular are still much more likely to become unemployed for over a year than any other group.

The question arises whether one should take unemployment duration as the single best indicator of the groups suffering worst from unemployment. The main arguments in favour include the well-known social and psychological demoralisation resulting from prolonged periods of enforced idleness, the disconnection from the labour market that results from long periods of unemployment and that, as shown in the last

---

[43]For a discussion of the role of working wives (albeit primarily on the unlikely assumption that it is wives' behaviour that determines the husbands' experience) see W. W. Daniel and E. Stilgoe, 'Where are They Now? A follow-up Study of the Unemployed', P.E.P. Broadsheet No. 572 (1977), Chs. 3 and 4.

section, hardship and poverty among the unemployed appears to be very heavily concentrated among the long-term unemployed. The fact that in this recession so many more of the long-term unemployed men are in families with dependent children would emphasise the use of unemployment duration as the best indicator since we now observe so many dependent children having to suffer the poverty induced by long periods of unemployment with its consequential effects on their upbringing and education and on their future lives.

The main argument against using duration as the sole criterion for assessing the burden of unemployment is the problems caused by recurrent unemployment which is primarily experienced by the young. However, the recurrent unemployed do not (by definition) experience labour market disconnection sufficient to cause severe lack of job offers nor do they appear to suffer the psychological demoralisation of long-term unemployment. The income losses of the recurrent unemployed are not known but it would be surprising if they were as large on a weekly let alone an annual basis as for the long-term unemployed. Moreover, for many young people a period of 'job swapping' with frequent but short spells of unemployment appears to be a conventional prelude to a stable working life without unemployment. Thus, Daniel and Stilgoe (1977) report not only that the young unemployed found unemployment less irksome than any other group (even though 17 per cent of their young unemployed—aged 18–24—had had 3 or more spells of unemployment in the previous 3 years) but that there was a sharp increase in the proportion of the group who reported their current job as being their normal job. In Daniel's original 1973 survey, only 54 per cent of the young reported their current job as normal, but this rose to 80 per cent in the 1976 follow-up.)[44]

The arguments above do not, however, dispose of the claim that the recurrent unemployed should be treated as a group of special concern like the long-term unemployed. To the extent that recurrent unemployment causes the individuals who experience it to have long spells either while still young (as suggested on page 77) or when rather older, then that is an argument for special intervention e.g. to provide training. However, this has by no means been firmly established even for broad groups, let alone for individuals. It is only if recurrent unemployment in itself is a good predictor of long-term unemployment for individuals that one can really make a strong case on economic grounds for preferential treatment of the recurrent unemployed such as I would argue is needed by the long-term unemployed. (There may, of course, be good non-economic arguments as well.)

Similar considerations relate to the labour market arguments for

[44]Daniel and Stilgoe, op. cit., Ch. 3.

preferential treatment for school leavers. For them the case for special provision is that leaving school for unemployment of more than a few weeks could mean that the school leavers so affected will miss out on the training (both formal and informal) that they would get in work. On the assumption that it may be very hard to catch up on this missed training later, unemployment at the start of a working life may thus threaten poor job prospects with repeated or long spells of unemployment in later working life. To the extent that unemployment at the very start of a working life is more damaging to morale and self-esteem than unemployment later, it could perhaps be argued that unemployment of 3–6 months for school leavers is equivalent in its demoralising effects to rather longer spells for older men and women. There are, of course, other powerful social and economic arguments in favour of special provision to prevent widespread or geographically concentrated unemployment of school leavers for long periods such as crime prevention and race relations.

When the current recession first had its impact on unemployment, it was the sharp rise in unemployment among young people in general and school leavers in particular that first became obvious. However, as the recession has continued, the statistical evidence has increasingly shown the swelling numbers of long-term unemployed and their changing composition towards prime age workers. In view of the provision that has been made for young people (e.g. under the Youth Opportunities Scheme) the group among the unemployed whose needs most appear to exceed current provision is the long-term unemployed. Discussion of how to meet the needs of the long-term unemployed has tended to focus on benefit provision. However, the financial needs of the unemployed are only part of the issue. To my mind the most serious problem is the lack of job opportunities for the long-term unemployed and their disconnection from the information networks of the labour market. Many (but by no means all) of the long-term unemployed are socially and economically disadvantaged but all have suffered the corrosively destructive process of long periods of unemployment, the stigma of which cannot but worsen their prospects in the eyes of employers. Thus, to my mind, the provision of job opportunities for the long-term unemployed is at least as important as benefit provision. This, however, is a very difficult task because of the large numbers of short-term unemployed from whom employers can choose and the unattractiveness to employers of the long-term unemployed.

5

POVERTY, GROWTH
AND THE REDISTRIBUTION OF INCOME

by Frank Field*
Child Poverty Action Group

Introduction

A shared assumption among many politicians and most of the electorate is that normal times in Britain are characterised by full employment and steadily rising national income. Memories are short, and it is to the fifties and early 1960s that most people look in support of this view. But if we take a wider panoramic view of the century a rather different picture emerges. Viewed historically, the boom years following the second world war are very much the exceptional period for Britain during this century. The title of this section of the Association's meeting suggests that this is now being recognised.

This paper explores three themes. The first section examines what is usually meant by the term poverty, how the numbers of poor have grown in the post-war boom years and the extent to which their rising living standards have been a consequence of rising living standards rather than of any redistribution. The second section argues that a relatively slow growth rate will increase the numbers of the poor and the ranks of those on low income will be swelled at the same time by demographic changes. Real incomes of the poor will therefore fall in the immediate future unless an increasing share of the GDP is allocated to them. The third section concludes on the note that a period of relatively slow growth will test the genuineness of the concern expressed by most shades of opinion about the poor in the post-war period. Will this concern be translated into action entailing a redistribution of income to maintain the present real income of the poor, let alone improve their relative position?

*I should like to thank Louie Burghes who undertook the main calculations for this paper and Chris Pond and Ruth Lister who commented upon it in draft.

1. The Post War Record

The Supplementary Benefits Commission's scale rates (plus an addition to meet housing costs) provide a minimum income for those people who are unable to work. Since 1965 Parliament has made an annual review of the scale rates and this officially approved minimum level of income for November of this year is given in the table below.

TABLE 5.1.
Supplementary Benefit Scale Rates—November, 1978

	Short-term rate £ pw	Long-term rate £ pw
Married or cohabiting couple	25.25	31.55
Single householder	15.55	19.90
Others over 18	12.45	15.95
16–18	9.55	-
13–15	7.95	-
11–12	6.55	-
5–10	5.30	-
0– 4	4.40	-

While the SBC provides a minimum income for those outside the labour market, the rates are far from generous. For example, a mother is expected to cover all the needs of a child under five on less than 63p a day. How many people in the years since 1948 have been living at this minimum level of income approved by Parliament? Table 5.2 sets out the numbers of claimants drawing National Assistance, or as it was renamed in 1966, Supplementary Benefit for selected years since 1948.

The broad picture which emerges from this table is as follows. The numbers of households dependent on Supplementary Benefit has risen from a little over a million in 1948 to almost 3 million by 1976. But these figures do not measure the total numbers of persons whose living standards are determined by Supplementary Benefit payments. If dependants are included with the numbers of claimants, the total rises to around 5 million. In addition there is a growing number of persons in households whose incomes are below the Supplementary Benefit level. The latest data are again for 1976. There were then 1,350,000 families containing 2,280,000 persons, living on incomes below the Supplementary Benefit level.

These figures tell us something about the size of poor households. Overwhelmingly they are small. Even if we examine only those house-

TABLE 5.2.

Numbers Receiving Supplementary Benefit, 1948–1976

Great Britain

Thousands

	1948	1951	1961	1970	1971	1972	1973	1974	1975	1976
ALL SUPPLEMENTARY BENEFITS	1011	1462	1844	2738	2909	2929	2675	2680	2793	2940
ALL SUPPLEMENTARY PENSIONS				1902	1919	1909	1844	1807	1679	1687
Retirement pensioners and National Insurance widows										
aged 60 and over	495	767	1075	1745	1816	1807	1747	1712	1586	1592
others	143	202	220	156	103	102	97	96	94	95
ALL SUPPLEMENTARY ALLOWANCES				836	990	1020	831	872	1113	1253
Unemployed										
With contrib benefit	19	33	45	73	129	94	48	73	135	654
Without contrib benefit	34	33	86	166	258	317	201	228	406	430
Sick and Disabled										
With contrib benefit	80	121	134	164	146	137	118	95	77	74
Without contrib benefit	64	98	133	159	159	161	162	165	165	169
NI Widows under 60	81	86	58	63	65	62	54	42	30	28
Other one parent families	32	41	76	196	213	227	228	245	276	303
Others	63	81	17	20	20	22	21	24	24	25

Source: 1948–1961 Frank Field, 'Poverty the Facts', C.P.A.G. (1975) Table 1.2.; 1970–*Department of Health and Social Security Annual Report 1970* (H.M.S.O. 1971) Table 113, p. 338; 1971–*Department of Health and Social Security Annual Report 1971* (London 1972) Table 111, p. 337; 1972–1976 Department of Health and Social Security, *Social Security Statistics*, Table 34.31, each year.

holds with children the picture remains very much the same. The majority of families with children drawing Supplementary Benefits in 1975, 69 per cent had only one or two children.

As well as showing a rise in the numbers dependent on Supplementary Benefits, the figures also illustrate how the face of poverty has changed over the past 30 years. In 1948 63 per cent of Supplementary Benefit claimants were retirement pensioners. By 1976 this proportion had fallen to 57 per cent. If the numbers of persons dependent on Supplementary Benefit are considered, as opposed to those claimants drawing benefit, the decline in the percentage of old people living at the officially approved minimum level of income is more marked. In 1955 retirement pensioners and their dependants made up 61 per cent of persons dependent on National Assistance payments. By 1976 this proportion had fallen to 42 per cent.

Some critics argue that the Supplementary Benefit levels should not be taken as a measurement of poverty over time. As living standards rise so too does Parliament increase the weekly payments made by the SBC. Politicians have not been slow to argue that an increase in the numbers of SB claimants is due to a more generous definition of poverty rather than an increase in the numbers of poor. For example, in the run up to the 1970 General Election, the present Secretary of State for Social Services, David Ennals, was involved in a dispute about whether the poor had become relatively poorer during the period of the first two Wilson Governments. The Minister did not reply directly to this charge made by CPAG, but asserted that 'the Supplementary Benefit scale rates have been raised every year since the Government took office. They are now, in real terms, 18 per cent higher than the 1964 National Assistance scale. One result has been to increase the numbers of people drawing benefit by 600,000.'[1]

What was not in dispute was that Supplementary Benefits had risen in real terms—comparing their value at the time of each uprating. But the Minister's argument that the numbers of poor had increased due to changes in the scale rates was only valid if their relative, as opposed to real, value had been increased. Did this in fact happen?

The evidence is somewhat confusing. If the value of Supplementary Benefit payments is expressed as a percentage of gross and net earnings for each year since 1948 the following two trends are discernable. Looking over the whole period it is clear that the value of the scale rate as a percentage of gross earnings, while fluctuating, has changed very little. A different picture emerges if we consider the value of benefits against net earnings. Because the tax burden has increased for working house-

[1]D. Ennals, D.H.S.S. press release dated 19 Apr. 1970.

holds the Supplementary Benefit poverty line measured against net earnings has increased substantially over the period. A major change occurred in 1965 in the value of what is called the ordinary scale rate. A similar rachet effect in the value of the long term rate took place in 1974.

However, an important study published recently suggests that the relative value of benefits has remained fairly constant in the post-war period. Last year the National Institute of Economic and Social Research issued a report by G. C. Fiegehen, P. S. Lansley and A. D. Smith entitled *Poverty and Progress in Britain, 1953-73.*[2] The authors were aware of the difference in the values of the Supplementary Benefit scale rates when measured against gross and net earnings but reworked the data on 'an equivalent net income basis'. After doing so their results showed that 'the relative living standards of the poor appeared to remain approximately constant between 1953/4 and 1971, at about 49 per cent of the median for the 5th percentile and about 58 per cent for the 10th percentile'. The Study went on to report: 'This reflects the much sharper rise between 1953/4 and 1971 in the direct tax burden of median households (4.3 per cent of gross incomes of 14.8 per cent) than of poor households (1.8 per cent to 3.2 per cent)'. And in their final comments the National Institute researchers observed: 'It is perhaps best to conclude that the evidence points to neither a significant deterioration nor an improvement in the relative income to the poor over this period'.[3]

If the relative income of the poor has not improved, in other words, if there has not been a redistribution to those on low incomes, to what extent, and by what means have the living standards of the poor changed in the post-war period?

This was also a question which concerned the N.I.E.S.R.'s poverty study. No one would dispute the fact that the living standards of the poor have risen during the post-war period. The extent of the increase can be seen from one of the N.I.E.S.R.'s calculations. When the real value of National Assistance for 1953/4 was held constant throughout the post-war period and up until 1971 the numbers of poor dropped from a total of 2.4 million to 300,000. Alternatively, by taking the real value of assistance in 1971, and applying it to households' incomes in 1953/4, the authors found a total of 10.6 millions poor in the earlier year.[4] On the basis of these calculations the study concluded that as 'the substantial rise of about 75 per cent recorded in the real income of the poor over the last two decades is not attributable to any appreciable

[2]T.C. Fiegehen, P. S. Lansley and A. D. Smith, *Poverty and Progress in Britain 1953-1973* (Cambridge, 1977), p. 29.
[3]Ibid. p. 29.
[4]Ibid. p. 29.

change in their relative standards it must reflect participation in a general improvement of living standards'.[5]

The Royal Commission on the Distribution of Income and Wealth undertook a similar analysis which was reported in its lower income reference. It concluded that the rise in the living standards of the poor was due to the general rise in prosperity rather than a redistribution of resources. Taking 1961 as its bench mark, and measuring the period up to 1974/5 the Commission found that the average real income of the lowest three tenths of family units increased by roughly 40 per cent in line with the growth of GNP of about 38 per cent.[6]

It also illustrated the importance of economic growth in raising the living standards of the poor. The Commission took 1961 as its base line and calculated the numbers in poverty in 1975 if the 1961 poverty line income was maintained in the real terms only. Their finding was that the proportion of family units below the 1961 level in 1975 was reduced by over a half to about a tenth, observing 'This shows how the growth of the economy operated over this period to permit the level of income of those on the lowest quarter to be raised'.[7]

2. Slow Growth and the Numbers of Poor

Research by the N.I.E.S.R. and the Royal Commission suggests that the increase in the living standards of the poor during the post-war period has not been due to a redistribution of resources. Rather, the rise in living standards of those on low incomes has occurred because they have shared in the country's increasing prosperity. A period of sustained slow growth could, therefore, result in a brake being applied to any improvements in the poor's living standards. There are four reasons, however, why a period of slow growth must be matched by a period of positive redistribution of resources towards those at the bottom of the income distribution.

The first concerns the actual standard of living on which a growing number of poor people are required to live. There is no dispute that the poor have shared in the increased prosperity of the last 30 years or so. But what has to be faced is whether the living standards of today's poor are at an unacceptably low level compared with the overall prosperity of the community in which they live. For example, a couple with two children on the ordinary scale rate receive a benefit valued at only 40 per cent of average earnings. Two pieces of research illustrate the need for an improvement in the relative incomes of those living around the

[5]Ibid. p. 29.
[6]Royal Commission on the Distribution of Income and Wealth, *Lower Incomes* (London, 1978), p. 18.
[7]Ibid.

Supplementary Benefit level, particularly if they have children.[8]

The first set of evidence comes from nutritionists who have cast doubt on whether poor families can feed their children adequately. In September 1975 Michael Church took the Supplementary Benefit scale rates for children aged between 5 and 11 and assumed that 75 per cent of this would be spent on food (although those on average earnings spend only about a third of their income on food). He then took the D.H.S.S.'s recommended intakes of nutrients for the U.K. and these were applied over the age band for 5 to 11 for the smallest and largest of children. The final stage was to work out the costs of providing energy for these different groups of children. Once this exercise was completed Church reported 'only the most efficient mothers [at shopping] with the smallest children, could even hope to provide enough energy for their children on the allowance'.[9]

A similar, but more detailed analysis was carried out by Caroline Walker together with Michael Church a year later. Data were taken from the 1975 National Food Survey on the food purchases of different socio-economic groups. The total energy value of the food consumed and its monetary value were then used to calculate the numbers of calories obtained per penny. These data were then updated to 1976.

On the basis of this work Walker and Church were able to challenge the very widespread belief about the consumption patterns for the poor. Their results showed that 'low income groups and large families tend to buy more efficiently than high income groups and small families'.

Their second finding, based on spending the *whole* of the Supplementary Benefit allowance for a 5 to 10 year old on food, was 'the present Supplementary Benefits allowance . . . . . . is inadequate to cover the food needs of the largest 8 to 10 year olds, even with the most efficient purchasing pattern'.[10]

The second set of evidence on the inadequacy of the living standards of the poor compared to the general standard of living comes from official surveys. The D.H.S.S. undertook research on the sick and disabled in 1972 and on unemployed beneficiariès in 1974. Both surveys sought to look at the standard of living afforded to claimants who were dependent on Supplementary Benefit income for a long time.

One part of the research was to examine whether claimants had

[8]For an explanation of how the calculations of family needs have always been underestimated, see F. Field, *A Changing Perception of Poverty? A Historical Review*, mimeograph (London, 1978).
[9]M. Church, 'Can Mothers Manage on Supplementary Benefits?*, Poverty 33 (London, 1976).
[10]G. L. Walker and M. Church, 'Poverty by Administration: a Review of Supplementary Benefits, Nutrition Scale Rates', *Journal of Human Nutrition* (xxx 1978).

clothing which brought their stocks up to the level laid down in the form BO/40 which is the official guide to Supplementary Benefit officers making exceptional needs payments for clothing. The guide lays down the following clothing stocks. For men and boys, the poor may be entitled to possess one overcoat or raincoat together with one jacket, 2 shirts, 2 vests, 2 underpants and a pullover together with 2 pairs of trousers or jeans. The list for women and girls is not dissimilar except for obvious differences. From what is known about average living standards, most people would have been unhappy to have to manage on such limited stocks, but both surveys showed many claimants' clothing possessions were below this level, particularly if they had children. 43 per cent of single sick and disabled claimants without children had stocks of clothing less than the BO/40 level and this rose to 61 per cent of claimants with two or more children. The equivalent figures for unemployed claimants were 49 per cent and 76 per cent respectively.

The surveys also reported on claimants who had fallen into debt since being on benefit. Again considerable numbers of claimants were found to be in this position. The surveys showed that the additional cash from borrowing was spent overwhelmingly on food, clothing, heating and meeting other household costs.

Reporting on the economies families had to make on benefit, as well as the extent of unmet needs, the official surveys concluded that the claimants with families were 'by several standards apparently more hard put to it than other claimants to balance their weekly budget. Some more subjective information gathered from the unemployed men also indicates that family men were the most hard pressed. The proportion of claimants who said that they had cut down on their usual expenditure since being on benefit was highest (93 per cent) for family men'. The unemployed men were also asked whether, in spite of cutting down, borrowing and using savings, they still felt that there was something they really needed and for which they were unable to find the money. The proportion who said they had unmet needs increased steadily with family size, from 59 per cent of lone claimants to 80 per cent of those with three or more children. 'The family men were more likely to say they had unmet needs the longer they had been on benefit'.[11]

The Supplementary Benefits Commission drew upon these official surveys in its evidence to the Royal Commission on the Distribution of Income and Wealth in order to comment on the adequacy of the Supplementary Benefit scale rates. Its conclusion was: "The evidence presented .... regarding the standard of living of Supplementary Benefit recipients strongly suggests that the Supplementary Benefits scheme provides, particularly for families with children, incomes that are barely

[11]Supplementary Benefits Commission, *Low Incomes* (London, 1977), p. 27.

adequate to meet their needs at a level that is consistent with the normal participation in the life of the relatively wealthy society in which they live".[12] And this 'barely adequate' standard of living was the end product, not of a period of slow or nil growth but of the post-war prosperity.

There is a second reason why a period of slow or nil growth should be accompanied by a policy of redistribution. Earnings data were first

TABLE 5.3.
Weekly Earnings of Manual Workers:
Lowest Decile as a Percentage of
Median Earnings, 1886–1977

Year	Manual Men	Manual Women
1886	68.6	-
1906	66.5	-
1938	67.7	64.3
1960	70.6	72.0
1963	70.7	68.5
1964	71.6	65.1
1965	69.7	66.5
1966	68.6	66.3
1967	69.8	66.1
1968	67.3	71.1
1970	67.3	69.0
1971	68.2	70.2
1972	67.6	68.9
1973	67.3	69.2
1974	68.6	69.1
1975	69.2	68.4
1976	70.2	67.8
1977	70.6	70.3

Source: Figures for 1886–1974 taken from *British Labour Statistics Yearbook*, 1974 (H.M.S.O. 1977) Table 52. Figures from 1975 taken from *New Earnings Survey 1977*, (London, 1978) Table 15.

collected for male workers in 1886. Data on earnings were then collected spasmodically up until 1970. What is of importance to our considerations is whether the value of the earnings of the poorest workers have risen compared to median earnings during a period of more rapid growth and

[12]Ibid. p. 28.

rising prosperity. The value of median earnings for manual men and women workers is given in the table above.

The figures show a remarkable stability in relative earnings. In 1886 the value of the lowest decile of manual men workers was 68.6 per cent of median earnings. By 1977 the value of the poorest manual men workers' wages had been edged up by two percentage points.

The first earnings data on manual women workers were collected in 1938 and the table shows a greater fluctuation in the earnings of the poorest women workers. For example, in 1938 the value of the lowest decile expressed as a percentage of the median earnings was 64.3 per cent while thirty years on this had risen to 71.1 per cent. Since then, however, the earnings of the poorest women workers shows the same kind of stability as can be noticed in the data on their male counterparts. By 1977 the value of the lowest decile was 70.3 per cent of median earnings. The overall impression given by the data is therefore clear: the prosperity of the post-war years has done little to improve the relative rewards of those who earn their poverty be they male or female workers. If the relative earnings of the poorest in work has remained fairly stable what has happened to the numbers who are low paid?

There are three ways of categorising low paid workers. The National Board for Prices and Incomes defined low pay as those in the lowest decile of the earnings distribution. While this approach has some advantages, its main disadvantage is that, with an unequal distribution of income, there will always be a lowest decile of male earners. It, therefore, holds no value for policy makers who wish to measure the success or otherwise of actions aimed against low pay. For this reason increasing emphasis is put on measuring the numbers of low paid as those who either earn less than their Supplementary Benefit entitlement, or who earn a wage packet which is less than a target figure of average earnings.

Data on the numbers earnings less than their Supplementary Benefit entitlement have been published for each year since 1972. However, the data for the two earliest years are not comparable with the sequence from 1974 when the self employed were included in the FES calculations for the first time. The numbers earning less than the Supplementary Benefit poverty line for each year since 1974 are given in Table 5.4. It is important to note, however, that the total of low paid workers will include those who have been unemployed or sick for less than three months and whose household income, when they were in work, was less than the SB rate. But it is also necessary to stress that the data excludes many low paid workers with working wives whose additional income brings the household income above the statutory poverty line.

While it must be emphasised that these FES data are open to a fairly wide margin of error, the trend from the table is nevertheless clear. The number of poverty wage earners has risen from 130,000 in 1974 to 290,000 two years later.

TABLE 5.4.
Incomes below Supplementary Benefit Level
of those Normally in Full-time Work or Self-employed

GREAT BRITAIN	Thousands	
	Income below Supplementary Benefit	
Year	Families	Persons
1974	130	**360**
1975	210	630
1976	290	890

Source: D.H.S.S.

The numbers earning less than the Supplementary Benefit payments which would be made to them if they were not working is but the tip of the low pay iceberg. An overall measurement of the extent of low pay comes from looking at the TUC 1974 minimum wage target which was set at £30 a week or two thirds of average male earnings. Although the TUC has been reluctant to revise this money target, the Government's latest white paper on inflation up-dates the target figure for 1977. Taking the two-thirds minimum wage target we see from the 1977 New Earnings Survey that 1.1 million men and 2.7 million women workers, a total of 3.8 million adult workers overall, earn below two-thirds of average earnings, even after taking into account overtime. If the earnings data were analysed without overtime the numbers rise to 1.7 million to 2.8 million respectively, a total of 4.5 million adult workers.[13]

The rising prosperity of the fifties and early sixties failed to eradicate low pay, however low pay is defined. The recession following the OPEC prices rises has resulted in a dramatic increase in the numbers who earn their poverty. The growing number of low paid alone makes a powerful case for redistribution. But there are additional reasons why a period of slow growth should be accompanied by an attack on low pay. Recently we have become aware of how low pay is not only an immediate, but also an indirect cause of poverty. Tony Atkinson summed up the evidence on this point by observing 'that low earnings are more important than

[13]For further details, see F. Field, 'Low Pay, Low Profile', *Low Pay Bulletin*, 18, Dec. 1977.

an analysis of the immediate causes of poverty would suggest. Low pay must be seen more generally as a disadvantage in the labour market, and as associated with high incidence of job instability and ill-health and with the absence of fringe benefits. The low paid worker is more vulnerable to the interruption or loss of earning power, and lacks the resources to meet such needs. Low earnings mean that people cannot save for emergencies or for old age . . . . . . In these and other ways low pay plays an important role in cycle of poverty'. To which he adds 'low pay is a thread which runs throughout people's working lives and beyond into retirement, and what may appear at first sight to be "bad luck" is likely to be related to labour market disadvantage. Poverty does not happen to just anyone'.[14]

But redistribution is demanded because a period of slow-quick will itself worsen further the low pay problem in the following ways. As Atkinson noted, those in low paying occupations and industries tend to be more vulnerable to unemployment. In part this is due to the fact that the low paid are concentrated in older industries employing outdated technologies which are more vulnerable to economic fluctuations. It is also due to the fact that unemployment is selective in its effects, bearing more heavily on women, the unskilled, coloured workers and those at the beginning or end of their working lives—all those groups in fact who are most likely to be found amongst the ranks of the low paid. Although we have very little information on the association between unemployment and wage rates at an aggregate level, these factors inevitably tend to depress the bargaining strength of workers who are already poorly paid.

Earlier we saw that a large number of workers on low basic rates of pay lift themselves and their families out of poverty by working overtime. The latest estimates, for 1977, suggest that three quarters of a million more people would have been low paid if they had not worked overtime. Indeed, the numbers of low paid men increase by over 60 per cent if overtime is taken out of the calculations. This being the case the cutbacks in overtime and shift working which inevitably accompany periods of slow or nil growth are likely to have a severe impact on the living standards of the low paid.

Moreover, we know that many families in which the breadwinner is low paid are forced to supplement these earnings through a second wage. Indeed, the Royal Commission on the Distribution of Income and Wealth cited evidence showing the proportion of working families in poverty would increase threefold if married women did not go out to work. Since married women are known to be highly vulnerable to unemployment,

[14]A. B. Atkinson, 'Low Pay and the Cycle of Poverty', in F. Field (ed.), *Low Pay*, Arrow, 1973.

the recession will again reduce the family living standards of low paid.[15]

The third reason supporting the case for a period of sustained redistribution is that the years of slow economic growth will be marked by an increase in the numbers made poor by unemployment. At the time of writing the numbers of registered unemployed stand at around 1.5 million. The latest estimates from the Department of Employment project a rise in the labour force both in the five years up to 1981 and in the following five yers. The projected increase in the labour force during the first five year period is put at a little under half a million (488,000). The projected increase over the whole period up to 1986 is put at a little over 1 million (1,047,000).[16]

On the assumption that the current job market is unaffected by technological changes such as the rapid introduction of micro-processing, what growth rate is required to create new jobs to match the projected increase in the labour force, let alone reduce the current record post-war level of unemployment? The estimates vary from 3 per cent from the Treasury to a 4 per cent growth rate from Terry Ward and the Department of Applied Economics at Cambridge. Against these figures we have to put the current growth rate of the economy of around 2 per cent which is unlikely to be maintained next year. It is on the basis of a growth rate substantially below the level required to match the expected increase in labour supply that practically all forecasting organisations project a rise in the numbers of unemployed. For example, the Cambridge Group has put the level of unemployment at 2.25 millions five years later. Unless there is a major programme of work sharing, or of early retirement, or of raising the age threshold to the labour market or of job creation, a period characterised by relatively slow growth rate will add to the numbers of unemployed. How will this affect the numbers of poor?

Unemployment causes poverty because it reduces the majority of workless to a low level of income. Loss of work is not countered adequately by National Insurance payments. In *Social Insurance and Allied Services* Beveridge spelt out the two key principles of his social insurance scheme. One was that "all the principal cash payments—for unemployment, disability and retirement will continue so long as need lasts".[17]

The Report laid down that to draw benefit the unemployed would be required to register for work and could be suspended from benefit if they left their previous employment without good cause or had similarly

[15]Royal Commission on the Distribution of Income and Wealth, op. cit.
[16]'New Projections of Future Labour Force', *Department of Employment Gazette* (June, 1977).
[17]W. Beveridge, *Social Insurance and Allied Services* (London, 1942), para. 20.

refused a job offered to them by the labour exchange. In addition Beveridge stipulated that the payment of benefit could be made conditional on the claimant's attendance at a training centre. Once these conditions were fulfilled (and they operate in today's scheme) Beveridge saw no objection to paying Unemployment Benefit for as long as unemployment lasted. Yet this aspect of the Beveridge scheme was not accepted. Up until 1966 a standard provision of seven months' Unemployment Benefit was made on top of which further days could be added depending upon the claimant's insurance record. The maximum period during which benefit was paid during any one time amounted to 19 months. The introduction in 1966 of an earnings related benefit for the first six months of unemployment was accompanied by a reduction in the duration of a flat-rate benefit for up to 12 months.

The second basic principle of the Beveridge scheme was the payment of insurance benefits at a level which put the claimant's income above the official poverty line. The Attlee Government brought the Beveridge scheme into operation in 1948 but insurance benefits were paid at a lower level than was originally envisaged. For example, in that year Unemployment Benefit was only 10p greater for a single person than the National Assistance scale rate. As claimants on the latter benefit would also have their rent paid, beneficiaries with no other resources than their National Insurance benefits would usually be eligible for National Assistance as well.

So despite the existence of the flat rate and earnings related Unemployment Benefit, increasing numbers of the unemployed during the post-war period are being pushed into poverty. Details on the numbers of unemployed claiming Supplementary Benefit are given in the table below.

The post war period has been characterised by two trends. The percentage of unemployed dependent exclusively on National Insurance benefits has fallen for most years irrespective of the level of economic activity. In 1948 71 per cent of the workless were dependent only on unemployment pay. By last year this percentage had dropped to 33 per cent and this total includes those drawing the earnings related supplement. At the same time the numbers of unemployed who were dependent exclusively on Supplementary Benefit rose from 10 per cent in 1948 to 42 per cent last year. The numbers made poor by unemployment will continue to grow as the total army of jobless increases unless major changes are made to the national insurance provisions for the unemployed. In a period of slow or nil growth these changes will need to be financed by a redistribution of income.

At a time when the numbers made poor by unemployment are likely to increase, demographic changes are taking place which will also increase **the number** of households living on low incomes. One major demographic

TABLE 5.5
Numbers of Unemployed
Receiving National Insurance and Supplementary Benefits

Great Britain   Thousands

Year (Nov)	Total Unemployment	Unemployment Benefit		Unemployment Benefit and Earnings Related Supp.		Unemployment Benefit and Supplementary Benefit		Unemployment and Supplementary Benefit and Earnings Related Supp.		Supplementary Benefit		No Benefit	
	No.	No.	%	No.	%	No.	%	No.	%	No.	%	No.	%
1948	327.9	233	71.0			19	5.8			34	10.4	42	12.8
1949	285.7	217	67.1			30	9.3			33	11.1	36	12.5
1950	302.0	174	57.6			38	12.6			39	12.9	51	16.9
1951	282.5	166	57.3			33	11.4			27	11.3	56	20.0
1952	425.3	233	57.2			59	14.5			43	10.6	90	17.7
1953	323.0	166	51.4			48	14.9			46	14.2	63	19.5
1954	263.1	120	45.6			30	11.4			50	19.0	63	24.0
1955	225.1	104	46.2			20	8.9			41	18.1	60	26.7
1956	265.1	125	47.1			30	11.3			43	16.3	67	25.3
1957	252.0	147	46.3			41	13.0			55	17.3	59	23.4
1958	528.4	268	50.7			66	12.5			85	16.1	109	21.0
1959	433.9	199	45.9			42	9.7			87	20.0	106	24.4
1960	351.4	146	41.5			31	8.8			76	21.7	98	28.0
1961	382.8	173	45.2			29	7.6			74	19.3	107	28.0
1962	545.3	259	47.5			55	10.0			95	17.5	186	25.0
1963	476.4	208	43.6			46	9.7			109	22.9	113	24.0
1964	350.1	146	41.7			26	7.5			85	24.2	93	26.6
1965	324.5	132	40.7			34	10.5			78	24.0	80	24.8
1966	484.3	234	48.4			36	7.4	5	1.1	84	17.3	130	26.9
1967	502.9	245	43.1			64	11.2	9	1.6	128	32.6	66	13.1
1968	555.0	235	42.3	90	16.2	53	9.5	7	1.2	136	24.6	131	23.6
1969	560.4	217	38.7	85	15.2	55	9.9	8	1.4	141	25.1	147	26.3
1970	596.0	243	40.8	97	16.3	52	8.8	6	1.1	149	24.9	152	25.5
1971	860.2	352	40.9	154	17.9	97	11.3	11	1.2	234	27.2	177	20.5
1972	790.1	268	33.9	116	14.7	76	9.6	9	1.1	281	35.6	165	20.9
1973	508.6	155	30.5	71	14.0	36	7.0	7	1.3	192	37.8	126	24.7
1974	617.7	208	33.7	95	15.4	55	8.9	11	1.8	212	34.3	143	23.1
1975	1079.3	406	37.6	206	19.1	90	8.3	29	2.7	389	36.1	194	18.0
1976	1200.5	446	37.2	214	17.8	110	9.2	31	2.6	444	36.9	200	16.7
1977	1346.8	440	32.7			98	7.3	23	1.7	561	41.6	248	18.4

Source: House of Commons Hansard, Vol. 923, 23rd June 1978, col. 63–6, 20/12/76 and Vol. 952, col. 288–90. *Social Security Statistics*, Table 1.32, *Social Security Statistics 1974 and 1976* (London 1975 and 1978).
Notes: Figures prior to 1959 are based on a 100 per cent count of National Assistance Board cases in December each year. Figures for 1965 are based on a sample enquiry in November. Figures for 1959 and onwards are based on a 5 per cent sample of total registered unemployed. The figures for total registered unemployed are grossed up from these sample figures in order to provide a consistent series and they may not therefore correspond to other published figures for total registered unemployed. The figures for 1976 are for May of that year.

change over the recent past which has affected the numbers of poor has been an increase in the numbers of elderly. However, projections over the next decade show the numbers of pensioners rising only moderately and that changes on this front are now unlikely to add significantly to the numbers on low incomes.

A totally different picture emerges if we look at the likely increase in the numbers of one-parent families. Recently single parent families have been increasing at a little over 6 per cent a year. If this rate of increase is maintained over the next decade the number of single parent families will grow from a total of 798,000 in 1977 to 1,390,000 by 1987. The corresponding increase in the number of children cared for in those families will rise from 1,436,000 to 2,503,000 over the same period of time. How will these projections affect the numbers of poor?

At the present time 60 per cent of one-parent families are dependent on Supplementary Benefit. If the same ratio is maintained over the next decade we find the following numbers of single parent families drawing benefit. By 1982 we estimate that 454,000 single parent families will be drawing Supplementary Benefit, a total rising to 599,000 five years later.

TABLE 5.6
Projected Number of One-parent Families on SB

Year	Numbers of families	Numbers of children
1977	343,938	619,000
1982	453,998	817,000
1987	599,277	1,078,700

There is, therefore, yet a further reason why a period of slow or nil growth will need to be accompanied by a redistribution in favour of the poor. All the projections cited above have been employed so that an estimate can be made of the likely repercussions on the social security budget. These projected social security costs in 1977 prices, taking account of demographic changes among pensioners and one-parent families, together with the cost of paying benefit to a growing army of unemployed, are presented in the table below.

TABLE 5.7.
Projected Social Security Costs (in 1977 prices)

Year	Unemployed £m	Pensioners £m	One parent families £m	Total £m
1977	2090.3	7,109	537	9,736.3
1982	3258.9	7,348	709	11,315.9
1987	5214.3	7,391	936	13,541.3

From this we can see that if the real value of benefits paid to these three groups of beneficiaries is to be maintained, the social security budget will need to rise from a current level of £9.7 bn for the three groups to just over £13.5 bn by 1987.

What will happen to the living standards of the poor during a decade characterised by a slow or nil growth rate? At the present time 10.8 per cent of GNP is spent on social security. If the real living standards of beneficiaries are to be maintained without a policy of redistribution GNP will need to grow by 16.3 per cent (or at 3.3 per cent a year in the years from 1977 up to 1982) and by 39.1 per cent (or at an annual rate of 3.9 per cent) in the years up to 1987. Few people predict a sustained rate of growth anywhere approaching these levels. A failure to achieve these rates will therefore mean a real cut in the living standards of the poor unless the coming decade is marked by a dtermined policy of re-distributing resources.

3. Conclusion

The post-war boom years may well prove to be an exceptional period for Britain during this century. They have, nevertheless, been a period characterised by an all-party agreement on poverty with both the Conservatives and Social Democrats supporting the view that improve-ments in the living standards of the poor should be one of the first calls on an ever-expanding national product. Social Democrats have gone further and argued that greater equality can and should be brought about by staking a disproportionate claim on the fruits of growth for those on low income. This central pillar underlying much of the ideo-logical consensus of the post-war years is now threatened by a period of slow or even nil growth. For there has been no political commitment to improving the living standards of the poor by means of a *redistribution* of income.

This paper has tried to show that the years of affluence have failed the poor in two very important respects. In the first place it has afforded them an unacceptably low relative standard of living. Moreover, it has done little to improve the relative earnings of the poverty wage-earner and has left an economy characterised by low pay.

On these grounds alone there is a powerful case for the next decade to be characterised by a policy of redistribution to the poor. But a period of slow or nil growth will itself add to the pressures for redis-tribution and thereby stand on its head the current political consensus about growth and rising living standards of the poor. A period of slow growth will see an increase in the numbers made poor by unemploy-ment as well as an increase in the numbers on low income as a result of demographic changes. In a period of slow or nil growth the living standards of what will become an increasing army of poor people will therefore be reduced unless the increase is matched by a policy of redistribution, for this rise in the numbers of poor will require a real increase in the social security budget.

Finally, what do we mean when we talk about redistribution? While there is a strong moral case for redistributing along traditional lines— from rich to poor—such a policy alone will be inadequate to meet the challenge of maintaining, let alone increasing, the relative living standards of those on low incomes. Redistribution must also be pursued horizontally from the childless to those with children. Redistribution will also need to take place from younger to older sections of the community and from the consumers to some low paid producers. And, in a period of rising unemployment, there will need to be a redistribution from those in work to the workless.

This plea will be met by the standard refrain that redistribution has already reached its limits. A period of slow growth will, therefore, need to be accompanied by a much more critical look at the extent to which redistribution has occurred during the post-war years.[18] The 'reaching the limits of redistribution' cry has allowed the privileged to become the convenient beneficiaries of their own propaganda—acting as a powerfull sedative on the conscience of the privileged in our society. A period of slow economic growth is to be welcomed if it results in a realisation that at any time, and particularly when national income failes to grow, the crucial political question revolves around what can be justified as a fair distribution of existing income.

---

[18]F. Field, 'The Limites to Redistribution', a contribution to the Colston Symposium, forthcoming.

6

CAPACITY ADJUSTMENT
IN A SLOWLY GROWING ECONOMY

by David K. Stout

Economic Director, National Economic Development Office

1. Introduction: More Food for the Long-distance Runner?

The earlier papers in this series have been mostly about the symptoms and causes of slow growth. I have come increasingly to take the view that British industrial investment behaviour itself has been much more of a symptom than a cause of our low growth rate.[1] In this paper I shall be looking at some of the implications for manufacturing investment of policies appropriate to a hitherto slowly-growing, mature economy which is trying to raise relative income. When discussing 'adjustment of capacity', I have in mind changes in the composition of plant and equipment (through investment) which follow from, and complement, structural policies. It is increasingly apparent that one of the most intractable of industrial policy problems is how to develop a strong alternative motive for investment, other than the motive which is normally dominant, namely adding to capacity in response to increases in demand.

To prescribe for a sluggish economy simply a larger slice of investment out of output is rather like admonishing an aspiring but seriously out-of-condition fell-runner to eat more heartily. Perhaps, whatever he does, he will never make a first class fell-racer. If, in the long run, he ever does, he will surely then demand and benefit from larger helpings of protein. In either event, it will not do to begin a new regime by feeding him like a hungry athlete. He sets out, after all, with little appetite and even less capacity to burn energy. Under-utilization is already a problem for him. He will not so much run faster as run to fat.

In the past fourteen years, the National Economic Development Council has met to discuss at least nineteen papers on the encouragement

---

[1] Professor Ed. Denison put the point clearly: 'growth may be rapid for reasons unrelated to capacity, but a rapid increase in capacity is induced by rapid growth'. R. Caves (ed.), *Britain's Economic Prospects* (London, 1969), p. 273.

of investment in industry. The slant of these papers, many of them reflecting changing official attitudes to the role of investment, has changed by degrees from seeking simply for *more* investment towards emphasising the contribution of investment to greater international competitiveness, greater product relevance to rapidly-growing markets, narrower specialization and fuller utilization.

In 1966, at a special N.E.D.C. conference on productivity held at Chequers, the keynote paper on investment stated: 'There is a strong relationship between a country's growth rate and the proportion of its income that is devoted to capital investment. On both these counts, Britain ranks lower than almost any other industrial country. A substantial increase in investment is the key to higher output per man and hence to faster growth.' Eight years later, at a meeting held in August 1974, the N.E.D. Office's background paper took a more subdued line: 'A faster rate of increase of living standards does not wait only upon a collective decision to build more plant and equipment across the economy. The productivity of labour in industry depends not simply upon the quantity of capital but upon the composition of the capital stock, how fully it is utilized and how far it embodies the most efficient available techniques.'[2] Since then, as industrial performance has come to be examined by tri-partite working parties representing individual sectors of manufacturing, investment programmes have increasingly been treated as complementary to more attractive product design, the exchange of technical information, standardization and improved liaison between producers and users.

In an economy in which relatively slow growth and declining manufacturing competitiveness are a century-old problem, spread across almost every sector, it is tedious but necessary to try to find out what has gone wrong market by market, and to direct policy to the recapturing of demand. Investment has its place in the vicious circle of slow growth, but it is not the right place to *break into* the circle when the productivity of existing capital is low.[3]

The advancement of economics on scientific principles naturally and rightly leads economists to search for encompassing general explanations

---

[2] D. K. Stout, *Industrial Performance in the Longer Term: An Approach Through Investment*, N.E.D.C. (74) 31 (Research Annex) (1974), p. 1 (mimeo N.E.D.O.).
[3] cf B. Moore and J. Rhodes: 'The slow rate of growth of demand has in turn been associated with a low rate of investment by the manufacturing sector and a low rate of expansion of productive capacity relative to other industrial countries. Low levels of investment imply a relatively slow rate of adaptation by industry to technical progress, particularly in growth industries, to changing demand in innovation in product ranges and to the need to modernise whole production and marketing provesses', 'The Relative Decline of the UK Manufacturing Sector', Univ. of Cambridge, D.A.E., *Economic Policy Review* (Mar. 1976).

of particular events. General explanations which have commonly found favour turn out either to be almost impossible to verify—like those referring to managerial incentives—or else to confuse effects, which reinforce the problem, with sufficient causes—like paucity of investment—or else to refer to a phenomen so vague and general as to be useless as a guide to policy without a great amount of detailed spade-work at the micro-economic level—like the pervasive and relentless decline in international non-price competitiveness.

It is (relatively) easy to prescribe for weakened incentives. It is difficult (but not impossible) to force through more investment, just as it is to restore international *price* competitiveness. But declining competitiveness in other respects breaks down into hundreds of separate missed opportunities in dozens of separate industries. The search by N.E.D.O. for a common thread through a tangle of O.E.C.D. trade statistics resulted in the finding of a low and declining added value per ton of UK exports within each individual product group relative to successful (and fast-growing) competitors (see fn. 17). But, from that observation alone, nothing operational follows, across the board, for industrial policy. In some cases, British producers have fallen irretrievably behind; in some, they have deliberately continued to produce too many elderly products; in some, they have been discouraged by institutional pressures or by lack of size, from introducing new techniques; in others, out of lack of confidence or lack of access to risk capital for long-term intangible investment, they have refrained from determined and persistent advance marketing in major customer countries. One thing that does *not* emerge from all this is a clear-cut proposition about the role of capital adjustment. What the aspiring fell-runner needs to begin with is appropriate training, not more food.

2. Trends in Manufacturing Investment and Utilization: Loss of Appetite and Lack of Exercise

In the 1970s the British economy—in particular its manufacturing sector—has been marked by both a decline in investment, a sharp annual rate of fall in the productivity of manufacturing capital stock, and greater under-utilization of this stock than in the 1960s.

Investment increased quite sharply (measured from peak to peak) in the later 1960s, reaching a maximum in 1970. Indeed, between 1967 and 1970 the growth rate of industrial investment matched that of Germany and France.[4]

---

[4]But while in France production grew almost at the same rate as investment, in Britain it grew at less than half the rate.

Between 1970 and 1974 manufacturing investment declined, dropped sharply in the next two years and recovered a little in 1977 and 1978. 1979 is likely to be a peak year, with investment running 6 per cent above the 1974 rate. For all that, measured at constant prices, it will still be about 3½ per cent below the level it reached nine years ago.

TABLE 6.1.
*Index of UK Manufacturing Investment
at Constant 1975 Prices (peak years)*

			Index	% growth p.a. from previous peak
1961			100	
1966			103.8	+ 0.8
1970			124.5	+ 4.7
1974			113.4	− 2.3
	(1975	102.0)		
	(1976	96.9)		
	(1977	103.5)		
	(1978	114.4)		
1979(est)			120.2	+ 1.2
1961–1979				+ 1.0

Source: Dept. of Industry and N.E.D.O.

The long-run fall in the share of manufacturing investment in GDP partly reflects the fall in the UK share of manufacturing markets themselves both overseas and at home; but it has been noticeably sharper than that drop in the share of manufacturing output itself.[5]

These figures are compatible with what we know from work at the individual industry level. With stagnant markets and a falling share of international trade, there has been little reason for much net investment in Britain. But on top of that, mechanization has proceeded much more slowly than in economies with an often quite similar pattern of manufacturing output.

According to some recent calculations,[6] it appears that slow growth

---

[5] If technical progress were 'Harrod-neutral', so that the equilibrium capital: output ratio remained unchanged at a given interest rate, the rate of growth of net investment should equal the rate of growth of output, of capital stock and (with a given labour force) of technical progress. In the UK, between 1961 and 1974, it grew less than half as fast.

[6] M. Panić *Capacity Utilization in UK Manufacturing Industry*, N.E.D.O., (1978).

TABLE 6.2.

Manufacturing Investment per Employee

(Current prices and exchange rates. Netherlands, Italy and France are for industry as a whole)

	UK	Neth.	US	Sweden	France	Japan	Italy
1970	604	1633	2145	1207	1439	1317	751
1974	920	2743	2785	2443	2288	2141	1469
1975	1006	3108	2947	2934	2682	1768	n.a.

Source: Brown and Sheriff, N.I.E.S.R. Conference on De-industrialization (1978).

has been accompanied by much more widespread and pronounced margins of excess capacity in the 1970s than in the previous decade, in spite of the low rate of investment. The subject is eating little, yet still putting on weight.

The increase in spare capacity reached a record level in 1976.[7] Three kinds of reason for it can be found. First, there may have been some increase in the desired normal margin of spare capacity. G. C. Winston[8] has described the circumstances in which planned utilization may fall. Among them, some that may have become more important are the increase in the relative cost of complementary labour (an input priced according to the time of day); increased uncertainty about the level of demand; and an increase in economies of scale when expected demand is growing. Second, either because of a slower growth of demand than was expected when capacity was laid down, or because of constraints on output on the supply wide (like shortages of certain skill categories) there is *unplanned* excess capacity. There appears to be the most likelihood of supply-side constraints when capacity expansion is the preponderant type of investment and when the investors do not pool information on their related manpower requirements.

Third, measured spare capacity may overstate the true reserve because technical advances or changes in the product composition of demand have rendered part of the capital stock irrelevant—effectively scrap. There is a widespread view among national economists from O.E.C.D. countries that the true scrapping rate has increased. As Lamfalussy first pointed out, the low scrap values which result from past failure to 'deepen' capital or to substitute modern and relevant plant, further deter investors from capital-deepening.[9]

[7] N.E.D.O., *The Margin of Spare Capacity and Constraints to Output Growth*, N.E.D.C. (77) 59 (1977).
[8] The Theory of Capital Utilization and Idleness, *Journal of Economic Literature*, Dec. 1974.
[9] A. Lamfalussy, *Investment and Growth in Mature Economies* (London, 1961).

A lack of correspondence between existing capacity in O.E.C.D. countries (perhaps especially the UK) and the plant and equipment appropriate to produce competitively the products where demand growth is strong and to which comparative advantage has shifted probably accounts in the main for the recent recovery of manufacturing investment in spite of the heavy under-utilization of the existing stock. But it also leads to hesitancy about long-term expansion.

3. Investment Ratios and ICORs: the Runner's Balance between Calorie Intake and Energy Output

Taking UK capital: output ratios as we find them, we can estimate the increase in the ratio of fixed capital formation to GDP which would be consistent with a long-term return to full employment. The figure works out at about 17 per cent.[10] It is now widely recognised that this sort of calculation begs most of the relevant questions. The past capital:output ratio is a disequilibrium one: witness the high under-utilization of the manufacturing capital stock. Furthermore, not only is the ratio likely to change with the bias of technical progress, but it is clear that it would *have* to change—and the productivity of the UK capital stock be increased —if the demand were to be forthcoming to generate and justify the corresponding investment.

It does not advance our understanding of the investment policies required for faster growth to rewrite $\Delta 0/0$ as $\dfrac{\Delta 0}{I} \times \dfrac{I}{0}$.

It is likely that the marginal productivity of capital will change if the investment ratio is raised.

Even in a closed economy, as Harrod has demonstrated,[11] it may be impossible, by demand management and in the absence of structural policies, to raise the investment ratio. The policies which are required to motivate additions to capacity may remove the real resource scope for increased investment. The fundamental point is that the correlation between the growth rate and the investment ratio holds for the UK only if export growth is added as a further determinant of growth[12]). The actions required to raise export growth go far beyond the encouragement of a larger volume of investment, which in fact waits upon that export growth. A larger share of investment is, at best, a necessary but not sufficient condition of faster growth.

A general subsidization of manufacturing investment, to the degree necessary to raise investment significantly, would be likely further to

---

[10]'This corresponds with an unpublished calculation for the O.E.C.D. 'Interfuture' programme by B. Molloy and D. Warner.

[11]'Are Monetary and Fiscal Policies Enough?', *Economic Journal*, Dec. 1964.

[12]D. Kern, 'An International Comparison of Major Economic Trends, 1953–76', *Nat. West. Bank Quarterly Rev.*, May 1978.

increase under-utilization, discouraging multiple shift working (Winston, *op cit*) and leading to the substitution of longer-lived capital of greater average age and further from best practice techniques. (See Fig. 6.1.)

In comparison with West Germany at the industrial order level, it turns out that relative output growth across industries in the UK is not significantly correlated either with the growth of the capital stock or with employment growth in recent years (1972–1976). In Table 6.3, the simple correlation coefficients for the UK have dropped almost to zero, while remaining quite high for Germany.

TABLE 6.3.

Simple Correlation Coefficients between Output Growth and the Growth of Capital Stock and Employment in UK and West Germany

Growth of Output	Capital		Employment	
	UK	WG	UK	WG
1954–59	0.76	0.37	0.82	0.75
1959–63	0.60	0.74	0.83	0.85
1963–68	0.80	0.39	0.66	0.62
1968–72	0.70	0.83	0.38	0.83
1972–76	0.04	0.77	0.08	0.68

Source: N.E.D.O., 1978.

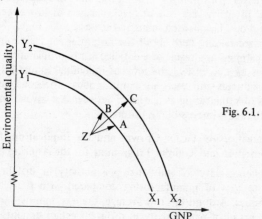

Fig. 6.1.

By way of illustration, assume, for simplicity that the earnings of an asset accrue all in the final year of its life, and that its useful life and the initial cost of the asset are positive functions of its chosen durability. In the diagram above, the present value of its expected future earnings $V(t)$ is $Q(t)e^{-rt}$ at the discount rate r. Optimum life is t^*, where net present value $Q(t)e^{-rt} - c(t)$ is maximized. If, through investment subsidy, the discount rate is reduced to r' the V curve shifts to $V'(t)$, optimum life to t'^*, and average age and vintage correspondingly rise.

The absence of correlation between capital stock growth and output growth at the industrial order level is a further indication of what we would expect in an open economy: that the growth of both the capital stock and employment depend upon the success of national industries in winning demand (as Germany did in 1972-76).[13]

From industrial comparisons with Germany there does not seem to be any straightforward argument for increasing capital intensity across manufacturing. In the industry comparisons carried out in N.E.D.O., above average increases in relative labour productivity were not associated with below average increases in capital productivity[14] Differences were due in general to the better or worse use of both factors of production in combination.

This is not to deny that increases in the manufacturing plant and equipment investment ratio (at a faster rate than would be likely to occur without encouragement) may help to increase productivity and demand. But the particular increases in capital intensity which fill this bill have to be carefully chosen so that external 'growth' economies are generated. The general principles of selection are well understood: where technical progress is embodied in capital and capital biased, where the rate of technical advance in the capital goods industry itself depends upon the level of domestic demand for investment, where the more rapid diffusion of (capital-intensive) product or process innovation is restricted in some way, or where important economies of scale, which entail greater capital intensity, are out of reach because of low expected growth of demand or a fragmented industrial structure.

We are talking here about the potential for discriminating increases in investment as a result of a detailed study of missed and future opportunities carried out at the level of individual industries and jointly by the producers and users of capital goods. The consequential relation, across manufacturing as a whole, between the investment ratio and the growth rate is impossible to estimate.

4. Transitionally Faster Growth and the Implications for Investment: the Nutrition and Training Programme for the Aspiring Also-ran

The average level of industrial productivity in Britain is now low in most sectors of manufacturing compared with the leading industrial economies. Around this low average, there is, in most industries, a fairly wide spread of productivity in different establishments. There appears

[13] In a comparison I made in 1975 between UK and West Germany of relative productivity growth, relative output growth and relative investment per employee, the ranks of UK indistries relative to their German counterparts were closely similar by productivity growth and by output growth; but quite unrelated to their ranking by relative investment per employee.

[14] N.E.D.O. Research Monograph No. 5 (ed. Panić, M.), *The UK and West German Manufacturing Industry 1954-72* (1975).

to be little movement of resources out of less efficient applications and little tendency for the average technique to move in Salter's terms closer to the moving horizon of best practice. In short, in most industries, faster productivity has increased in Britain at about the background rate of technical advance. That is what one would expect it to do in a technologically pace-making economy like the United States where the level of productivity is already high. The experience of what is now the large majority of Northern European economies suggests that there are several ways in which an extended disequilibrium phase of unusually fast or catching-up growth can be managed without dramatic changes in the *broad* structure of output: that is to say without large-scale shifts of resources out of low productivity sectors of the economy.

In contrast with Britain, in Germany and France and, with rather less consistency in Belgium and Sweden, the growth of productivity has been faster than the underlying pace of technical progress, without wide relative output shifts between broad industries.[15]

The most obvious way in which growth of this kind can happen is during a period in which a technological gap is closed. The potential for this exists both in mature economies which have lagged behind (like Belgium) and in economies like the fast growers in SE Asia as they apply the new technology of more mature economies to a traditional manufacturing base. Another route to unusual growth, which equally entails resource mobility, is one where a change in product structure leads, so that the output of an industry is composed of products for which international demand is growing fast and dynamic economies of scale follow the changed products and marketing policies.

The demand for resources and the direction and quality of new investment are conditioned by the effect upon future expectations of the past performance of the economy, and by the policies and attitudes which have been protectively assumed in response to that poor performance. The failure over twenty years to find a way to emulate the extended episodes of unusual growth in neighbouring economies has introduced further obstacles to change and deeper doubts among investors about the value, or even the possibility, of comparable success. These obstacles lie in the organisation of the supply of external finance (lenders being both more conservative and less industrially committed than in economies with unusual growth experience); in cautiousness about process innovation and new product development instilled by long experience of cycles, slow growth, and competitive disadvantages due to domestic inflation; in industrial relations where they inhibit changes in the organisation and composition of production or in the speed of

[15]UN Economic Commission for Europe, *Structure and Change in European Industry* (UN, 1978), ch. 1.

mechanization; in pricing and other conventions where they attenuate competition, preserving an industrial structure where so many separate firms or products share what growth there is that economies of large-scale continuous operation are denied.

On the other hand, the recognition of industrial decline and the disenchantment with macro-economic remedies have made it possible to satisfy to some extent one condition of rapid transitional growth which is usually met only in the context of a national economic plan: a significant reduction in the barriers to the flows of technical and market information between domestic companies both within industries and between vertically related companies. The contribution of information exchange and of joint ventures to speed of diffusion of new processes in industries where concentration is low is recognised in several of the tri-partite working parties which now set objectives for exports and import substitution for their own sectors and recommend what they should do to achieve them.

The faster diffusion of a new process is itself the most obvious cause of an episode of unusually fast growth.[16] What can we say about the implications for investment of such an episode? In particular would investment need to be selectively encouraged at its beginning?

I believe that it would. The expenditure on re-equipment that is required when a manufacturing industry has fallen as far behind, in terms of product quality and technical vintage, as have many sectors of UK engineering, are dauntingly large. Many O.E.C.D. economists are doubtful now whether even the flow of investment decisions required to expand capacity in line with increases in permanent sales expectations and changes in utilization will be sustained, given worldwide growth pessimism and the uncertainties about inflation, raw material and energy prices, the growth of competition from newly industrializing countries and the spread of protectionism. In countries like Britain, France, Sweden and Italy, where investment is no longer regarded simply as a necessary macro-economic adjustment of capital stock, but as required to increase international competitiveness as well as to assist in the return to full employment, investment economists are increasingly sceptical of the adequacy of market adjustments and are convinced of the need of one form or another of specialised investment incentive.

[16]G. F. Ray in L. Nabseth and G. Ray, *The Diffusion of New Industrial Processes* (Cambridge, 1974), pp. 5–6: 'If, in a country, the rate of diffusion had been rather slow for some time, and it then speeded up in all or most industries, that country could for a while grow faster than others where there had been no such change. The scope for such transitional increase in the growth rate . . . depends on how long it takes in the various countries to absorb any new innovation completely. One of the most striking observations in the studies reported here is that quite frequently the diffusion process may last for many decades; there is thus plenty of scope in practice for temporarily falling behind or catching up in the rate of growth of industrial output per head.'

In the British economy, when contemplating the investment requirements both to improve international competitiveness and to reduce
industrial unemployment, the problem of motivating sufficient investment looks very formidable indeed. Worries about utilization, low
current profitability and the financial constraints faced by hitherto
unsuccessful firms with a large potential for improved performance can
lead them to postpone even that level of replacement which would be
undertaken by a company that was already close to best practice
techniques.

The more it proves possible for unusual productivity growth to take
the form of increase in the *quality* (and value) of existing levels of
output with unchanged inputs, rather than of sharp increases in physical
productivity of homogenous products, the greater the employment
effects and the less the resistance to be expected from workers from
changes in technique.[17]

The case for re-equipment to develop new products and to speed up
the diffusion of new techniques is at its strongest when traditional
investment incentives are at almost their weakest. Between 1970 and
1976, and in spite of exchange rate movements which improved the
index of trade competitiveness, the volume of manufactured exports
grew at only three-fifths the rate of imports, which themselves grew
twenty times as fast as manufacturing production. Spare capacity was
exceptionally high over most of those years and investment extremely
depressed. The caution thereby engendered about any investment at all
is understandable. Investment will have to spring from what are usually
subsidiary motives which have had little influence when the two principal
forces—pressure of demand on capacity, and confidence in future
demand growth—have been weak: motives like meeting competition,
applying major innovations, responding to a changed composition of
expected demand and increasing the rate of scrapping and replacement.

5. The Absence of Dynamic Economies of Scale: No Bursts of Adrenalin at the Check-points

One of the fast runner's greatest advantages is that his rapid progress
improves his spirits. The bonus of fast growth is not just that the average
age of the capital stock is thereby automatically lowered, but that
lower uncertainty premia, increased scrap values, and lesser resistance

---

[17]One of the more striking features of British international industrial backwardness
is the relative decline and present low level of value per ton, product group by
product group, of exports compared either with the exports of competitors or
with value per ton of imports. In N.E.D.O., *International Price Competitiveness,
Non-price Factors and Export Performances*, N.E.D.O. (April 1977), Appendix B,
and D. K. Stout in Blackaby (ed) *De-Industrialization*, Heinemann (1979)
there is a fuller account of this effect.

to labour-saving innovation increase the likelihood of greenfield invest-ment in integrated plant, instead of piecemeal additions and replace-ments. Conversely, there are well-established vicious circles involved in the process of slow growth.

Poor runners who sprint to the first check-point, however, are likely to find that the burst of adrenalin they get does not compensate for their breathlessness. The benefit to productivity and the positive feedback effect of a younger capital stock and a more promising set of employment opportunities are too small and slow-acting to make a consumption-led burst for growth a sensible policy option.

There are many comparative studies of performance at the level of the individual industry which show the importance of unrealised scale economies in the UK.[18] British Industry is not only handicapped by a low long-term rate of growth of output, but such growth as there is is often spread between a large number of particular products and small markets served by a fragmented industry. The indivisibilities which attend such new processes as special presses in paper making, tunnel kilns in brick-making or shuttleless looms in the textile industry call for a greater concentration of production of fewer items in fewer plants than in a faster growing economy.[19]

Unrealised static economies of scale, the indivisibilities associated with many new processes, the stubborn persistence of wide dispersion of productivity at the establishment level in many industries, and the relation between industrial concentration and the rate of diffusion of new techniques all suggest that, provided the discipline of competition can be guaranteed by keeping the economy as open as possible, we should not strive too hard to prevent increases in concentration at plant level. In many industries, the effectiveness of investment in raising long-term obstacles to industrial growth is likely to be greater if there are fewer plants than now operate. Generalisations are dangerous because in some industries there are severe offsetting plant diseconomies of scale above a level well below the engineering optimum, as the organisation of work becomes more difficult and the costs of interruptions or bottlenecks increase.

---

[18]See, e.g., W. Beckerman, *The British Economy in 1975* (Cambridge, 1965), ch. 1; N. Kaldor, *Causes of the Slow Rate of Economic Growth in the United Kingdom* (Cambridge, 1966) and 'Conflicts in National Economic Objectives' (Presidential Address to Section F of the British Association), *Economic Journal* (Nov. 1971); A. Lamfalussy, *Investment and Growth in Mature Economies* (London, 1961), ch. 6.

[19]L. Nabseth and G. Ray, *The Diffusion of New Industrial Processes* (Cambridge, 1974), ch 11, and D. K. Stout, *Industrial Performance in the Longer Term: An Approach Through Investment*, N.E.D.C. (74) 31 (Research Annex) 1974, p. 1 (mimeo N.E.D.O).

6. The Inducement of 'Autonomous' Investment: More Meat and Less Potatoes

If a laggard industrial economy is to run faster to begin to catch up with the growth rates of its more successful competitors, it cannot wait for reflexive investment in capacity expansion to carry it forward, least of all at a time of world-wide unemployment and excess supply. What is required is sustained autonomous investment, that is to say, investment that complements increases in market share and helps to create sales of new products. It is difficult to set out the conditions for such an investment programme. The determinants of the rate of replacement and modernization are poorly understood since the flexible accelerator is the dominant force in explaining investment even in cross-section studies.[20] Very few of the variables that we should expect to influence non-accelerator investment—such as relative wage change, labour constraints, or changes in tax rates—play a significant role in any gross investment functions. Yet it is only by scrapping and replacement that either the vintage of capital, the composition of output or capital intensity can be radically altered.

Much investment in modernization and industrial restructuring involving the substitution of integrated plant, and accompanying the redesign and manufacture of more sophisticated products, while it may be favoured or hampered by background conditions like current cash flow, is really 'autonomous' in the sense that it may be expected to result from consensus planning in which the decision-taking function is shared (and risks, costs and returns shared) by many participants, including the government, workers, other vertically related producers and financing authorities. Such decisions remain essentially profit-seeking, since they are not centrally imposed; but the surplus they look for is more widely diffused and may take account of longer-run effects, including security of industrial employment and the faster growth of domestic demand contingent upon improved international track performance.

The recent 'supply side' approach to industrial policy[21] has led to a

---

[20] R. Eisner, 'Components of Capital Expenditures, Replacement and Modernization Versus Expansion', *R. E. Statistics* (Aug. 1972); and M. S. Feldstein, 'Tax Incentives, Stabilization Policy and the Proportional Replacement Hypothesis: Some Negative Conclusions', *Southern Economic Journal* (April 1974). A partly successful exception is the attempt by Ando, Modigliani, Rasche and Turnovsky, ('On the Role of Expectations of Price and Technological Change in an Investment Function', *International Economic Review*, June 1974) to allow for variable replacement investment, in response to expected changes in product and input prices.

[21] The policy is briefly outlined in my paper (D. K. Stout, 'De-Industrialization and Industrial Policy', in Blackaby (ed.), *De-Industrialization*, Heinemann (1979) to the N.I.E.S.R. Conference on De-Industrialization.

number of industry-based schemes of selective investment assistance and to one or two broader-based measures of help with investment costs, like the recent Product and Process Development Scheme. The main contribution of other participants than the corporate decision-taker in such uncharacteristically motivated investment, if it occurs, will be towards the reduction of the uncertainties which otherwise discourage all investment, but especially investment ahead of pressure of familiar demand upon existing capacity. The main expressed inhibitory doubts are about the acceptability of the new investments to the workers who must man them, about the supply of certain key categories of complementary skilled workers, about relative future changes in unit product and factor prices, about the rate of inflation and its possible policy consequences, about the exchange rate and the pressure of competition from imports and about the limits to government intervention and the continued voluntariness of micro-economic planning. It is a mistake to add together these various kinds of uncertainty and subsume them under a lower expected growth of demand, since what is under consideration is 'autonomous' investment. This (together with complementary research and development, product design and marketing decisions) is aimed at creating demand rather than reacting to it. Neither are these uncertainties satisfactorily caught by a notional premium added to the cost of capital, since some threshold levels of uncertainty will absolutely prevent investment, whereas changes in the cost of capital tend at most to affect its timing.

What essentially is involved is exchange of information about intentions and contingent commitments by those directly affected. So far as the two sides of industry are concerned, the establishment of areas of common interest is possible, with goodwill, at the industrial sector working party) level. Investment decisions themselves, however, require understandings between employers and workers at company level. More participative planning procedures at company level could significantly reduce the uncertainty attaching to innovational and 'catching-up' investment.

So far as the government is concerned, its main contribution ought not to be as a partner in individual decisions nor probably as a contributor of discretionary assistance at the industry level. Rather it should be to undertake to maintain a helpful and stable framework of macro-economic conditions and legal and institutional arrangements, so far as the constraints upon the balance of payments permit. In order to do this, governments would have to be seen to be continuing, over many years, to give a very high priority to industrial recovery and to the conditions for restructuring investment on which an extended episode of unusual growth would depend. The problem for a government is of course that it can be held accountable and expected to be able to deliver its part of a growth bargain; but no corresponding entity exists that can make a promise on behalf of an industry about investment or about manning. The best that a government can do is probably to announce macro-economic policies which will provide a benign and sustainable background for the necessary non-accelerator investments. The object should be to remove uncertainty about the long-run practicability of intensive export marketing by making a commitment to a stable real exchange rate, to a tax structure which will increase rather than diminish the savings available for replacement investment, and to trade policy which will generate continued British access to world markets. The government cannot guarantee to deliver a specific growth rate and should never pretend to, since that growth rate will depend upon how successful industries are in catching-up, as well as upon the growth of world demand, and the balance of payments policies of major competitors and customers.

Nor, of course, can any government commit its successor. The most important advantage of tri-partite industry committees is that they may reach conclusions about policy which are industrial rather than political and so may help to take industrial policy out of the arena of adversary politics. If that happens, we may enjoy some of the continuity of policy which an erstwhile 'also-ran' like France experienced when moving out of the pack at the back of the field to the elite group at the front through the fifties and sixties.

Summary

In order to enjoy a period of abnormally fast growth (as Germany and France have done) and to get closer to the moving horizon of maximum output per head, the British economy needs a quite different kind of investment diet from that which is enjoyed by economies in long-run equilibria. It needs not the investment induced by an expected growth of sales, but investment which modernises both the processes and the products of its industries. The programme is one which consensus planning at industry level and participative decision-taking at company level will help.

The British economy is like an ill-conditioned jogger who wants to become a successful fell-racer. It does not help to eat like a hungry athlete. His appetite for investment has been weakened by past lack of exercise. Nor can he rely upon the automatic shots of adrenalin that the leader of the pack gets by virtue of his success.

The rebuilding process requires close attention to diet and a rigorous long-term training programme with the subject's full cooperation. The government cannot control the weather but must guarantee no breaks in training. There is no guarantee that the subject will become Fell Racer of the Year but he may be able to break away from the ruck at the back of the field.

7

HOW RAPID PUBLIC SECTOR GROWTH
CAN UNDERMINE THE GROWTH OF
THE NATIONAL PRODUCT

by Walter Eltis*
Exeter College, Oxford

All economies have a sector which produces a surplus off which the rest of the economy lives. This is one of the oldest propositions in economics. It has always been understood that if the surplus is large, the economy will be able to support strong but unproductive armed forces and an extensive state establishment which meet their material needs from the extra output of agriculture, industry and commerce. If the surplus is small, the country cannot afford to employ many non-producers and if it attempts to finance them, it will push taxation to the point where agriculture, industry and commerce fail to function as they should. Their output will fall and tax revenues with it and governments will then find it increasingly difficult to finance their spending. If they push up rates of taxation as their surplus producing sectors decline, they will put these under increasing pressure and force cuts in output and employment until the conflict between the demands of government and the needs of the sector of the economy which must finance it becomes intolerable. An economic crisis then results characterised by rapid and accelerating inflation, growing unemployment, and a cessation of growth.

The surplus creating sector of economies is the market sector. This is because marketed output—output which is sold—must supply a nation's entire export needs since all exports are marketed. In addition, capital equipment is always sold to firms so all physical investment goods must come from the market sector. Finally all the consumer goods and services which are bought privately are marketed. Hence the marketed output of industry, agriculture and services taken together must supply the total private consumption, export and investment needs of all nations.

Much marketed output is required by those who produce none. The

*The author is grateful to Robert Bacon for extensive comments and help with the statistical work.

armed forces, the civil service, government employed teachers, doctors, nurses, policemen, dustmen and pensioners all produce no marketed output. They eat and require clothing and housing and most drive cars and work in buildings which have to be constructed and maintained: These are all marketed goods and they must be provided by the workers of the market sector, or obtained through international trade from the market sectors of other economies. Thus the market sector must produce marketed output in excess of its own needs to provide for all the requirements of those in the non-market sector. The market sector must therefore provide a surplus and the non-market sector lives off that surplus.

The transfer of resources from the market to the non-market sector is most efficiently achieved through the tax system. The market sector pays taxes and the non-market sector lives off the revenues obtained.[1] Market sector employment is therefore self-financing and the ultimate source of all tax revenues, while non-market employment is tax-financed. If the budget is balanced, the aggregate taxes paid in the market sector will equal the *net* taxes required to finance the non-market sector.

The market sector includes government controlled companies which market their output as well as privately owned corporations, and government companies can finance social services from the taxes derived from their surpluses (provided they earn them) in basically the same way as privately owned companies. The vital borderline is therefore not the traditional one between the public and private sectors. Instead the vital distinction is between the self-financing companies in the *public* and *private* sectors which market their output, and the tax-financed non-market sector which the market sector finances through the taxes that companies and their employees pay.

Where governments finance their spending through deficits instead of taxation, the position is basically similiar. Here part of the non-market sector may be financed through the voluntary savings of the market sector workers who buy government secutities which allow the state to spend. Alternatively, the state finances some of the spending of the

---

[1]Some do not perceive this basic fact because non-market sector workers also pay taxes, so everyone appears to be a taxpayer. A civil servant with an income of £20,000 must rely on others for his entire marketed output needs because he produces none, but he is not entitled to buy £20,000 worth of marketed output because he pays perhaps £7,000 of total taxes out of this. Hence the net cost to the market sector of employing him is at most £13,000 and not £20,000 and the basic fact is that the market sector must give up £13,000 of marketed output if he is to be employed at a salary of £20,000. Once the taxes paid by non-market sector workers and pensions are deducted from their gross pay, it is clear that where the budget and international trade are balanced, the total net taxes paid by the market sector must equal the total net of tax incomes received in the non-market sector plus purchases of capital goods and materials by the non-market sector.

non-market sector through the printing press. The latter has the same effect as a *tax* on all cash holdings. If printing money raises prices 10 per cent, market sector workers with cash of £100 will find they can only buy real goods and services which used to be worth £90. The other £10 their cash can no longer buy can then go to soldiers, pensioners and civil servants. Ultimately therefore, the great bulk of the non-market sector is tax-financed, whether the budget is balanced or not, but the tax will be an inflation tax on cash balances rather than a more obvious method of taxation where governments have to resort to the printing press because regular taxes will not suffice to finance non-market spending.[2]

1. How Smooth Growth to a Larger Non-Market Sector can be Achieved

The fact that the market sector ultimately finances the non-market sector does not mean that it is more important to the wellbeing of a society. Welfare and civilization depend on the efficiency of agriculture, industry and commerce, and equally on the effectiveness of education, health services, welfare systems, crime prevention and much more that is not bought and sold. In 1759 François Quesnay also listed "the beautification of the Kingdom" among the objectives of an economy:[3] he was right, and such eighteenth century objectives which cannot be measured in monetary units are often ignored by today's economists.

The expenditure patterns of the wealthy show that on average they spend more than the poor as a fraction of income on education, health, personal security and the arts. Therefore, it is reasonable to assume that as economic resources per head increase, the average citizen will expect a higher fraction of a nation's income to be spent on the improved education of his children, better medical treatment, greater security for his family and his property, and more opportunities to enjoy the theatre, music and opera which the wealthy value. It is consequently to be expected that a society will spend an increasing fraction of its resources in these directions as real incomes grow. If education and health are not marketed, and to a great extent they are not in modern societies, then non-market expenditures can be expected to grow, decade by decade, in relation to marketed output. If they did not, societies would be failing to raise consumption in the ways that consumers prefer when, like the wealthy, they are free to choose.

In addition, increasing numbers in many countries have come to

---

[2]The argument that excessive printing of money acts as an inflation tax on cash balances was set out by Keynes in his account of the German hyperinflation in *A Tract on Monetary Reform* (London, 1924) ch. II, 'Inflation as a Method of Taxation'.

[3]*Quesnay's Tableau Economique*, M. Kuczynski and R. L. Meek (eds.) (London, 1972), 3rd ed. (1759), p. 20.

consider that the co-existence of extremes of poverty and wealth in the same society are unacceptable. Hence there has been growing pressure to raise standards of support for non-producers such as pensioners and the unemployed, in relation to the average earnings of employed workers. This has necessarily raised the ratio of transfer payments to the National Income.

The fact that a growing share of resources to the non-market sector makes economic and social sense does not mean that the rule that the non-market sector must be financed from the surplus of the market sector can be broken. This rule must always be followed by any society which seeks to avoid economic breakdown. A failure to finance the non-market sector from the surplus of the market sector can only result in balance of payments collapse as efforts are made to use the resources of foreigners to provide what a population is unwilling to pay for, or physical shortages of capital as a society consumes its seed-corn in the form of extra social services, and so fails to maintain the employment creating capacity of its capital stock.

There are various ways in which economies can be destroyed by a failure to finance the non-market sector from the surplus of the market sector, but before these are explained in detail, the model of an ideal development of the non-market and market economies through time will be set out.

Suppose that for the reasons which have been explained, as a society becomes richer its population wishes to raise its spending on the resources the non-market sector provides one-and-a-half times as fast as on private consumption. Then whenever output per worker rises say 10 per cent, non-market spending per worker will rise, for instance, 12 per cent, while spending on the products of the market sector will then increase 8 per cent. Therefore, as the society progresses, each 10 per cent rise in average output per worker will allow social spending per family to rise 4 per cent more rapidly than private spending.

Over a longer period in which output per worker doubles, a rise in the non-market sector's share of marketed output of about 5 per cent from say 35 to 40 per cent will suffice to raise the resources available to the non-market sector about one-and-a-half times as fast as those which go to the average market sector worker, and this is illustrated in Table 7.1. The overall tax rate would need to rise by about 5 per cent in the market sector in the twenty to fifty year period over which output per worker doubles in this table, because the market sector is able to purchase 70 per cent of its own output at the beginning of the period and only 65 per cent at the end.

This example shows the effect of assumptions which are extremely favourable to the non-market sector, namely that a community wishes to increase unmarketed public services and pensions one-and-a-half times

TABLE 7.1.
*The Non-Market Sector Grows
One-and-a-Half Times as Fast as the Market Sector*

			Increase
Net Output per Worker	100	200	100%
Purchased by the Market Sector per Worker Employed	65 (65%)	120 (60%)	84.6%
Purchased by the Non-Market Sector per Worker Employed	35 (35%)	80 (40%)	128.6%

Non-Market Purchases rise 1.52 times as Fast as Market Sector Purchases

as fast per worker as the marketed output that is consumed privately by those who produce it. If the preference for unmarketed public services is weaker than this, taxation will need to rise less quickly than in the table. It will not need to rise at all if there is no desire that public services should grow faster than private consumption, and this will presumably be the case at some very high income level, because no population is likely to wish to increase taxation indefinitely, when its social services are already extensive.

The principal condition which must be fulfilled if a continuous transfer of resources from the market to the non-market sector of the kind illustrated is to be achieved is that the increase in taxation should be realized without damage to the underlying structure of production in the economy. What this requires is that extra taxation should be paid without damaging those economic activities which finance necessary imports and the capital investment which is indispensable to growth and long-term job creation. Taxation must therefore be paid from the surplus of the market sector and not with the economy's seed corn. If extra taxation leads to the substitution of public for private *consumption*, there can be no damage to the underlying structure of production. Workers produce for the non-market sector what they would otherwise produce for the market sector, and the government allocates what would otherwise be distributed by market forces. As private consumption foregone pays for extra public consumption, there is no damage to the balance of payments or to investment in job creation and growth. The economy can, therefore, grow as fast, provide as many jobs, and pay for the same imports, but services are given away which would otherwise be paid for, including pension rights which would otherwise require private insurance policies.

For this transfer from private consumption to the 'social wage' to be achieved, workers must either acquiesce in the continuous increase in rates of taxation that is needed or alternatively governments must have adequate powers to ensure that workers will not pass the extra taxes on so that they fall on capital investment or the balance of payments.

It is, of course, vital if such acquiescence is to be achieved that the output of social services should rise as rapidly as expenditures upon them. If there is a preference for extra education, and taxation is raised continuously to finance it, while each generation of children is worse educated than the one before, either because the extra money is spent on administration instead of teaching, or because teachers fail to teach the technical skills which later life will require, taxpayers may not regard the extra 'social wage' as adequate compensation for private consumption foregone. In the ideal conditions assumed, it is therefore necessary that the non-market sector be as efficient as the market sector. A society will then be substituting unmarketed public services which are as efficiently produced as private goods and services for the extra private consumption it would otherwise obtain. Workers then obtain a combination of private and public goods and services which they can sensibly prefer to alternative combinations where there are fewer public goods and services. If the non-market sector is consistently less efficient, it is unlikely that combinations which take increasing fractions from this inefficient sector will be rationally preferred.

Finally, it is not enough that a continuous relative shift of resources into the non-market sector be acceptable to the average worker. Workers with above average incomes may regard the increasing 'social wage' they obtain (which will generally be no greater than the increase in the average worker's 'social wage') inadequate compensation for the above average taxes they will be expected to pay with progressive taxation. Ideally the increasing equality involved in an ever growing non-market share will need to be acceptable to a whole community and not merely to a majority, or to workers with average or below average incomes. Dissatisfied minorities of the better off can disrupt and interrupt a smooth progression to an ever growing non-market sector.

Difficulties have arisen in a number of countries since 1960 because the growth of the non-market sector at the expense of the market sector has not taken this ideal form. The difficulties that can arise are best illustrated by considering three general cases where economies or regions within economies have been destablized because extra rapid non-market sector growth prevented the market sector from growing as it should. These cases are first the British one where the non-market sector grew far more rapidly than in the example which has been illustrated, with the result that it grew largely at the expense of capital investment and not consumption. The second case is that of New York City where extra rapid growth of the non-market sector produced a destabilizing movement of market sector employment out of the city and of welfare receipients into it to produce all but insoluble social and financial problems. Finally, something will be said about the abortive revolutions in Chile and Portugal where attempts to superimpose a vastly greater non-market sector on a market sector which was simultaneously reducing output led to financial collapse and a loss of power by those who sought to produce a new society.

If the world's market sectors grow more slowly in the 1980s and 1990s than in the 1950s and 1960s as is now widely expected, other countries will be destabilized in similiar ways if they fail to reduce the growth of their non-market sectors to the new and slower rates which their market sectors can finance.

2. The Destabilization of Britain

The British case with which this examination of modern error will begin is illustrated in Table 7.2.[4]

TABLE 7.2.
*The Shift from the Market
to the Non-Market Sector in Britain: 1964–73*

	1964	1973	Increase
Net Output per Worker	100	126.6	26.6%
Purchased by the Market Sector per Worker Employed	66.0 (66.0%)	76.2 (60.2%)	15.5%
Purchased by the Non-Market Sector per Worker Employed	34.0 (34.0%)	50.4 (39.8%)	48.2%

Non-Market Purchases rise 3.1 times as fast as Market Sector Purchases

This shows that the average rate of taxation on market sector output rose considerably faster than in the previous example in Britain from 1964 to 1973, the last full year before the start of the world recession. The non-market share rose a great deal more from 1973 to 1976 but this was partly due to lack of growth of market sector output because of exceptionally unfavourable trading conditions during the recession. The period 1964–73 shown in the table was uninfluenced by such adverse factors and 1964 and 1973 are both expansion years which can safely be compared—and this period shows disproportionate non-market sector

[4]The statistical methods used to arrive at the split between market and non-market sector purchases in Britain were set out in general terms in R. Bacon and W. Eltis, *Britain's Economic Problem: Too Few Producers*, 2nd ed. (London, 1978), pp.243–7, and refined in their 'The Measurement of the Growth of the Non-market sector: and its influence' *Economic Journal*, Vol. 89, June 1979.

growth. In the previous example, non-market purchases of goods and services increased one-and-a-half times as quickly as market sector purchases per worker. But in Britain from 1964 to 1973 they actually increased over three times as fast. Personal preferences may give priority to public services over private consumption, but it is not plausible that many will wish the public services to grow over three times as fast. The increase in taxation involved in what occurred averaged about 6 per cent in the nine years in which output per worker rose 26.6 per cent in contrast to the previous example where a smaller increase in taxation was needed in a period over which output per worker doubled (about twenty-seven years at the British rate of growth) and the non-market sector grew one-and-a-half times as quickly as the market sector. Britain therefore compressed over twenty-seven years of increased taxation into a nine year period. The average worker with ordinary earnings was expected to pay the increased taxes like the rest of the community, and deductions from the average worker's paypacket increased by 6.7 pence in the pound from 1964 to 1973,[5] slightly more than the 5.8 per cent increase in average taxation indicated in the table.

It is reasonable to suppose that what occurred went much further than actual preferences in the community for higher public consumption. British workers wanted extra private consumption also. Many were unable to afford car ownership: many ate far less meat than they wished even before Britain joined the European Economic Community; many aspired to house ownership (55 per cent of British families live in houses they own) and house ownership was becoming increasingly expensive. Certainly more public services were desired, but it was desired that private consumption should rise rapidly also. It is probable that politicians of all British political parties appreciated this, but they made two major errors of analysis which led to the position illustrated in the table.

The first error was due to the Keynesism that dominated British economic thought and analysis across the whole political spectrum from 1964 to 1973.[6] There were thought to be unemployed resources in most years from 1964 to 1973, so few British politicians or civil servants or academic economists believed that extra growth of the non-market sector cost anything. On the contrary, all had been taught or themselves taught that each extra pound sterling spent by the non-market sector increased total incomes by between two and three pounds

---

[5] The statistical basis for this calculation is set out in Bacon and Eltis, op. cit. pp. 210–3.

[6] The line of argument set out here is developed more fully in Walter Eltis, 'The Failure of the Keynesian Conventional Wisdom', *Lloyds Bank Review* (Oct. 1976). See also Lord Kahn's reply 'Mr. Eltis and the Keynesians' (Apr. 1977), And my Rejoinder (July 1977).

(to follow Keynes's own estimate of Lord Kahn's multiplier—the concept which taught two generations of English speaking economists that you can expand your cake and eat it faster at the same time), so the British happily allowed the non-market sector to increase at rapid rates in relation to the growth of the remainder of the economy whenever they wished to expand demand and production. It rarely occurred to those in power or their advisers that extra social spending would eventually need to be paid for. Therefore at election time, all political parties promised more expenditure on the social services and more private consumption also without ever indicating that taxation would need to rise to pay for the enlarged non-market sector. Voters never actually chose the growth imbalance which occurred. Instead they voted for more of everything many times.

The second error Britain made was that where governments actually made· long-term expenditure plans, the rate of growth on which the plans were based was overestimated. The long-term rate of growth of British expenditure on the social services was consistently based on the assumption that Britain would achieve a rate of growth of final output of around 4 per cent.[7] In reality, production grew by only 2.8 per cent a year from 1964 to 1973. An economy growing at 4 per cent could have financed the increases in social expenditures which occurred with much smaller increases in taxation, and far more growth of private consumption than was actually achieved. It will be seen that the rapid non-market sector growth itself contributed to the slow growth of the economy which undermined the financial foundations of the social services.

Britain's third error was to fail to ensure that the non-market sector would be managed as efficiently as the market sector. In fhe hospital service, for instance, there was a 51 per cent increase in the number of hospital administrators from 1965 to 1973 and an 11 per cent fall in the number of beds they were administering.[8] It took longer for the sick to get into hospital as waiting lists grew from year to year, but the real cost of administering each bed grew over 60 per cent. In British state education, employment grew 54 per cent from 1964 to 1974, but only 51 per cent of those employed actually taught anyone. The other 49 per cent administered, cleaned, served meals, but did not directly educate.[9] Vast sums also went on prestige projects, for instance, Concorde, instead of on goods and services which would have genuinely raised

---

[7]See *Growth of the United Kingdom Economy to 1966* (H.M.S.O., 1963); and *The National Plan* cmnd. 2764 (H.M.S.O., 1965).
[8]See Dr. Max Gammon, *Manpower and Number of Beds Occupied Daily 1965-73, UK N.H.S. Hospital Service*, St. Michael's Organisation (London, 1975).
[9]*Department of Employment Gazette* (1974), p. 1141.

the 'social wage'. These are just examples of what occurred. There was a widespread belief that much of the non-market sector was not giving full value for the taxes deducted to finance it.

Whether for this reason, or because it was allowed to grow far faster than workers' preferences for public goods, there was a clear departure from the ideal conditions for non-market sector growth which have been outlined. Workers did not acquiesce in the increased taxation that was needed to finance the extra-rapid growth of the non-market sector, and they therefore made every effort to increase their private consumption at rates almost as fast as public consumption was growing. Private real market sector incomes grew about 1.6 per cent per annum for each worker employed from 1964 to 1973 which was a far slower rate of increase than workers had obtained in the previous decade, and continued to expect. Each individual group of workers could only increase their private consumable income at more than 1.6 per cent per annum by gaining wage increases which were larger than those that other groups of workers were obtaining or by raising wages exceptionally at the expense of profits. Union leaders who were particularly likely to push for exceptional wage increases without inhibitions about the methods used to obtain them were therefore increasingly elected to positions of power in the labour movement, and these were often on the extreme left politically. Individual trade unions then went on to exploit each particular advantage they possessed regardless of the damage they were causing to the economy and the rest of the community. The coalminers demonstrated that the country could not function without electricity and obtained very large wage increases after long and significant strikes which set a lead for other settlements. The dockers also demonstrated their power and extracted for their members (partly in the form of high redundancy payments) a high fraction of the potential surplus value resulting from the technical advance of containerization. Most of the unions with the opportunity to obtain exceptional wage increases by disrupting the productive process did so with the result that money wages started to rise far faster than before. There is some rate of unemployment which would have checked this inflation—monetarists call this the 'natural' rate of unemployment—but the greater militancy of the trade unions raised this critical unemployment rate. Hence successive British governments were faced with the choice of either far more inflation than before if they maintained traditional unemployment rates, or else a much higher unemployment rate to check inflation. They found both of these alternatives unacceptable and introduced a series of official 'incomes policies' in their attempts to avoid having to choose between intolerable inflation and intolerable unemployment. In these the trade unions agreed to wage restraint for two years at a time, but only in exchange for a series of concessions which included price controls that severely reduced profits.

The unions managed to raise the share of wages in two additional ways. More militant union leadership at the local level meant that much of the surplus value resulting from technical advance which previously went to profits now went to wages instead, for workers only agreed to work new plant if much higher wages were paid or they were compensated in some other way. In addition, the more militant trade union leadership that resulted from workers' frustration increased the political power of the working class in the Marxist sense with the result that a considerable amount of legislation was passed which reduced companies' property rights. Companies therefore found it more difficult to choose the employment level of a factory (since they were often obliged to continue to employ workers whom they would have preferred to declare redundant), and they could not easily obtain possession of a factory or goods in it against the wishes of the unions in their area. This meant that companies earned lower profits from a given capital stock than before. As they also earned lower profits from the introduction of new technology, and less profit as a result of the government price controls which were frequently introduced, the share of wages rose markedly at the expense of the share of profits. In fact from 1964 to 1973 the share of profits fell by almost precisely the 5.8 per cent of output by which the non-market share rose, while the share of wages and salaries in the National Income increased.[10] Workers were therefore able to compensate for some of the 6.7 pence in the pound increase in taxation which fell on them by squeezing the share of profits, and raising the share of wages and salaries in the National Income. Their private consumption could therefore rise almost as fast as output, while the cost of financing the rapid growth of the non-market sector fell largely on profits. The non-market sector was therefore financed, not at the expense of consumption, but to an increasing extent at the expense of investment and the balance of payments, because the profits squeeze soon led to an investment squeeze. This was especially the case in industry where union pressures were strongest and profits were squeezed most,[11] and net industrial investment actually fell 46.2 per cent in 1964-73. In Industry the link

[10]In 1964 British Industrial and Commercial companies earned trading profits domestically of £3530m net of stock appreciation of £238m and capital consumption of £1072m, while the net national income was £26981m. In 1973 profits were £4268m net of these, while the national income was £57451m so that the share of net profits on this basis fell from 13.1 per cent of the national income in 1964 to 7.4 per cent in 1973. (*National Income and Expenditure* (H.M.S.O., 1964–74), Tables 1, 34 and 35.)

[11]See Bacon and Eltis, op. cit. (1978), pp. 231–8 for a comparison between profits in manufacturing companies and in British companies as a whole. The results are illustrated in Charts 11.1 and 11.2, pp. 21–2.

between investment and job creation is especially strong. It sometimes pays to put up buildings which provide little extra employment,
but new factories always need to be manned. It will be seen that the
fall in industrial investment had extremely serious consequences for the
economy.

It is to be noted that if the non-market sector's share in marketed
output rises as it did in Britain, while the consumption share of market
sector workers does not fall correspondingly, then the share of investment
and net exports (that is, exports less imports) must necessarily fall—as it
did in Britain. What actually happens is partly that the accompanying
profits squeeze may immediately incline companies to spend less on
investment, on research and development and on product promotion in
home and overseas markets—and this happened in Britain to a certain
extent. If, however, companies persist in expanding investment, despite
the profits squeeze, simple arithmetic decrees that the current account
of the balance of payments must then move sharply into deficit, for the
share of government and workers' consumption cannot rise without a
corresponding fall in the share of *net exports plus investment*. What
happens here in practice is that when output is near to its capacity limits,
investment *plus* net exports are crushed between the irreducible shares
of government and workers' consumption. If investment does not give
way of its own accord because profits are being squeezed, there is
absolutely certain to be a large import surplus corresponding to the
increased share of government and workers' consumption. If the import
surplus cannot be sustained, and this has been persistently the case in
Britain, governments necessarily respond by deflating the economy
which pulls job-creating investment down. Hence when the non-market
share of output rises, job creating investment falls, either because profits
are squeezed, or because of the effects of balance of payments deficits
on government policies and the adverse effects these will then have on
investment. In the simplest possible terms, investment and net exports
together must give way at full capacity working if the government and
workers together insist on taking a larger share of marketed output. If
the current account of the balance of payments must be balanced over
a period of years—and this was certainly the case in Britain—then the
cost of an increase in the government share must fall in one way or
another on investment. There is no other possibility.

Hence, Britain's non-market sector grew, not at the expense of the
economy's consumable surplus which any society can afford, but instead
at the expense of investment in job creation, the economy's seed-corn.
The effect of what happened was that employment in British industry
fell at a rate of 155,000 a year from 1966 until 1973, the final year
before the world recession. Therefore even before the beginning of the
recession, British industry had already lost 1,087,000 jobs. It lost these

partly because of the fall in investment that resulted from the profits squeeze and the deflationary policies which followed balance of payments weaknesses, and partly because the union pressures which have been outlined made labour extremely expensive to companies so that they had strong incentives to substitute capital for labour. Hence such investments as firms managed to make created fewer jobs than before because each new job cost far more in real terms, and the new jobs were therefore insufficient to make good all the jobs any economy must lose each year because of the obsolescence of plant, wear and tear and technical change and improved designs in the rest of the world. An American study has estimated that 57 per cent of industrial jobs are lost each decade throughout the USA for these reasons, and these have to be made good through the creation of new jobs which will often involve new designs and new technologies.[12] The position in Britain is almost certainly comparable, and there was simply too little investment to create enough new jobs to make good those that were lost. Hence the industrial part of the market sector employed fewer and fewer people. Fortunately the private services raised their employment slightly so that overall market sector employment fell less than industrial employment—in fact by 625,000 from 1966 to 1973, but in the same period non-market employment rose by 810,000 so that in a mere seven years—and seven years of world expansion at that — self-financing employment fell over half a million, and tax dependent employment rose almost a million. Table 7.3 shows what would happen in Britain if that trend continues, and the total British labour force grows at the rate which is now expected.[13]

TABLE 7.3.

British Employment if the Trends of 1966–73 Continue

	1966	1973	1976	1980	1987
Total Labour Force	25,066,000	25,545,000	26,136,000	26,466,000	27,388,000
Self Financing Employment	20,707,000	20,082,000	19,467,000	19,457,000	18,832,000
Tax Dependent Employment	4,078,000	4,888,000	5,337,000	5,698,000	6,508,000
Unemployment	281,000	575,000	1,332,000	1,311,000	2,048,000
Number of Market-Sector Workers Available to Finance each Non-Market Worker	4.75	3.68	2.92	2.78	2.20

[12] See G. Breckenfeld, 'Business Loves the Sun Belt (and Vice Versa)' *Fortune*, June 1977.

[13] This Table is derived from data in the *Department of Employment Gazette*, the *Annual Abstract of Statistics, Economic Trends* and *National Income and Expenditure*. Table 1.11. It is assumed that the labour force will grow 0.5 per cent per annum from 1973 to 1987.

The continuation of past trends clearly produces an intolerable outcome, both because unemployment can be expected to rise to over
three millions by 1987, and because the number of market sector
workers who will be available to finance each non-producer of marketed
output will fall from 4.75 in 1966 to 2.20 in 1987. From 1966 to 1973
British taxation had to rise sharply because the number of market sector
producers available to finance each non-producer of marketed output
fell from 4.75 to 3.68. If the same trends continue, only 2.78 producers
will be available to finance each non-producer of marketed output in
1980 and only 2.20 in 1987. It is to be noted that the previous trend
continued unchecked until 1976 when only 2.92 producers were available to finance each non-producer of marketed output. In 1966 there
were 4.75. If this trend continues further, taxation will need to rise
drastically for another decade, which would certainly mean that British
governments would turn increasingly to the printing press with its
consequent inflation 'tax' of cash balances to finance their expenditure.
There were already tendencies in this direction in 1972-6 a period in
which the non-market sector's share increased very rapidly. Conventional
taxation just could not be increased to the extent needed if rapid non-
market sector growth continues at the rate indicated in the table. If
workers again succeeded in passing extra taxation on to companies as in
1966-73, profits would virtually disappear—they had become extremely
low by 1974—and market sector employment would fall by more than
the 89,000 per annum indicated, so unemployment would rise still
faster than in the table. Soaring unemployment with a total collapse of
company profitability and massive money printing by the government
would certainly produce a crisis for British capitalism at some point in
the 1980s.

This was well understood in Britain by 1976—at least in official
circles. Early in that year the authorities decided that further growth in
non-market employment would cease for a time. A glance at the table
will show that this by no means suffices to correct Britain's growing
structural imbalance. If tax-dependent non-market employment ceases
to grow while market sector employment continues to decline by 89,000
a year, unemployment will grow all the faster.

In 1976 the British economy was in a trap. Employment in the
market sector had been declining for ten years, but it is precisely the
market sector which must ultimately finance the non-market sector and
the consumption of the unemployed. Britain's Labour government of
1976 therefore had to attempt to reverse the decline of the market
sector. To continue to expand the non-market sector, a Keynesian
solution, through government inspired and financed job creation
schemes, or further expansion of the public services, would have been
no solution because it would have involved still higher taxation and

worker frustration, or ever growing deficits involving an increasing use of the printing press to finance them.

The decline of market sector employment from 1966 to 1973 was largely due to the profits squeeze which reduced the real rate of return on British capital to as little as 3 or 4 per cent by 1973. Since 1973, the market sector has continued to cut employment, partly because of the world recession which began in 1974, and partly because it just could not afford to finance enough jobs to compensate for those lost as a result of technical progress and international competition. The government therefore had the urgent task of raising profitability in the market sector. It did this by deferring company taxation on profits that are the counterpart of inflation in the value of inventories, and by presiding over incomes policies in 1975-7 which cut the real wage by about 10 per cent so that profitability could be restored. British workers accepted the real wage cut because a collapse of the currency which few wanted was the obvious alternative. If these policies to raise company profitability are reinforced rather than reversed in 1978-80 and an internationally competitive currency is maintained so that British industrialists can earn adequate profits in export markets, British market sector employment could start to grow again after 1978 and the structural balance of the economy can start to be restored after this. Once it is, every four new market sector jobs created will provide the finance for one extra public service job at unchanged rates of taxation, so the creation of extra market sector jobs will have a multiplier effect on employment. It has already been pointed out that the belief that extra non-market jobs had a sustainable multiplier effect on employment contributed to Britain's policy errors and those of other English speaking countries.

The attempt to cure Britain's structural imbalance in 1976-7 was painful. In 1976-7 non-market employment fell 2 per cent as a result of the government's necessary economies, and market sector employment has continued to fall because government policies to help the market sector can only act slowly. Unemployment therefore increased to over 1,400,000 and the country has seen the government destroying public sector jobs at the very time that industry and commerce were also employing fewer people. That was a clear result of the imbalances of 1964-73. In that decade non-market sector growth was financed at the cost of investment instead of personal consumption. In consequence the market sector was unable to provide a sound financial foundation for growing non-market employment and jobs were destroyed in every sector of the economy in 1976 and 1977 because of this error. Once the market sector starts to expand again, employment in the non-market sector can begin to be restored, for the key point which Britain forgot and is painfully relearning is that it is a growing market sector which finances social welfare.

3. The Destabilization of New York

The imbalances created by rapid non-market sector growth in Britain have an extremely close parallel in North America, for New York's problems have been fundamentally the same. Non-market spending has increased still more rapidly in the United States than in Britain in recent decades.[14] There is, however, an important difference. In Britain the vast growth of non-market spending was predominantly financed by increases in national taxation because only a little over 10 per cent of total British taxation is local. In the United States over two-thirds of the increase in public spending and taxation from 1964–1974 was local—by states, cities, counties and townships. Federal taxation increased hardly at all as a share of output.[15] The difference would be immaterial if local taxation increased uniformly throughout the United States, but this is not at all what occurred. Taxation and public expenditure increased a great deal in some areas and hardly at all in others. In particular taxation and spending increased far more in the North and especially the North East than in the sun belt states. According to official United States statistics, a family of four paid about 10 cents in the dollar more in taxation in the four high tax cities, Boston, Buffalo, Milwaukee and New York, than in Houston, Jacksonville, Memphis and Nashville.[16] This difference is made up of higher state income taxes, higher property taxes, and higher local sales and corporation taxes. Companies to some extent compensate their workers for living in high tax areas like New York, so they earn less profit there, both because they are taxed more heavily themselves and because they have to pay higher salaries. Capital therefore tends to move out of the high tax neighbourhoods, so these acquire a diminishing ratio of market sector jobs. The expensive local non-market sector therefore has a diminishing productive base to support it as in Great Britain.

New York is a high tax city and real take home pay *fell* 3.5 per cent after all taxes in 1966–76[17] so workers paid for some of the rapid growth of its non-market sector, and companies have been expected to pay for the remainder. But their response has been to move more and more jobs out of New York, and market sector employment in the city fell from 3,130,000 in 1960 to 2,664,000 in 1976, a reduction of 15 per cent. The city's taxable surplus out of which its social services are

[14]See the statistical comparisons set out in Bacon and Eltis, op. cit. (1978), Ch. 6.
[15]See the *Statistical Abstract of the United States*, US Department of Commerce, Tables 418 and 425 of the 1976 edition, and equivalent tables in earlier editions.
[16]See the *Statistical Abstract of the United States*, US Department of Commerce, Table 450 of the 1976 edition.
[17]See the account of a New York State Labour Department study in the *New York Times* on May 15th, 1977.

financed has been moving South. In the same period non-market employment in New York City increased over 30 per cent. From 1960 to 1974 non-market employment actually increased 42 per cent. Then came the financial crisis and in the next two years public sector jobs had to be cut back by 50,000 at the very time that market sector jobs were also declining—by over 200,000.[18] The extra rapid initial expansion of non-market jobs with consequent local tax increases therefore contributed to a situation where market sector jobs were lost as firms moved out and contracted employment—until in the end both sectors were forced to cut employment at the same time exactly as in Great Britain.

There is a further important effect. United States evidence suggests that the better paid salaried workers move out of the high tax areas towards low tax ones.[19] At the same time, the poor move into the high tax and high public benefit areas. A former mayor of Houston put it colourfully. "Houston is a good place to be if you want to work. If you don't want to work you might get a better deal in New York."[20] As the rich and potential high earners move out of the high tax areas and the poor move in a vast unstable movement begins. The potential high tax payers congregate in areas where there is a wealth of skill in the population, and few poor people to support. In other areas, the unskilled and the deprived congregate, and there are a diminishing number of skilled workers to pay the taxes to support them, and to provide a magnet to market sector industry and commerce. These trends are slow but they are socially devastating. In New York City which has suffered from both a loss of market sector jobs and an influx of would-be beneficiaries from New York's fuller social services, unemployment increased from 4.8 per cent in 1970 to 10.6 per cent in 1976. In addition, employment in the 16-19 age group fell from 30 per cent in 1970 to a disastrous 22 per cent in 1976.[21] Among the ethnic minority groups, employment fell to a mere 14 per cent in this age group so the young had extremely few lawful opportunities to achieve living standards above the welfare minimum.

By contrast, in low tax Houston, aggregate employment grew rapidly in both the market and the non-market sector and employment in the 16 to 19 age group rose from 41 to 47 per cent from 1970 to 1976.

The destabilization of New York illustrates a general problem. In an

[18]See the *Thirteenth Interim Report* of the Temporary Commission on City Finances, New York City (May 1977), p. 15.
[19]See, for instance, J. R. Aronson and E. Schwarz, 'Financing Public Goods and the Distribution of Population in a System of Local Governments', *National Tax Journal* (June 1963).
[20]See Breckenfeld, op. cit.
[21]See the accounts of a United States Federal Government study in the *New York Times* on August 2nd and 7th, 1977.

economic area like the United States where capital and people can move freely, any region which offers non-market standards which are more expensive than companies and the better off wish to pay for is liable to suffer the gradual erosion of its productive base. Capital will leave a region where net of tax returns are below average. Some of the better off will leave an area where the benefits from the non-market sector social services are less than tax costs at their income level. The conditions for a smooth transition to a larger non-market sector which were out-lined earlier are breached where the better off do not accept the re-distributive element in higher taxation and have the power to react against it. Once capital and the better off start to depart, the high tax and high benefit areas must either cut public sector employment because they are losing the tax revenues which finance it, or they must raise rates of taxation still more. The latter will drive yet more taxpayers out and bring the final financial crisis nearer.

It is to be noted that if a combination of high non-market expenditure and high-taxation was attractive to the skilled and highly paid, they would move into the high tax areas and not away from them. The studies quoted suggest that what deters them from doing so is the redistributive element in the taxation that they are asked to pay. They can finance their own social services and have something left over in a low tax area. A further point is that, as in Britain, high taxation and high public expenditure often involves a proliferation of administrative expenditures and not the output of more public goods.

New York is the obvious example where instability due to these effects has gone furthest, but there are other cities and provinces which face similar difficulties. The Californian electorate has sought to avert them, well in advance, by passing the now celebrated proposition 13 to limit local spending in California. In Canada, Quebec has income tax rates which exceed those in the remainder of Canada by 6 cents in the dollar or more at the higher income levels, regulations which seek to enforce a higher minimum wage and further restrictions (obligations on Quebec based companies to do business in French) which are unattractive to many employers. Capital is therefore leaving Quebec which already has an unemployment rate one-and-a-half times the Canadian average.

Quebec like New York needs growing market sector employment so both are under overwhelming pressure to reverse the policies which have persuaded companies to locate elsewhere, and if the pressure is not obvious now in Quebec's case, it soon will be. If the European Economic Community continues to move towards truly free labour and capital mobility, Europe too will have its New Yorks and Quebecs. The problem is fundamentally that no city or province or country within a large economic union where labour and capital is free to move can afford to be relatively unattractive to the companies which create market sector jobs. These jobs will leave at a rate of 1 or 2 per cent a year and this will suffice over two decades to remove the foundations on which the financing of the non-market-sector rests.

4. The Destabilization of Chile

A final example of how rapid non-market sector growth can destabilize an economy is the case of a mismanaged revolution. Chile provides an example where statistics are beginning to emerge, and it is likely that Portugese figures will tell a similar story once they become available for the revolutionary period.

After Allende was elected President of Chile in September 1970, the rate of growth of government final consumption (which increased more slowly than government expenditure as a whole) rose from 2.2 per cent per annum for each worker employed to 7.0 per cent per annum. This would have involved increased taxation in itself but not necessarily an unacceptable rate of increase in taxation, at least in the short term, given the fact that many had voted for significant change—and that tax revenues would grow 2.2 per cent per annum for each worker with unchanged tax rates if the previous rate of growth of productivity of 2.2 per cent per annum was maintained.[22] What would have happened in 1970-3 would then have been something like the outcome set out in Table 7.4.[23] With this pattern of growth, the non-market sector would have grown about fifteen times as fast as the market sector.

What actually happened was far more serious for the market sector. For various reasons the previous rate of growth of productivity of 2.2 per cent per annum was not maintained after 1970. Indeed, according to ILO data, productivity fell 4 per cent in 1970-3. It fell for a number

[22] See the United Nations *Statistical Yearbook* for 1975, Tables 189-90, and the ILO *Year Book of Labour Statistics* for 1971 and 1976. Table 17 in the ILO Yearbook indicates that Chile's overall rate of growth of labour productivity was 2.2 per cent per annum in 1961-70 and −1.3 per cent per annum in 1970-3. It is inferred from this series and the United Nations' Table 189 that employment rose at a rate of 2.5 per cent per annum in both 1961-70 and 1970-3, and this information is needed to infer the rate of growth of government consumption *per worker* from the data in Table 189. It is assumed that the increase in government consumption in 1970-4 occurred entirely in the Allende years of 1970-3 for which a separate figure is not available.

[23] The basis for the assumptions about productivity growth and the growth of government spending in this table is set out in note 22 above, and the growth of government spending is if anything understated by using the growth of government consumption as a basis (see Table 201 of the UN *Statistical Yearbook* for 1975). The ratio of non-market purchases to market output is set at 25 per cent in 1970 because the ratio of total government spending to the National Income was 25.8 per cent in that year (Tables 201 and 185) and there is insufficiently detailed data to permit a breakdown between market and non-market purchases in the case of Chile.

TABLE 7.4.
What Could Have Happened in Chile in 1970-3 with Unchanged Productivity Growth

	1970	1973	Increase
Output per Worker	100	106	+ 6.7%
Purchased by the Market Sector per Worker Employed	75 (75%)	76.1 (71.3%)	+ 1.5%
Purchased by the Non-Market Sector per Worker employed	25 (25%)	30.6 (28.7%)	+ 22.4%

Non-Market Purchases rise 14.9 times as fast as Market-Sector Purchases

of reasons including in particular a cessation of capital accumulation in some factories and farms, with indeed failures to renew capital in many cases. In addition, the function of managing many of Chile's farms and factories was taken over by the working class and its elected government before the necessary skills to manage the nation's capital equipment successfully had been acquired. The ILO's statisticians do not suggest that this destroyed the market sector—merely that productivity fell about 4 per cent on average instead of rising by 6.7 per cent. Table 7.5 shows that this was quite enough to destabilize the economy in three years, given the 22.4 per cent increase in non-market spending which was now more than a declining economy could sustain.

TABLE 7.5
What Happened in Chile in 1970-3

	1970	1973	Increase
Output per Worker	100	96	— 4%
Purchased by the Market Sector per Worker Employed	75 (75%)	65.4 (68.1%)	— 12.8%
Purchased by the Non-Market Sector per Worker Employed	25 (25%)	30.6 (31.9%)	+ 22.4%

The market sector which produces all investment all exports and all private consumer goods and services had 12.8 per cent less per worker in 1973 than in 1970. In consequence exports, private consumption and investment all fell. Investment per worker fell 16 per cent, while exports fell 8 per cent.[24] The fall in exports played its part in Chile's

[24]These figures are derived from Table 189 of the United Nations *Statistical Year-book*, the growth of employment being inferred as in note 22, p.136. It is inferred that the reductions in exports and investment in 1970-4 were concentrated in the three years, 1970-3.

balance of payments crises and the rapid destruction of the inter-national value of the currency, but this was also due to the government's increasing resort to the printing press to finance its expenditures for conventional taxes could not be increased by 6.9 per cent of the National product in a mere three years. The fraction of expenditure financed by conventional taxes in fact fell from 87 per cent in 1970 to 65 per cent in 1973,[25] so up to one-third of the government's soaring expenditures were being financed by the printing press and consequent inflation taxes of cash balances by 1973. Conventional taxes might have financed an adequate proportion of expenditures if productivity had risen 6.7 per cent instead of falling 4 per cent in 1970-3, so this was a vital factor.

It is evident from the fact that exports per worker fell 8 per cent and investment 16 per cent that Chile failed to finance its increased social spending from the market sector's surplus. By presiding over policies which simultaneously reduced productivity and raised the real wage (where this includes the 'social wage'). the government destroyed most of the economy's surplus so that there was too little left for investment and the balance of payments. The Soviet Union was careful to precede its successful five year plans with the New Economic Policy which involved some use of capitalist managements in the early 1920s. Chile's and Portugal's Marxists in contrast preferred immediate reforms which sacrificed productivity and therefore most of their economies's potential surpluses of marketed output. If Marxists are to make more successful use of any future opportunities which European electorates may give them in the next decades, they will need to ensure that there are sufficient market sector surpluses in the period of transition to their preferred society for job creating investment and the provision of enough exportables to pay for necessary imports. If this is again forgotten, the New Left with its enthusiasm for immediate worker control, even at a cost of surplus destruction, will find that it has an infallible recipe for economic failure, and this is likely to be followed by political failure also, as in Chile and Portugal.

5. Conclusion

The world's viable economies are those which have an adequate market sector surplus to finance both the needs of the non-market sector and the job creation the economy requires. The examples of Britain, New York and Chile illustrate the slow or rapid destabilization which results if investment in job creation is neglected, or the surplus is destroyed.

The world's rate of growth of output has been much slower since 1973 than in the three previous decades. This may merely be the result of a recession which might conceivably prove temporary. Alternatively, the

[25]See the United Nations *Statistical Yearbook* for 1975, Table 201.

world may now have to face two or three decades of far slower growth. If the world's non-market sectors continue to grow at the rapid rates to which they became accustomed in the prosperous decades which followed the second world war, many countries will follow Britain, New York and Chile along the road to destabilization. A typical "successful" economy had a rate of growth of marketed output of 4 or 5 per cent per annum in 1950-73, and a rate of growth of real non-market expenditure of 6 or 7 per cent in this period. Hence non-market spending increased as fast as in Britain, but the economy's productive base typically increased about two-thirds as fast as rapidly growing non-market spending so taxation increased at an acceptable rate, given the rapid rate of growth of the National Product. Moreover, with 4 or 5 per cent real growth per annum, the market sector as well as the non-market sector obtained a rapid increase in real resources. If the rate of growth of marketed output now falls to 2 or 2.5 per cent in the typical "successful" economy, and real non-market spending continues to be expanded at 6 or 7 per cent each year, then a British style imbalance will begin to emerge in economies which have hitherto achieved balanced growth. 6 per cent non-market growth will cream off the entire growth of the economy if marketed output is only growing 2.5 per cent per annum, and this will leave no scope for increased private consumption in the market sector. If workers begin to pass on the consequent tax increases as in Britain, investment and the balance of payments will be undermined after a few years.

Therefore, if the 1980s and the 1990s prove to be decades of slow growth, the world's governments will have to become accustomed to far slower expansion in their own expenditures than in the prosperous 1950s and 1960s. If they continue to increase spending at the former rates—and this is bound to appear socially desirable to many—instead of the new and slower rates which market sector taxation will finance at tax rates workers are prepared to pay, destabilization will follow as surely as in Great Britain and New York. Other countries are certain to follow Great Britain's and New York's unwillingness to face the extra taxation needed to finance a sharp increase in the non-market sector's share. Like Britain and New York, they will therefore be drawn towards deficit financing, massive borrowing, and then the printing-press—which New York never had access to. Destabilization will certainly spread if it is not appreciated that when world growth decelerates, public expenditure must advance more slowly also.

8

THE MANAGEMENT OF THE WORLD ECONOMY

by C. J. Allsopp
New College, Oxford

1. Introduction

This paper concentrates on some aspects of the present situation in the industrialised countries and the policies being proposed to bring about a return to full employment growth without inflation. The difficulties faced are depressingly well known. But it is just a question of putting together some coherent package at the international level, or are the problems more deep seated? Were capitalist economies bound to run into serious problems sooner or later?

It is argued that the problems are, for the most part, neither surprising nor theoretically insuperable. The greatest difficulty is a straightforward failure of demand management policies. But the demand management problem is posed in a context which is unfamiliar in two important respects. The first, obviously enough, is that it is an international demand management problem with all the difficulties entailed. Secondly, and equally importantly, the demand management problem is medium term in nature. The purposeful management of demand for growth may be substantially more difficult than short term stabilisation policy. In the important case of generally sluggish investment and adverse expectations, short term policy, unless very carefully managed, may appear actually perverse from a medium term viewpoint.

Of course the demand management problem is far from being the only issue faced at the present time. Indeed it is now more usual to put the control of inflation first as a policy priority. But concentration on growth may be justified in that, already, many countries would prefer higher output and faster growth in spite of inflation. More fundamentally, it seems far from clear that the control of inflation would become any easier in a slow growth world rather than under fast growth with increasing living standards. For individual countries, a major difficulty is external constraints on domestic action. For balance of payments reasons more than any other, countries are locked into the international situation with little room for manoeuvre.

At the heart of much of the confusion and conflicting policy prescriptions is a question which is as old as economics. Are free enterprise economies basically stable and self righting, tending apart from the trade cycle, to generate full employment growth, or are they unstable without intervention or good luck. This question underlies much of the debate between Keynesians and monetarists, and at the political level divides those who favour a market solution—emphasising micro economic flexibility—from those who believe that macro economic intervention is essential. The view taken here is that free enterprise economies are, left to themselves, potentially unstable; that cumulative disequilibria may be very damaging; but that economies may be controlled by appropriate intervention, and in some circumstances may be stabilised by forces of a semi-autonomous kind. If, then, instability is a problem—if sustained growth is fragile—the present difficulties and the greater difficulties of the inter war period look like the normal case, and the hard thing to explain is the rapid and reasonably stable growth of O.E.C.D. countries in the 1950s and 1960s.

2. Post War Growth

It is of course well known that, despite many studies, the explanation of rapid growth since the war remains highly contentious. The various studies differ greatly in methodology and coverage, and the subject is bedevilled by apparently irresolvable problems of cause and effect. The thesis developed here is that the process always looked fragile but that a combination of favourable factors on both supply and demand sides meant that the problem of policy for growth never really had to be faced. Thus the idea gained ground that relatively minor policy interventions could be effective, that the medium term would look after itself, and that the proper domain for policy action was the domestic economy.

The facts are not seriously in dispute. In the two decades 1950 to 1970, the industrialised countries on average grew at about 4½ to 5 per cent per year. But within the group performance diverged markedly. In the United States and Britain, output per employee grew at about 2 per cent per year on average. In most of continental Western Europe productivity performance was much better—4½ to 5 per cent per annum in the major countries. And in Japan, productivity growth was nearly 8 per cent per year. Very broadly, one could say that the UK and North America maintained their relative position in terms of income and output per head, whilst Japan and most continental European countries went on to approach North American levels of income per head and productivity.[1] The process of convergence can be regarded as natural, in which case it is the poor performance of the UK and some other countries

[1] For a longer historical perspective see A. Maddison's contribution to this volume.

that stands out, or the rapid growth in Europe and Japan can be looked at as the exceptional phenomenon. At the very least there is a question about what it was that accounts for the success stories, and the high average rate of expansion.

Eclectic views of the process of growth usually start by stressing various facilitating factors on the supply side. In most of the fast growing countries, vast changes occurred in the disposition of the labour force between sectors, and between rural and urban occupations. It is often argued that these movements were a necessary condition, for the growth achieved—more rarely that it was causal.[2] Also on the supply side, the development of technology, and for many of the fast growers, the existence of a backlog of technical opportunities are regarded as important in explaining the rapid rates of growth of productivity achieved.[3] Morevoer supplies of raw materials and food were plentiful and available at stable or declining terms of trade. But such a characterisation of the potential that existed after the war—which is not too hard with hindsight—hardly explains how it was that the potential was realised. There are too many examples of economies with potential that did not grow fast in particular historical periods.

In order to go further towards an explanation of the growth that was achieved, it seems essential to turn to the expenditure or demand side of the growth process, and its complex dynamic interaction with supply side elements like technological and organisational change and the development over time of productivity. One obvious explanation is government policy and commitment to growth. After the war, most governments took responsibility for high employment, and in many cases reconstruction programmes provided an initial stimulus to growth and investment. As time went on and it came to be believed that the authorities could and would pursue policies of full employment and growth, government policy per se may have become less important than the expectational climate generated by success. High and rising investment expenditures are one of the most conspicuous features of post-war expansion, and were simultaneously a demand side factor making for rapid growth, and by their influence on productivity and organisational change, a factor making for the rapid development of potential. And of course, for successful countries, the development of exports was

[2]See, for example, N. Kaldor, *Causes of the Slow Rate of Growth of the United Kingdom* (Cambridge, 1967); G. P. Kindleberger, *Europe's Post-War Growth— The Importance of Labour Supply* (Cambridge, Mass., and Oxford, 1967).
[3]See S. Gomulka, *Inventive Activity, Diffusion and Stages of Economic Growth* (Aahus, 1971), and Gomulka's contribution to this volume.

favourable to demand and to industrial change.[4]

It may be useful to sketch the process of growth in a rapidly growing successful country in terms of the 'virtuous circle' or 'cumulative causation' theses that are well known in the literature.[5] There are a number of elements. Rapid growth, once started, is conducive to buoyant expectations and high investment. High investment, economies of scale, and the rapid diffusion of technology lead to rapid rises in productivity in the crucial manufacturing sector, and facilitate organisational change elsewhere. As growth proceeds, labour is drawn out of low productivity sectors such as agriculture and relocated in higher productivity and expanding sectors. The elastic supply of labour to the leading sectors means that expansion is not frustrated, and may be a factor reducing wage inflationary pressure. Another element is the rapid rises in living standards which defuse problems of income distribution. And fast rates of growth of productivity combined with low inflation mean that—particularly under fixed exchange rates which ruled through most of the period—that export competitiveness improves. Fast growth and undervaluation are in turn favourable to profitability and investment.

The characteristic of such a process is of course the absence of constraints, on the supply side and on the demand side, combined with self-reinforcing tendencies due to expectational factors, due to economies of scale (or more generally of growth) and due to the tendency for high investment and growth to generate high profitability. An obvious problem with such explanations is, of course, that it is much easier to explain the maintenance of rapid growth than the initiating factors that started the process off. The other point is of course that the virtuous circle could be broken at almost any point—due to supply side constraints, due to inflationary pressure, due to inappropriate policy responses, or due to balance of payments problems. Once broken, it would be very difficult indeed to sort out cause from effect and one would observe a combination of unfavourable elements.

Such a combination of unfavourable circumstances appears to have applied in the United Kingdom, and accounts for the controversy over the cause of Britain's relatively poor performance. Some have argued that labour constraints were the fundamental factor. Others that external problems relating to the balance of payments and competitiveness were

---

[4]Many writers on the subject have stressed the interaction between investment, expectations and exports as an explanation of the rapid growth achieved in countries with extensive supply potential. See, for example, W. Beckerman, *The British Economy in 1975* (Cambridge, 1965); Kaldor, op. cit.; Kindleberger, op. cit.
[5]Beckerman, ibid.; Kaldor, op. cit.; B. Moor and J. Rhodes, 'The Relative Decline of the U.K. Manufacturing Sector', *Cambridge Economic Policy Review* (Mar. 1976).

the most important constraint. Or, the process of slow growth, initiated by supply problems, may over time have led to such poor productivity performance, that the problem changed, and became, in the sixties, one of competitiveness which ultimately led to difficulties in generating full employment. And as is well known, more qualitative explanations such as inflationary pressure, or poor management, or a lack of innovation also suffer from the difficulty that they could equally plausibly be cause or effect.

But returning to the international picture of generally high rates of expansion, I want to make some points which may be important in understanding how it happened, and how it might be reproduced. The first is about the autonomous elements making for expansion. The second concerns the absence of very serious balance of payments or exchange rate problems over much of the period. And the third is concerned with the difficulty of assessing the role of policy action in general, and demand management policies in particular.

In considering a growth path it is extremely difficult to make a meaningful distinction between those components of expenditure that are induced and those that are autonomous. In short run models of the Keynesian kind, the autonomous components are typically taken to be government expenditure and (in the short run) investment, and for an individual economy, exports as well. For the aggregate of many economies, exports cannot be taken as exogenous or autonomous. And of course, the extent to which investment is autonomous is highly problematic. Much investment, perhaps most, depends on expectations of growth—the need to expand capacity to meet expected increments in demand. And in the long run, the extent to which trends in government expenditure are autonomous is severely constrained by the need for national budgets to be financed. Everything appears to depend on everything else.

This problem is well known enough in the theoretical literature on growth. Appeal is often made to "animal spirits" as the ultimate driving force behind investment; even more often the problem is suppressed by dropping the ideas of an independent investment function and assuming full employment growth.[6] But in applied economics it does seem that some distinction between autonomous and induced components of demand is still useful. Tentatively, one might define a semi-autonomous component as one which is relatively independent of the trade cycle, and relatively independent of the general course of expansion.[7] Looked

---

[6] For a survey, see A. K. Sen (ed.), *Growth Economics* (Harmondsworth, 1970).
[7] This is similar to the procedure adopted by M. Kalecki in 'Trend and Business Cycles Reconsidered', *Economic Journal* (June 1968), who uses the term 'semi-autonomous' to characterise those components of expenditure which are invariant over the cycle.

at in this way, it does appear that there were some fairly strong autonomous forces of expansion in the post war period: reconstruction programmes initially; a rapid rate of technical change; and, for many countries, a backlog of profitable investment oportunities no doubt increased the 'autonomous' elements in investment. And, probably much more important than generally assumed, social and political forces making for an expansion in public expenditure generally and, in the 1960s, on welfare and income maintenance in particular.

Of course autonomous expenditures have to be financed – which is one reason why no major expenditures are fully autonomous in the long run. But if induced expenditures react quickly then the autonomous expenditures may become self-financing or at least profitable according to conventional criteria. An increase in government expenditure may, if other expenditures react, be self-financing as tax revenues swell with growth. And the revenue of an investing firm will rise as others get in on the act. And as expectations of continued growth develop and stabilise it becomes more and more difficult to separate out the autonomous elements from the induced effects. The main autonomous element becomes, in effect, the continued expectation of growth.

One of the financing problems that could be expected to arise concerns balance of payments adjustment. With the interwar difficulties in mind, the architects of post-war policy expected trouble. And given that exchange rates after 1949 turned out to be much more fixed than had been intended or expected, there is an interesting question as to how it was that, despite strains, the international payments system worked as well as it did. Part of the explanation is surely that in the early part of the period, there were many direct controls which were dismantled only slowly. Another reason may be that, at the beginning of the period, the overriding need for reconstruction in Europe meant that the payments problems that did exist were not allowed to get in the way of domestic objectives. Moreover the dominant role of the United States must have been important; the widely feared dollar shortage did not materialise, and ultimately became the problem of a dollar glut.

But another reason appears to have been that undervalued countries tended also to be countries with vast supply potential, so that as they became more and more competitive, macro economic and payments balances were preserved by rapid growth. Thus fast growing countries such as Japan, Germany in the fifties, and Italy (also in the fifties) did not on the whole generate unsustainable surpluses. It is not often enough recognised that fast growth may, at least for a time, be a substitute for revaluation. In general one would expect balance of payments adjustment to become more difficult when there is less flexibility in growth rates.

Turning now to the question of policy and its role, there are a number of interrelated points that I want to make. The first is well enough known—that it is difficult to explain the generally higher rates of employment by the direct effects of demand management policy of a Keynesian kind. Even for the United Kingdom where such policies were most consistently applied, government action appears much too small to explain the generally high level of employment.[8] The key difference, in the United Kingdom as elsewhere, appears to have been the high level of investment. Macro economic balance was achieved not by government dissaving and budget deficits, but by the generally high propensity to invest.

But of course, as noted, the indirect effects may have been very important. With a commitment to growth and full employment, and apparently, the means to achieve it, the expectational climate is favourable. Longer term investment plans become geared to the expectation of continued growth which both stabilises the business cycle and tends to raise the level of investment. Thus paradoxically, a successful demand management strategy means that it has only to be lightly applied. And for competitive countries, the external sector may operate in a powerfully stabilising way. Buoyant exports maintain demand and output directly. And if balance of payments surpluses result from domestic recession, these offset and over time may reverse the domestic forces that led to recession. Kalecki described budget deficits as artificial export surpluses.[9] In the context of post war growth it might be better to say that export surpluses were artificial budget deficits.

But the stabilising influence of buoyant world trade could not have occurred if the international business cycle had been synchronised. The trade cycle was not eliminated in individual countries (though it often took the form of decelerations and accelerations in growth), but by and large it was not coincident between major areas of the world economy. Thus world trade grew steadily. Until recently, the most nearly coincident cycle was the recession of 1958. But at that time policy actions were taken in major countries, early on, and recessionary forces were quickly reversed. The lack of synchronisation meant both that individual economies were stabilised, and that demand management policies were easier to apply. The multiplier applying to individual countries was lower (because of the import leakage) than that which would apply to the system as a whole. Each bit was stabilised by all the rest.

The lack of coincidence—of movements in demand and output, and of policy problems—is hard to explain. Why did the international

[8]R. C. O. Matthews, 'Why has Britain had Full Employment since the War?', *Economic Journal* (Sept. 1968).
[9]M. Kalecki, 'Determinants of Profits', in *Essays on the Dynamics of Capitalist Economy* (Cambridge, 1971).

transmission mechanisms work so much less strongly than in the interwar period? One obvious reason is simply that as time went on many more countries were important in trade. A more subtle reason, which has elements of both cause and effect, might be termed national autonomy. As already noted, the overriding importance of domestic objectives, combined with fairly strong interventionist policies meant that countries were able to pursue their own policy priorities. And as rapid growth developed, and the international business cycle was attenuated, countries really could have a fair degree of national economic sovereignty. And it happened that the sum total of domestic actions—whether appropriate or not—did not seem to add up to any very large destabilising influences for the world economy.

Viewed from the present most of the features of the growth period are rather worrying. Expectations can turn sour. International transmission effects, unless offset, seem almost bound to lead to problems of synchronisation and external constraints. In a more constrained world economy, balance of payments adjustment problems appear likely to be a real issue. And above all, the weapons of policy were not really tested in adversity.

3. What Went Wrong?

After the oil crisis, the industrial countries went into the deepest recession since the war, and inflation rose until it was on average about 15 per cent per year. They are now faced with a combination of high unemployment, continuing high inflation, serious payments imbalances, exchange rate instability, sluggish investment, problems of structural adaptation to higher energy and raw material costs, and an accelerating drift to ad hoc forms of protectionism. The recovery, rapid in 1976, now looks fragile and hesitant at best. This long list of problems—which do not of course apply with equal force in all countries—should not be surprising. It is the natural result of an international system in serious disequilibrium.

But what were the main reasons for the breakdown, and how fundamental were they. There are of course, many views—the oil crisis, fiscal and monetary irresponsibility, wage push inflation, or even bad luck. A recent study—the McCracken Report—points both to shocks in the early 1970s—harvest failures and the timing of the explosive rise in oil prices—and policy errors.[10] They conclude: 'our reading of recent history is that the most important feature was an unusual bunching of unfortunate disturbances, unlikely to be repeated on the same scale, the impact of which was compounded by some avoidable errors in economic policy'.

[10] P. McCracken et al., *Towards Full Employment and Price Stability* (O.E.C.D. Paris, 1977).

This basically optimistic position is moderated within the report by two important qualifications. The first is the recognition that the problems were getting more difficult through the sixties, even before the commodity price boom and the oil crisis. The second is that the starting point is now one of disequilibrium, and to get back to something like the past will present quite unusually great difficulties.

It is difficult not to agree with their emphasis on shocks and policy errors. But this does not mean that the errors were easy to avoid, nor that similar problems will not arise in future. The policies followed had a kind of inevitability about them, and if it is accepted tht the previous period of rapid growth looked fragile, the recent instabilities are not hard to account for. It is not possible here to rehearse the history of the last decade.[11] But there are some general features which are worth bringing out as they mark a contrast with the previous period.

The most obvious feature of the last decade is the acceleration of inflation. Though this is often presented as a continuous process, such a characterisation is misleading. The rise in inflation in Europe and America in the late 1960s is in fact hard to account for. Even in the United States, where the usual explanation runs in terms of excessive demand pressure, the trade-off was worsening, and there appear to have been social and political forces at work as well. It was a time of protest and militancy. In Europe, conventional explanations in terms of demand pressure or monetary expansion fail. There was a series of wage explosions in different countries, and the rises coincided with shop floor unrest. In Europe, certainly, the rise in inflation appeared to be due to wage push pressure, and the phenomenon raised the old fears that full employment and growth might be incompatible with a reasonable degree of price stability.

One possible explanation of increased inflationary pressure is that the unemployment and underemployment in Europe and America in the fifties acted as a dampening factor, and that as the balance between supply potential and demand changed over the longer run, inflationary pressure was bound to increase. Another, which would be difficult to distinguish from the previous one, is that it was inevitable that expectations and aspirations would catch up with the actuality of rapid growth. The combination of expected real rises in living standards and the assumed ability of governments to guarantee full or near full employment would eventually mean that the inflationary problem, disguised for a time by unexpectedly good performance, would reappear. In support, it could be argued that a number of the wage explosions had followed periods of slower growth and apparently frustrated expectations. And slower growing countries such as the United Kingdom had always

---

[11] See McCracken et al., op. cit.

appeared to have had difficulties with cost push pressure.

By contrast with the late 1960s, the inflation of the subsequent boom period was initiated in product markets—it was set off by the commodity price boom, and in many cases by real estate price rises as well. It was of course made much worse by the steep rise in oil prices at the end of 1973, which added 2 to 3 per cent to price levels in most countries.

The controversial question after the oil price rise was not whether inflation would rise in the short term, but what the appropriate policy response should be in order to avoid a continuation or acceleration of inflation as rapid rises came to be expected and as wage earners attempted to get money wage rises sufficiently high to protect their real living standards. One obvious response was to seek to contain inflation by restrictive policies and rising unemployment. But in many countries it was argued that such policies had not been successful in the past, that the effect on income standards would be magnified rather than diminished, and that the best chance lay in maintaining demand and output and in seeking some sort of incomes policy or social consensus so that the relative price changes could be absorbed over time in a reasonably rational way. On this view it was an advantage that many oil producers would not be able to spend their surpluses, so that the real impact on potential living standards was necessarily delayed. Of course, even in countries where that was the dominant view, it was recognised that there was excess demand in the world economy and within some countries, which would need to be eliminated. At the very least it was necessary that the commodity price rises should be stemmed, if not reversed. As can be seen, different views turned on the question of how best wage inflation could be controlled in a situation where relative prices and income differentials had been greatly disturbed, and where expectations of inflation were very volatile. The same question is still at the root of much of the present controversy about the appropriate stance of policy, nationally and internationally.

Another feature of the recent period is the increased instability of the world economy—which illustrates well the difficulties that are faced when it moves approximately in phase and the international transmission mechanisms are strong. A major reason for the over rapid boom in 1972/73 is that individual responses in particular industrial countries, which looked appropriate in terms of domestic objectives, when summed up for the group as a whole had too great an impact. Although forecasting procedures should in principle capture the interactions, national authorities had become accustomed to the framing of policy in a rather more stable world economy. An aspect of the boom was, of course, that monetary policy was very expansionary and was an important element in the speculative forces that developed. Importantly, this appeared to be due to the breakdown of the Bretton Woods system of fixed exchange rates and the desire in Europe and Japan to avoid re-valuations. By the early 1970s the advantages of undervaluation had become widely recognised. Thus the impact of the dollar outflow was not offset. Again, the main point is that the policies followed seemed justified from the narrow point of view of domestic objectives.

After the oil crisis the instability of the world economy was again seriously underestimated. The demand effects of the oil price rise could have been offset, as was well understood at the time, and the main reason for the policies followed was the anti inflation objective. But the recession went much further than expected or generally intended. There are many technical reasons for this, but very broadly the increased instability reflected the power of the transmission mechanisms, and the adverse expectational climate that developed. Two stabilisers that had been important in the past—the expectation of continued growth, and governmental commitment to growth, no longer operated to anything like the same extent.

The interesting question is really why the recession was not larger, given the policies followed and the adverse factors. Again there are many reasons—the industrialised countries were stabilised by the third world, some countries tried to offset or lagged the downswing—but the major reason was the classic stabiliser of government deficits which rose in nearly all countries to record levels.[12]

The recovery that set in in the second half of 1975 depended on a reversal of the stock building cycle, and a recovery of consumer durable demand from exceptionally depressed levels. Its distressing feature was that it did not become soundly based with a recovery of business invest-ment, which lagged more than usual, and has been hesitant and sluggish at best. But the slow response of investment is hardly surprising in view of the increasingly pessimistic expectations of business, and the degree of excess capacity in the world at large. As the natural but temporary factors in the upswing faded, and as policy became more restrictive,[13] the world recovery faltered and growth in 1977 and 1978 has been in the 3 to 3½ per cent per annum range—a rate that implies an increasing degree of slack for most countries. And with the slow-down, longer term expectations are being revised down, further contributing to slow and cautious investment.

But the most notable change of all in the 1970s has been the dimi-nution of national economic sovereignty, and the gradual recognition

---

[12]In 1975, General government net landing was over 4½ per cent of GDP/GNP for the major seven countries combined. See *O.E.C.D. Economic Outlook*, (July 1977), Table 14.
[13]Budget deficits were substantially reduced in 1976 and 1977. See *O.E.C.D. Economic Outlook* (July 1978).

that the scope for domestic policy action is, in all but a few countries, [14] severely constrained by the external environment. The lesson to be drawn is not the failure of demand management policies, but that the appropriate domain for policy action to raise demand is now the world economy.

As noted, there was considerable disagreement after the oil crisis about the appropriate strategy for the world economy and for individual countries. Those that did not want to accept the recession domestically, and who assumed that the world recession would be offset or short lived were most vulnerable. They were dragged into the recession due to automatic effects and increasing external difficulties. And the shock of discovering that other countries did not operate rationally (from their point of view) should not be underestimated. If they had assumed a recession on the scale that actually developed, their optimal policies would presumably have been different.

There is a further complication. Particularly for a country in a weak external position, the best possible situation is, often, to have a relatively cautious policy, and to rely on world demand to provide the domestic stimulus. But if many countries take the same view, the strategy is in ruins and general deflation and slow growth results,—which may be far worse than the cooperative solution of joint reflation. If countries feel themselves weak, the cooperative solution of maintained growth is very fragile. If it does not happen, the costs to those who assumed it would are great. Even if it does happen for a time, it may pay a sufficient number to break ranks. And once the expectation of continued co-operation and growth is broken, a return to a cooperative strategy may be very difficult to achieve.

The obvious reason for the external constraint on so many countries is the uneven pattern of payments balances that developed due to the O.P.E.C. surplus, and the deflationary policies initially followed by the strongest countries. In fact, deficits have remained concentrated on the smaller and weaker countries,—and on the non-oil producing countries— and the problems are cumulative. The uneven pattern imparts a severe deflationary bias to the world economy.

But of course the problem is not just one of payments imbalance. The most serious problem is the interaction between domestic policies, the exchange rate, and inflation. Reflationary moves may, in a world of floating exchange rates, lower the value of the currency, raise the price of imports, impart a mechanical impact to the price level, and feed through into the wage bargaining process. There is the possibility of a nightmarish spiral of declining exchange rates and rising inflation. Thus domestic moves to reflate or offset may, quite genuinely, be very

[14]Notably Germany and Japan.

dangerous for inflation, even if the faster growth *per se* were not, or even if growth were actually helpful to wage moderation. For this reason more than any, even large countries such as Britain, Italy and France, feel that they are very constrained in their demand management policies. A disturbing feature of the situation in 1978 is that the United States is no longer immune from the pressures other countries face. The weakness of the dollar combined with a tendency for inflation to rise, means that the policy of maintaining demand and output and going for growth looks increasingly vulnerable.

The essential point about most of the external factors that constrain domestic policy in so many countries is that they apply to individual countries rather than to the world economy. They arise from relative conjunctural positions, and from the effect of domestic monetary and fiscal policies on international financial markets. It is not surprising that the freedom of any region of the world economy is constrained by what is happening in the others. It is the normal case. The abnormal situation was the fragile situation that existed in the past, when national objectives and international balance did not come seriously into conflict. The micro-macro paradox is of course well illustrated by the obvious point that there can be no such thing as a payments problem for the world economy as a whole, or even more graphically by the point that exchange rates cannot spiral downwards relative to each other. Thus the problems of individual countries cannot be problems for the world system as a whole. There are, however, two problems that do remain for the industrial countries in aggregate. The first is the relationship between wage inflation and pressure of demand and growth. The second, which bears analogy with the balance of payments problem for individual countries, is the real price or terms of trade of commodities, which interacts with the problem of inflation.

4. Strategies

It can of course be maintained that the present slow growth in the world economy is desirable, that the pressure that exists on individual countries forces them into an appropriate policy stance, given world inflation, and that slow growth is inevitable until inflationary expectations are finally broken. This is not a view I accept. Moreover, O.E.C.D. governments have repeatedly affirmed their determination to get back to faster growth, and to manage world demand so that, at least, there is no further reduction in the utilisation of potential. In spite of that commitment, summit meetings have come and gone, with little in the way of positive action, and as the failure to agree has become obvious, longer term expectations of businessmen, consumers and governments, have been affected. Now, in 1978, many are projecting slow growth, in the 3 to 3½ per cent range for the foreseeable future – that is if they are not even more pessimistic. This expectational climate is dangerous. In an obvious sense, such expectations may be self validating. I shall argue later, that there is a danger that they may not be, and that the likely outcome would be even slower growth, with cumulative problems of disequilibrium.

Soon after the oil crisis, it became recognised that the problem of getting back to more acceptable developments in the world economy would take time to solve. It was a medium term problem. This recognition was reflected in the normative scenarios that were prepared, principally by the O.E.C.D. and the policy statements of governments.[15] There has been a substantial shift away from short term stabilisation policy towards more medium term objectives and planning. And by and large, such normative medium term plans for the world economy have been endorsed by national governments. Why do they then appear to be failing?

The obvious reason is the policy stance in Germany and Japan. The US alone even approached the targets set. With major countries falling behind, and with an objective in most of the others of lagging the cycle for balance of payments or anti-inflation reasons, a shortfall was bound to occur, and as it occurred it became reinforcing both because of the transmission effects and because of the downward pressure on the weaker countries. The targets could only be met if the tendency to overshoot was as strong as the tendency to undershoot. This is a familiar problem in indicative planning. The strategy has to be credible, and except in 1976, it did not appear credible.

There has been a shift in 1978, towards more generalised expansionary moves, and some small overall stimulus can be expected. The reason for this is, first, the pressure towards domestic reflation within many of the weaker countries—and increasing diplomatic pressure on Germany and Japan. In diplomatic terms German compliance is being bought for progress on protectionism, and on exchange rate instability. The fragility of the deal is obvious, but it is too early yet to rule out cooperative moves of reflation. But a major difficulty is a lack of understanding of the implications of managing demand for the world economy in a purposeful way so as to produce a steady sustained upswing from the present, which obeys 'speed limits'.[16] The next section considers some of the theoretical difficulties, and the succeeding one some of the practical implications of these difficulties.

[15]See for example, 'A Growth Scenario to 1980', *O.E.C.D. Economic Outlook* (July 1976), and McCracken et al., op. cit.
[16]One of the judgements expressed in McCracken et al., op. cit., is that the speed of the 1972/73 upswing was very inflationary, and that, in future, rapid upward movements should be avoided. Hence their prescription of a steady recovery along a 'narrow path' which obeys 'speed limits'.

5. The Demand Management Problem

5.1. Macro-economic Consistency in the Medium Term

Standard forecasting models are principally designed to track short term fluctuations in the economy, and to serve as a tool in assessing the short term effects of economic policy changes. In the longer term they depend upon the development over time of exogenous variables. I have already noted that they are not particularly well adapted to an understanding of the growth process. If a supply side approach is taken, policy and other parameters have to be geared to an assumed growth of productive potential. If a more demand oriented approach is favoured, then the problem is that none of the assumed exogenous variables is really exogenous—as noted in discussing the past, even the most autonomous trends are only semi-autonomous.

In considering the development of demand in the medium term there is a lot to be said for going to the other extreme and regarding all demand components as induced in a closed macro system. This means basing the analysis on Harrod,[17] rather than Keynes, and the central concept is not the consistency of plans at a moment of time, but the stronger condition of macro-economic balance along a growth path.

The central relationship in Harrod's analysis of a closed economy, with no government sector, is between investment and growth. If for formal simplicity, a constant capital output ratio is assumed, the relationship is that the investment output ratio for the economy (I/Y) depends upon the growth, or rather the expected growth, of the economy,

$$I/Y = v_r g_e \qquad (v_r \text{ is the capital coefficient})$$

If this relationship is combined with a particular propensity to save, s, which as a matter of accounting must be equal to the investment output ratio (at this level of simplification) there is a unique rate of growth, the warranted rate, which is consistent over time with the maintenance of equilibrium. As well known, that rate of growth had the magnitude s_r/v_r, where s_r is the desired, or required, savings ratio of the economy.

The significance of that particular path is that macro economic consistency is possible along that path, and along no other path (unless the parameters change). Any other path must be a disequilibrium path in the sense that either savers are not saving what they want to save— and thus would react through the multiplier process—or the investment that is going on is not appropriate to the growth that actually results. Another way of putting it is that given the assumed behaviour of savers

---

[17]R. F. Harrod, 'An Essay in Dynamic Theory', *Economic Journal* (Mar. 1939). See also, R. F. Harrod, *Economic Dynamics* (London, 1973).

and investors, there is a unique rate of growth which if expected, would be consistent with the maintenance of that expectation over time. Any other expectation would not be self validating.

Even at this level of simplicity, for formulation of the problem of growth leads to two difficulties of the greatest significance for practical policy. The first is that there is no a priori reason for supposing that the path which is consistent with macro economic equilibrium over time is consistent with the growth of supply potential of the economy. The second is that the path appears unstable, in that an expectation of a faster rate of growth would tend to lead to even faster growth. Most of the growth theory literature since Harrod has been concerned with dodging the implications of these two problems.

There are many ways out of the first problem. Formally either the savings behaviour of the economy, or the capital coefficient (i.e. investment behaviour) could change. The warranted rate need not be unique. Of if supply potential is not the datum in practice that it is usually assumed to be, the problem may not arise. Harrod himself has no doubt that policy to affect either savings or investment would be necessary in practice. Turning immediately back to practicalities, I noted in an earlier section that in fact the fast growth period after the war, macro economic balance was achieved by high investment and growth, rather than by deficit support to consumption. The growth achieved had some characteristics of a warranted path without extensive intervention. And a major reason that this was possible was flexibility on the supply side.

The question of instability is more intricate. How can a growth path which is unstable, which could only be achieved by chance, and which would not be sustainable except by chance be of the slightest significance for policy? The phenomenon of instability is, of course, suggestive of the trade cycle, but the moment lags are built in one seems to get models of the trade cycle which do not grow, and the warranted rate concept disappears.[18] Such views misunderstand the nature of the warranted path. It is not a model of growth, but a consistency condition. Looked at in this way, there is no reason why one should not have a warranted path which was perturbed by a reasonably short run and predictable cyclical movement. The easiest way to conceptualise this particular version of trend and cycle is to posit two levels of expectation. If the longer term expectation is correct and at the warranted rate (strictly an expectation of growth on average along a particular warranted path) there is no reason why short term movements of a cyclical kind should not occur, which would be powerfully dampened by the continued

[18]For a formal analysis of the view that multiplier/accelerator models can explain cycles or growth, but not both, see L. L. Passinetti, '*Cyclical Fluctuations and Economic Growth*', *Oxford Economic Papers* (June 1960).

expectation of growth. If demand fluctuates in the short term, business-men do not in practice immediately revise their longer term expectations.

But what I have done, in effect, is to introduce an autonomously growing component of demand—based on expectations—into a short term cyclical model of the trade cycle, a familiar enough construct. Despite some assertions to the contrary in the literature, growth at the rate of growth of the autonomous components is (assuming that the cyclical component is unimportant, or has died out), growth at the warranted rate in Harrod's sense. This needs some justification. Very broadly conventional multiplier accelerator models of the trade cycle are inconsistent with the warranted rate concept because the introduction of lags means that the consumption income ratio, and the realised capital coefficient are not independent of the growth rate. If the lags are retained, but the expectation of growth is built into the relationships, the problem disappears, and the growth rate is warranted. But the intro-duction of the autonomously growing component does something else. Within limits, the warranted rate is now variable, and the system can, in principle, track onto the rate of growth of autonomous expenditure. It is the equilibrium share of the autonomous components that provides the necessary degree of freedom. This is a useful result in that the unique-ness problem is diminished.[19]

But the problem of the uniqueness of the warranted rate has not totally vanished. The autonomous components are not completely auto-nomous, whether based on longer term expectations, or on policy, or on other factors such as technical opportunities. The moment the autonomous components of demand are linked to either output (as a share) or to the growth rate (as with investment) or to tight financing criteria, the uniqueness of the warranted rate comes back. And that re-introduces instability as a kind of longer term cumulative problem. If growth falls below expectation, then as the semi-autonomous compon-ents react, so even slower growth may result.[20]

The concept of the warranted path can be further weakened and made more realistic by the recognition of induced changes in savings behaviour, or by induced changes in the capital coefficient. It can be generalised to include sectoral, regional or balance of payments effects. Many realistic modifications, which take into account financial effects

---

[19]Though the warranted rate is variable, this does not mean that the approach to a warranted path would necessarily be stable if expectations and the level of output were initially wrong.

[20] The analysis here is probably closest to Kalecki's views of the determination of trend and cycle (Kalecki, op. cit.). For Kalecki, the 'semi-autonomous' components of demand were autonomous investment, and an autonomous component of capitalists' consumption. These, ultimately, in his model, determine the growth of the system.

or sectoral balances suggest that measured profitability ex post is a function, inter alia, of the level of investment and the rate of growth.[21] But the key point is that the concept brings together financing considerations—such as savings/investment balance—or balance of payments flows, and the real side, which is concerned with the share of particular expenditure components, such as investment or consumption, and their consistency or otherwise with a particular growth path. A few illustrations of a practical kind will serve better than a long theoretical discussion.

In the first place, macro economic balance may be achieved either by high growth and high investment, or by low growth and deficit finance. If the savings ratio is given and the capital coefficient given, this must be so. Thus, a priori, a closed economy that had to slow down for, say, supply side reasons, would have to run public sector deficits (to increase the share of consumption), and have a slower development of public expenditure. And it is notable that the combination is not particularly inspiring politically. But unless the deficits were incurred, even slower growth and even larger deficits would result—that is the instability problem. Thus demand management is much more important in a supply constrained economy. The transition would however be easier, if either investment kept up as a share in spite of lower growth—in which case, the capital output ratio would be rising—or if lower investment induced lower proportionate savings.

For an individual economy, there is an extra degree of freedom in the balance of payments and in export growth. In the first place, if export growth is rapid, because the economy is competitive, this is an autonomous source of stimulus. If investment is lower than domestic savings and the budget is balanced an export surplus must result. If the supply potential is adequate, a combination of government policy, expectational effects and financial effects is likely to result in higher growth and higher investment. Macro economic balance may then be achieved by higher domestic investment and no surplus results. If the economy slows down (for supply side reasons, perhaps) a structural balance of payments surplus would tend to result unless, as before, deficit support of consumption fills the gap, or a relaxed monetary policy

---

[21]The most well-known model which gives this result is the Kalecki multiplier process which pre-dates Keynes. For Kalecki, in most of his formal models, savings were made out of profits, and workers' savings were 'definitely unimportant'. With savings out of profits the only stabiliser (leakage) in the system, the result that profits (ex post) depend on investment is self-evident, and no more 'paradoxical' than any other multiplier result. Similar results are obtained if it is company savings that are important. Savings out of a business expense such as savings out of wages, or savings out of oil revenues reduce profitability (ex post) for a given level of investment.

can either raise investment or lower savings. If deficit or monetary support to demand is not sufficient, two things could happen. If the economy is competitive, continued export expansion may generate the required growth, but with a structural surplus on the balance of payments. If the economy becomes less competitive—perhaps because of exchange rate changes, the growth of exports falls (though the surplus may not initially), and this further reacts on investment and there is a danger of a cumulative process as exports and investment simultaneously weaken. I need hardly add that there may be a tendency for such a process to occur in Germany.

As a final illustration of the requirements for macro economic balance over time, consider the oil price impact. The impact on O.E.C.D. countries as a group of the surpluses the oil producers were bound to run (if demand and output were maintained) was of the order of 40 billion dollars—or 1½ per cent of GNP. The increase in effective savings (ex ante) requires, other things being equal and ignoring expectational effects, a similar decrease elsewhere in a system of ex ante savings, or an increase in investment. This can be seen as a requirement in two areas—the first is that balance of payments deficits of the required magnitude have to be acceptable. That was well appreciated initially. Secondly, corresponding to the worsening on external account, the increase in borrowing, or the decrease in saving has to be acceptable domestically *within* the various economies. The receipts versus expenditure position of either households, or companies or government has to worsen. Households might have decided to borrow to maintain real expenditures—it was unlikely and in the event they saved more. Companies could have stabilised the system by maintaining investment and employment, in spite of a deterioration in cash flow—and, this is important, lower measured profits. In effect they would have been borrowing from the surplus OPEC countries at reduced profitability. Again, unlikely. In practice it would have to be governments who took the impact on the public sector deficit. I am not, of course, arguing that the oil price impact should have been offset in this way—only that it could have been if it were desired to maintain macro economic balance at that time. Any other policy towards the oil impact per se, would have been bound to lead to macro economic disequilibrium of one kind or another.

Of course, though the oil impact may have been simple, the short term policy problem was not. The world economy was in disequilibrium in a number of respects. There was excess demand. Inflation was having an unpredictable effect on domestic savings/investment behaviour. Expectational factors had changed greatly. And national targets for the level of output and its rate of growth had changed. Many countries foresaw a need for real adjustments in the balance of payments. The combination of short and medium term problems was particularly adverse. And the appropriate stance of short term policy to achieve medium term aims is not simple even in theory. I will illustrate the problem theoretically before turning to the difficulties presently faced.

5.2. Short-term Policy for Medium-term Aims

In terms of Harrod's consistency condition, it is easy to see what the requirements are for a *change* in the medium term growth trend. If the target growth rate is to be lower,[22] it will usually be true that investment has to fall as a proportion of output—corresponding to the lower growth rate. Somehow or other, savings have to be brought down to match. If it is not expected to happen automatically the normal way of doing it would be a step increase in the public sector deficit, to produce a step rise in the level of consumption, followed by a lower growth in consumption in line with the new target. This is just the policy of lowering the warranted rate in line with the new target. It has three elements. The rise in consumption, the fall in investment, and the slower growth in both of them. Since it is easy enough to lower investment, and to raise consumption, it is fairly plausible that such a policy can be carried out. But even here, there is a snag. The change in the structure of demand from investment to consumption will have real effects—excess capacity in the capital goods producing industries, deficient capacity in the consumer goods industries. In practice the structural problem will be mitigated. Some investment, such as housing and much public sector investment is not closely geared to the growth rate—and one could add defence. And for an individual country substitution of consumer goods for capital goods through trade may greatly increase flexibility.

There is no serious inconsistency between likely short term responses, and medium term requirements in the case of a slow down in target growth. The main danger is one of overshoot. The reason that short and medium term requirements are not in conflict is that the policy instruments to lower investment and to raise consumption exist. Turning however to the problem of raising growth from a depressed rate, in line with a target of more rapid expansion, the difficulties are much more acute.

If growth is to *rise* the requirements in the medium term is a fall in consumption, and a rise in investment.[23] It appears that taxes should be raised to make room for the needed investment. If investment is directly controlled, there is no problem, other than the need to squeeze consumption, and a possible short run deficiency in capital goods producing sectors. But in practice the difficulty is obvious. Investment tends to lag and if it does not immediately respond, there is a deficiency

---

[22]For example, the authorities may revise downwards the expected long-run potential growth rate of some limiting variable, such as the labour force.

[23]Retaining the simplifying assumption of a relatively fixed capital/output ratio.

of demand, and even lower growth results in the short term, further weakening the incentive to invest. The medium term requirement appears inconsistent with the short term response. The requirement that the warranted rate should be made equal to the target rate is, in fact, dangerously misleading. If investment cannot be controlled except indirectly by going for growth and waiting for the response, the only alternative, in a closed economy, is to go for the growth first by public sector expansion, or by consumption. One or both of these components has to rise, relative to existing levels, in spite of the medium term requirement, that they should fall. The control problem is quite tricky. In fact it is all a matter of timing. As the investment response comes through, so the other components of demand have to be curtailed. If this is not done then upward instability—which could be inflationary, would result. Consumer or public sector led booms may be highly unstable. But they do have one advantage in a period of depressed investment and pessimistic expectations. Short of other instruments of control over the private investment decision, they are the only way.[24] And if the control problem is fully understood it should be possible to time the impulses correctly and to avoid the danger that 'if it is enough, it is too much'.

This analysis may give a clue to the British problem of stop-go cycles. But though I would argue that the world economy now faces this problem, it was not always so. If investment intentions are buoyant, if expectations are favourable, then there may be no problem in generating the investment response that is required without recourse to rapid growth of the public sector or of consumption. Many of the fast growing countries were in that fortunate position. And a key factor is the competitiveness of the export sector. If the response to recessionary trends at home is booming exports, and surpluses on the balance of payments, investment is directly maintained and stimulated, and there is no need for "dangerous" macro economic experiments. I believe this accounts for the success of relatively non-interventionist policies in some countries.[25] But though the problem may be best solved for a firm, or for a region, or for an individual country by being in a competitive position and being brought up by external demand, it is self evident that this is a micro-economic solution to a macro-problem, and that for

[24]Clearly, housing investment is not typically a lagging component of demand, and can, moreover, be affected by monetary policy. The problems outlined do not apply. Under present conditions, however, the house price rises that would tend to go with a monetary stimulus to housebuilding could add to expectations of inflation and money wage pressure.

[25]As an illustration one may cite the German experience of using deficit finance to get out of the recession of 1967. Not for the first or last time, the strength of exports was underestimated, and the boom was overstrong. The simple answer, is that time they did not need that kind of demand management policy.

the world as a whole the problem does not disappear. Everyone cannot become more competitive relative to everybody else. And not all countries can wait for export led growth, to solve the presumed problem of low investment—tempting as that may be, even for surplus countries.

6. Dangers in Strategies for the Medium Term

In nearly all countries, the policy problem is now seen as medium term in nature. A typical objective is steady growth at about the rate of growth of productive potential, or a little more if possible to bring down un- employment. It is not always realised how high such targets are in aggregate. The McCracken Report has a target of 5½ per cent per annum over five years. To achieve such a target is a demand management problem in that in most countries the present degree of slack means that there is adequate supply potential—though structural bottlenecks may be a problem in some. And it is well recognised that over a 5 to 10 years period it is necessary to pay attention to the structure of demand. It is possible to guess at investment requirements—and as a matter of fact, most countries believe these have risen. For many countries also, there is a requirement for a diversion of resources into the balance of pay- ments. If the sums are done, the scope for rises in consumption and public expenditure together can be derived as a residual. Again, as a matter of fact, there is an objective in many countries that the medium term growth in public expenditure should be curtailed—to make room for extra investment and exports, or to allow private consumption to rise faster—often with the anti-inflation objective in mind. In real terms macro economic consistency is guaranteed by the procedures used.

Such medium term assessments may be thought useful or not. They vary greatly in their degree of sophistication, and the number of be- havioural relationships that are implicitly or explicitly involved. But a general characteristic is that they contain normative targets for key variables such as investment, consumption, exports or public expenditure over the medium term. And the political focus tends to be diverted away from short term problems to longer term aims. Often such a change in emphasis is justified by the view that fine tuning did not work in the past, or was unnecessary.

An emphasis on medium term aims is entirely laudable, and is indeed an essential framework for the formulation of short term policy. But the dangers are obvious, and may add up to a deflationary bias over and above the obvious one of international uncertainty and interconnected- ness. Most obviously, since the components of demand that can be controlled tend to be consumption and public expenditure, there is great danger that these targets will be met, but that in a situation of low growth and poor expectations, investment and exports will not come through. If they do not come through, demand is weak, and a further downward reaction in investment is likely. For a world as a whole, trade declines as well if the problem is generalised.

Secondly, gearing any component of demand to GNP or its growth, increases instability since they become less autonomous. The process is quite subtle. As governments take a more pessimistic view of world prospects and domestic growth, plans for the growth of expenditure components also tend to be revised down. In aggregate the problem is increased. The mechanism may be most obvious with the spending plans of nationalised industries. Poor international prospects may lead to the curtailment of investment schemes, intensifying the problem. The government and state industries start to act like the private sector.

Thirdly, there is a danger in financial targets—e.g. for the public sector deficit. In any case, in the medium term, deficits or surpluses may be necessary. Balance would only be appropriate if the private sector (at the assumed growth rate) itself tended to zero balance. And it seems probable that the required medium term balance has changed for a number of countries, and old rules of thumb may not be appropriate. But whatever the medium term requirements, the short term requirements may be quite different. If investment is sluggish, and lagging, then support to other components of demand—consumption or public expenditure—is necessary. In order to generate a turn round in investment in the medium term, in line with the target, the share of consumption and/or the share of public expenditure, has to rise in order to fall eventually. And deficits, already large because of low investment, may need to rise further in the short term, so that they can come down later. Politically, such movements may be hard to justify, not least because of the expectational effects on financial markets.

These various domestic problems reinforce the international difficulties. It is much more acceptable to run a balance of payments surplus, rather than a public sector deficit. And export demand may seem a good way of bringing up investment, whilst controlling the development of consumption and public expenditure in line with longer term targets.

A continuation of slow growth would be likely to require a continuation of larger public sector deficits than governments are used to, or believe to be desirable. Attempts to lower them, other than by raising them initially, could lead to a cumulative slow down. And, especially in the short term, the excess capacity that results from a downward inflexion in growth (quite apart from level changes) could, as expectations became more pessimistic, increase recessionary forces in the short term, and lead to even greater excess capacity.

7. Concluding Remarks

I have argued that if the period of past growth is regarded as special and somewhat lucky, then the difficulties that have set in since are reasonably

easy to understand. Rapid growth was favoured both by the expectational climate—which owed a lot to governmental policy—and by
favourable factors on the demand and supply sides. One result of this
period is that the policy weapons that were used were easier to apply.
Many countries appeared to be in some sort of corridor within which
economic responses were not too destabilising, nor too difficult to offset.
Indeed, it can be argued that within such a corridor, fine tuning may
have been overdone, and more reliance could have been placed in some
countries on automatic short term stabilisers. But although it is possible
to describe the world economy as being on some kind of warranted
path, the equilibrium was far from being a full equilibrium in the sense
that that term is usually used.

The supply side was, I have argued, permissive—which meant that the
theoretical difficulty of adjusting growth to some target based on supply
potential did not have to be faced. And of course, the divergence in
performance between countries can hardly be regarded as a long term
equilibrium phenomen. As potential diminished, and as divergent performance continued under fixed exchange rates, the demand management
problem and the problem of payments adjustment were both bound to
become more difficult. In a more constrained world economy it would
in theory be necessary to adapt to some large changes in important
relative prices. In the broadest possible terms, one could characterise
the rapid growth period as one in which quantity changes — reflected in
growth performance — were the principle adjustment mechanism. The
situation now can be regarded as more normal in that both quantity
adjustments and relative price adjustments appear to be necessary.
Individual countries need real devaluations, or revaluations. And
the world economy as a whole has to adjust to a changed relative
price for energy — and in the long run — probably for commodities as
well.

The need for relative price adjustments interacts with the problem of
inflationary pressure within countries, and this in turn means that floating
exchange rates do not remove the external constraint on weaker countries. Indeed, for some it may increase their problems, or appear to.
And the experience of the past suggests that structural adaptation to
changed relative prices, such as exchange rates, is difficult and may take
a long time.

The most obvious reason for sluggish growth performance at the
moment is the international difficulties in putting together a coherent
strategy for the world economy. The external position of many countries
means that they have little freedom of action on their own, and the
scope for the use of demand management policies for domestic ends is
severely limited. There is a kind of game theoretic problem in putting
together a credible strategy, and making sure that national self interest

does not so weaken the coalition that it fails before it has started. But an even more serious barrier to international cooperation is that the kind of strategy that is required may not be fully appreciated. I have argued that the required short term response may look dangerous. Politically it may appear to run counter to medium term aims that are widely agreed. But given a starting point of disequilibrium, policy may need to be rather cleverly designed if it is to succeed at all. An active demand management strategy may be much more necessary now than it was in the past.

The greatest difficulty of all is, perhaps, that the desirability for policy action of an expansionary kind is very far from being universally agreed. The fundamental disagreement between economists of different schools is about whether free enterprise economies are, in the medium term, self-stabilising or not. If they are, there is a case for riding out the recessionary period. Even those who are not so optimistic about the fundamental mechanisms of capitalist growth can argue that the present situation is appropriate to the control of inflation, and that a longish period of low growth and high unemployment is necessary and inevitable.

But the cure may be worse than the disease. If slow growth continues, capacity is bound to adapt to the growth that is achieved, and if that happens, faster growth would genuinely risk running into supply constraints—which would be inflationary. After nearly five years of recession, the world economy is moving towards that situation. Moreover, the supply potential of important commodities would be curtailed in line with lower growth and weak markets. The search for energy substitutes and the pressure towards conservation would diminish. Slow growth could indeed become structural, and hard to change.

Even now, an expansionary strategy for the world economy could run into structural bottlenecks, and it is likely that the faster growth would be accompanied by a higher real price for commodities. As this came through it would be called inflation, even though the most important change were a change in relative price of a longer term kind. The key question then would be whether the inflationary spiral could be controlled, in a situation where income relativities were disturbed, and people were worse off because of the food and raw material price rises. If higher commodity prices are necessary, but cannot be absorbed, if they just lead to spiralling wages and prices, the world economy would become supply constrained by commodities, even though technically it need not be. That kind of model is well known in the literature, where it is normally called structural inflation. It arises from inflexibility in relative prices.

For individual countries, and for the world as a whole, important relative price changes may have to be absorbed. Oil and commodity prices may not be in long term equilibrium. Many countries may need a real devaluation. Slow growth may, for the world economy, or for individual countries, be a substitute for some of these changes. This means that there is an insidious danger in slow growth. Longer term price signals are suppressed.

The difficulties involved in joint action to overcome world recessionary trends may seem so great that slow growth is inevitable. It is unlikely that it would turn out to be very slow, because then domestic pressures would become irresistible. But a continuation of the present degree of hesitant cooperation must be regarded as likely. There are some pressures towards greater expansion. Germany and Japan fear overvaluation. They also fear the increasing trend towards protectionism. The exchange rate changes that have already occurred may improve the position of some countries giving greater freedom of domestic action. But the evidence suggests that such changes are slow—and are unlikely to offset the many forces making for cautious responses and slow growth.

Finally, however, there are other things that could be done. The greatest failure of international cooperation after the oil crisis lay in not effectively offsetting the linkage effects, and in not taking seriously enough the need to preserve some semblance of national economic autonomy. I have argued that, in the past, the pursuit of domestic objectives was one of the reasons for the rapid growth that developed. In the much more disturbed situation after the second world war, the desirability of promoting national economic sovereignty was well appreciated—and was in marked contrast to the situation after the first world war. In fact, in the recent period, remarkably little has been done. It was and is, absurd that less developed countries should be forced to take on excessive debt, or to restrict development efforts because of the inflation problem in industrial countries. More generally, the cycle could have been attenuated by appropriate policies if so desired. The history of recycling schemes and the like, which could have helped in giving countries greater freedom of domestic action, is not encouraging. The moment that it became clear that the international payments system was not actually going to fall apart, the more radical suggestions were quietly shelved. And of course there was no major increase in aid flows or compensatory finance. Reliance on private capital markets greatly increased the linkage effects, and is a major factor now behind the instability in exchange markets. But above all, what is needed is a change in attitude to deficits and surpluses. The accounting identities must be respected. Until surplus countries have a duty to adjust—or to make sure that deficits elsewhere are acceptable and willingly run – the bias will remain. And domestically, public sector deficits to offset an excess of private sector savings, must be accepted as inevitable and desirable.

If the political will were there, there is, moreover, a way that approximates to export-led growth for all industrial countries – a massive increase in foreign aid flows to facilitate expenditure by those who do want to invest more than they can save.

9

BRITAIN'S SLOW INDUSTRIAL GROWTH–
INCREASING INEFFICIENCY VERSUS
LOW RATE OF TECHNICAL CHANGE[1]

by Stanislaw Gomulka
London School of Economics

1. Introduction

In spite of much research and debate, the extent of agreement as to the causes of the wide variation among nations in economic performance appears not very high, even at the level of general qualitative relationships, and is embarrassingly low as to precisely how important various possible causes, in fact, are. Originally, the theory of growth stressed the role of the quantitative changes in labour and capital, the main factor inputs. However, numerous empirical studies over the last thirty years or so have shown fairly conclusively that the international differences in the growth rates of outputs are largely the result of differences in the rate at which the productivity of the (joint) factor input changes. Since capital inputs (as well as intermediate inputs) are themselves outputs of the production processes, productivity changes of the non-producable or primary inputs, especially labour, appear vital. This brings us to the field of technical and organizational innovation where, it is now realized, rather complex mechanisms are at work, in which the purely economic factors may not play the dominant role, thereby limiting the usefulness of the formal economic analysis.

This paper is primarily an attempt to search for the major causes of the UK's slow industrial growth in the long term, with emphasis on the

[1]An earlier version of this paper was presented to a number of university seminars, and I owe a great deal to the critical reactions of many of the seminars' participants. I wish to thank in particular Wilfred Beckerman, Walter Eltis, Philip Hanson, Mervyn King, Alan Marin, Stefan Markowski, Kikunosuke Ohno, Mica Panic, George Ray, Jack Winkler, and Peter Wiles, for their comments, suggestions and references, which I used freely to broaden the empirical base of the paper and to sharpen the argument. I also wish to thank Ray Richardson, who encouraged me to think about 'British problem'. and Jan Rostowski and Andrew Threipland, who advised me in matters of grammar and style, as well as substance.

postwar period. To this end, we shall first of all survey international evidence on the productivity performance, foreign trade characteristics, the age of machines, and labour-and-capital utilization levels.

The present debate on Britain's slow industrial growth is unfortunately seriously hindered by the lack of statistically representative and reliable empirical evidence from major industrial countries concerning the technological levels of productive equipments and outputs, and the rates of utilization of employed labour and capital. Consequently, several different interpretations of Britain's slow industrial growth may be offered.

The first interpretation accepts that utilization rates are likely to be different between countries—in particular, that overmanning in the UK could be much higher than, say, in Germany—but it also assumes that these differences are stable over time. This 'neutral' position concerning the dynamics of the utilization rates implies that while the international differences in labour productivity *levels* may partly be accounted for by differences in labour utilization rates, the observed wide variation in the *growth rate* of labour productivity is approximately identical to, as well as implied by, the corresponding variation in the rate of organizational and technical change. It therefore focuses attention, firstly, on the evidence which suggests a slow assimilation of innovations in the UK compared with Western Europe and Japan and, secondly, on the economic and social causes of this relative slowness.[2]

The second interpretation (implicitly or explicitly) assumes that both the level of technological advance and the rate of technical change are more or less the same in all major industrial countries. It postulates that differences between these countries in labour productivity and in its growth are caused primarily by differences, respectively, in labour utilization rates and in their changes over time. In particular, it postulates that the UK's much lower labour productivity level, equal to about 40 per cent of the US level, can be fully explained by higher overmanning (more men employed on each machine than actually needed) and more underproduction (less output from each machine per unit of time than is optimally possible).

Another development in the debate was the recent contribution by Bacon and Eltis (1976). They accept the latter position about the causes of lower productivity change, but they also draw attention to the fact that since 1966 there has been an outflow of workers from industry into the sector producing community services. They believe that this outflow has been not an effect but a (government-originated)

---

[2]Notably Pratten argues that the 'relatively inefficient operation of new plants and equipment and slow innovation are the most important causes of the relatively slow progress of the British economy'. See his 'The Reasons for the Slow Economic Progress of the British Economy', *Oxford Economic Papers* (1974).

cause of slower growth of output, which has created a 'structural imbalance' in the UK economy. Their argument rests on the notion that erosion of the industrial base was associated with taxes increasing less than the 'social wage'. This resulted, they say, in an increase in the consumption share in total industrial output at the expense of exports and investment, which contributed to the balance of payments difficulties, and to a further eorsion of the base. We shall comment on this theory later in the paper.

All the three explanations of the UK's slow growth outlined above focus attention on the supply side of the economy. Several authors, notably Beckerman, and Lamfalussy, argue that the expectations of the business community concerning the *long-term demand* prospects are the key variable which determine both the level of investment activity and the rate of productivity change, and which thereby differentiate the output growth rates of 'reasonably advanced' countries. The expansion of exports is thought to be the variable which forms those expectations in most countries and which, therefore, is capable of inducing and sustaining economic growth at a particular rate. The ability to expand exports is in turn linked with the degree of 'competitiveness', which is defined as 'basically the question of price and technological superiority', but including also 'all sorts of secondary characteristics such as packaging, punctuality of delivery, after sales service, credit terms, and so on'.[3]

An important characteristic of this view of the growth process, and one which I find most open to question, is that lower export prices are given equal standing with technological and organizational change in stimulating productivity growth. The implication of this view is that the UK's slow productivity growth may be the result of the pound having been overvalued.

Recently A. P. Thirlwall reported that, according to his estimation, the UK income elasticity of demand for imports is not particularly high in relation to her main trade competitors, but the world income elasticity of demand for UK products is much lower compared with most of her competitors. If correct, these findings can be construed to support the demand-oriented explanation of slow growth and, indeed, provide 'an alternative explanation of the UK's deteriorating macro-economic performance since 1965, in which the growth of the non-marketable output sector is seen as the result of a much deeper structural malaise relating to the inability of the industrial sector to grow in line with its potential owing to a balance-of-payments constraint'.[4]

[3] W. Beckerman, 'Demand, Exports and Growth , in W. Beckerman and Associates, *The British Economy in 1975* (Cambridge, 1965).
[4] A. P. Thirlwall, 'The UK's Economic Problwm: A Balance-of-Payments Constraint?', *National Westminster Bank Quarterly Review* (Feb. 1978).

The Paper's Interpretation in Outline

The interpretation suggested in this paper is somewhat different than those outlined above. Apart from the world's leaders in technological advance and in the current research activity (now in most cases the. USA), the central role in the growth processes in all countries is attributed to the economic, cultural and institutional factors which influence the rate of diffusion of foreign-made innovations. Important among the economic factors are the relative technological (and organizational) gaps between a particular country and other countries, which are indicative of the potential growth reserve, and the country's own level of technology, which is a proxy for its absorptive capability. The non-economic factors, though less tangible, appear quite powerful. These are sometimes referred to as the 'X-efficiency' factors, such things as the innovative dynamism of managements, their ability to motivate workers and to make them an ally of technical and organizational innovations, and the traditions, institutions and ideologies affecting the extent of the loyalty of both, workers and managers, to their firms.

According to this view, then, low export prices help to expand exports, and may even lift the balance-of-trade constraint, but they are not likely to stimulate productivity growth. The policy of achieving competitiveness through 'real' depreciation may be effective in sustaining full employment, but at the price of lower real wages.[5]

The unusually low world income elasticity of demand for UK products, giving rise to the demand constraint on growth, and the low labour and capital productivities, resulting in low wages and investment, are argued to have the same underlying causes: the innovation-resisting characteristics, cultural and institutional, of the industry itself. The UK problem is neither exclusively of the supply type nor of the demand type. The causes underlying increasing inefficiency and slow innovation affect at the same time the supply potential and the demand prospects. The positive relationship between productivity growth and export growth, observed by some authors, is interpreted to be one of association and not of causality.

The paper also suggests that in contrast to the *level* of technical advance, and despite her highly productive R and D sector, the innovation *rate* in the UK industry has been significantly lower than in Japan and Western Europe since at least the beginning of this century. Inevitably, with a lower trend rate there would have to come a time when also the level itself is lower, and, for most UK industries, this time has arrived in the post-war period. The loss of superiority in the non-price elements of international competitiveness, for an increasing number of UK products,

[5]The standard of living may however increase, since, under less-than-full employment, the positive employment effect may outweigh the negative real-wage effect.

has made the UK shares of world and home markets fall somewhat faster than would otherwise have been the case.[6] This has forced many UK firms to adopt 'rationalization programs', entailing cuts in employment and output. Where these cuts were opposed by the trade unions or the government, increased overmanning and lower profitability would be the side effects. (It is not suggested, however, that this is the only mechanism leading to high overmanning).

The conclusions flowing from this interpretation of the UK's slow growth can be summarized as follows. The phenomenon of wide and still increasing relative gaps in productivity (especially) and technological levels between the UK and Western Europe and Japan is essentially unrelated to post-war government policies. In this area the government's role is limited to finding second-best solutions of probably marginal beneficial effect, especially in the short term. Examples of these are: lower personal taxation to stimulate effort and attract talent, more risk capital at low interest rate, or outright gifts, to stimulate product innovation and more rapid expansion of proven products, greater incentives to attract foreign management expertise, especially from Japan, to assist in the diffusion of attitudes stimulating innovation and effort. However, as the productivity and technological/organizational gaps increase, the rate of innovational diffusion from the outside world is rising automatically, (almost) irrespective of what the government does or does not. This 'natural' process will, with time, lead to freezing the relative international gaps. The growth rates of the productivity levels and of the technological/organizational levels will then be the same in the UK, Western Europe, the USSR and Eastern Europe, Japan, and the United States. Only the levels themselves will be different, with the UK levels probably much lower than in Western Europe, Japan and USA. Therefore the problem of a relative slowness in the expansion of productivity and wages will gradually disappear, but the problem of a

---

[6] It appears that the UK's share in world exports of manufacturers had been increasing during the first century of the industrial revolution to reach a maximum about 1880, when it stood at 41.1 per cent. It fell to 29.9 per cent in 1913, to 22.9 per cent in 1955 and 7.5 per cent in 1973. Some of this fall after 1880 was an inevitable consequence of the spread of the revolution to other countries. It is interesting, however, that West Germany's share in 1955, at 19.2 per cent, was comparable to the UK's, but in 1973 it stood at 22.4 per cent, or about three times the UK's share. It appears that it was about a century ago when Britain was the dominant industrial power and the technologically most advanced economy. The period from 1880 to 1914 set the stage for the present relative decline. See D. H. Aldcroft, 'The Entrepreneur and the British Economy, 1870–1914', *Economic History Review* (Aug. 1964), A. Lewis, *Growth and Fluctuations, 1870–1913* (London, 1978), and C. Barnett, *The Collapse of British Power* (London, 1972). See also A. Singh, 'UK industry and the world economy: a case of de-industrialisation?' *Cambridge Journal of Economics* (June, 1977).

lower standard of living will acquire an added emphasis. At the same time, the downward pressure on the UK share in international and home markets will be increasing. If widespread import restrictions are ruled out, the size of exports sufficient to halt deindustrialization and maintain high employment can be secured only by lowering export prices (through real depreciation of the pound and/or export subsidies) to compensate for the poorer non-price characteristics of the UK products' competitiveness. The UK would have to adopt, though possibly on a much smaller scale, the protective practices which are used widely by the developing countries of the Third World and Eastern Europe now or by Japan until recently. Such practices will further reduce the real wage in the UK in comparison with the more competitive industrial nations. This should be considered as being just a reflection, hopefully an acceptable one, of the cultural and institutional differences among nations.

2. International and UK Industrial Growth: the Stylised Facts

The economic performance of a country is conventionally judged by the level of the Gross National Product per capita and by the growth rate at which that level changes over time. Similarly, economic performance of a country's industrial sector is judged by the level of labour productivity and by its growth rate, denoted in this paper by y and g_y respectively.

Differences in both y and g_y among nations have always been very substantial. It will be convenient to begin this paper with a brief survey of the extent of that diversity among selected market and centrally planned economies in the postwar period.

The basic industrial growth data are given in Table 9.1. Most of these data refer to the period 1951–74. They have certain qualitative features that are worth noting.

(i) The output per unit of capital (capital/output ratio) is fairly constant over time, but the output/labour ratio (labour productivity) increases systematically.

(ii) There is a considerable and persistent diversity among nations both in the level of labour productivity and in the rate at which the level has been increasing. The average of this growth rate in the period 1951–74 for the selected market countries was in the range from about 3 per cent (UK and USA) to about 9 per cent (Japan). The corresponding range for the centrally planned economies in somewhat smaller—from 4.2 per cent for Hungary to 6.9 per cent for Rumania—and it lies within the range for the market economies.

(iii) Industrial output in the seven centrally planned economies as a whole has been expanding more rapidly than that in the market economies. However, the difference is due primarily to a slower labour productivity growth in the US manufacturing sector.

TABLE 9.1
*Basic Facts of Industrial Growth Performance
in 14 Countries in the Period 1951-1974*

(Columns 1-2: thousands US dollars, 1970 prices, columns 3-5: per cents)

No	Country	1 x_{1950}	2 x_{1974}	3 g_x	4 g_L	5 g_Y	6 $\dfrac{Y_{1974}}{Y_{1950}}$	7 $\dfrac{x_{1974}}{x_{1950}}$	8 $\dfrac{v_{1974}}{v_{1950}}$
1	USA	7.7	15.7	3.0	1.0	4.0	2.57	2.03	.90
2	Germany, West	3.2	10.6	5.1	2.2	7.5	5.60	3.33	1.00
3	Japan	1.1	8.7	8.9	5.0	8.9	25.20	7.75	.90
4	France	2.6	9.7	5.6	.5	6.1	4.10	3.73	
5	Netherlands	2.5	8.6	5.3	.4	5.7	3.80	3.42	
6	Italy	2.2	6.1	4.4	2.7	7.2	5.60	2.81	
7	UK	2.9	5.7	2.8	.0	2.8	1.96	1.96	1.15
8	USSR	1.8	7.5	6.2	3.3	9.7	9.19	4.23	1.15
9	Germany, East	1.4	6.5	6.5	1.6	8.2	6.67	4.50	
10	Poland	1.4	5.6	5.8	3.5	9.5	8.83	3.86	.70
11	Czechoslovakia	1.6	5.4	5.3	2.3	7.7	6.00	3.43	.60
12	Rumania*			6.9	5.6	12.9	5.48	2.55	
13	Bulgaria*			6.4	4.1	10.7	4.13	2.39	
14	Hungary	1.4	3.9	4.2	3.0	7.5	5.67	2.70	1.05

*Period 1961-1974

Notes:

Columns 1-2: x is gross value added per worker in thousands of US dollars, 1970 prices.

3: g_x is growth rate of x, average annual.

4-5: g_L is growth rate of employment, g_Y is growth rate of (gross) value added. Both rates average annual.

6: Output in 1974 in terms of output in 1950.

7: Output per man in 1974 in terms of that in 1950.

8: Capital/output ratio in 1974 in terms of that in 1950.

Sources: UK, compiled by the author from UK Statistics. USSR data of Soviet origin taken from S. Gomulka 'Soviet Postwar Industrial Growth, Capital-Labour Substitution, and Technical Progress: A Re-examination', in Z.M. Fallenbuchl (ed.), *Economic Development in the Soviet Union and Wester Europe*, Vol. 2, *Sectorial Analysis* (New York, 1976), Table 1. Other countries, Tables 2 to 7 in S. Gomulka and J. Sylwestrowicz, 'Import-led Growth; Theory and Estimation' in F. L. Altmann, O. Kyn, H. J. Wagener, (eds.) *On the Measurement of Factor Productivities: Theoretical Problems and Empirical Results* (Gottingen-Zurich, 1976). The productivity levels adopted are based partly on the levels of physical productivity (surveyed by L. Drechslar and J. Kux) and partly (for countries 2-6) on the levels implied by the official exchange rates; see Tables 2 and 5 in S. Gomulka and J. Sylwestrowicz, op. cit.

(iv) The post-1948 substantial increase in the rate of labour productivity
was more or less a universal phenomenon in Europe. However, in the
UK the increase was delayed by about 10 years and at 4 per cent
per annum the post-1961 new trend rate remains still about 1.5 per
cent below the corresponding trend rates for France and West
Germany, and about 5 per cent below the Japanese trend rate. Since
1950 these three countries have considerably reduced their (relative) labour productivity gap to the United States. In contrast,
the productivity gap between the USA and the UK was increasing
until 1962.

It is interesting that the higher growth rate of labour productivity
since the early 60s has been associated with a significant reduction in
the growth rate of employment and with no increase in the growth rate
of output. Both these facts are at variance with the so-called Verdoon-
Kaldor Laws (See Section 6).

The long-run trends in labour productivity are given in Table 9.2. It
is seen that UK's labour productivity growth was relatively low, not
only in the post-war period but also in the years 1890-1938.

TABLE 9.2.
*Four Countries, 1890-99 to 1974: Percentage Changes
in Industrial Output per man, average annual*

	Period 1	Period 2	Period 3	Period 4[1]
UK	0.3	1.8	2.5	3.5
USA	1.6	2.0	2.5	3.4
Germany[2]	2.2	2.6	5.1	4.7
Sweden	2.3	3.9	3.8	5.4

Period 1: 1890-99 (in Sweden, 1892-99), through 1913.
Period 2: UK 1924, USA 1920, Germany 1925, Sweden 1921, all through 1938.
Period 3: UK 1947, USA 1946, Germany 1950, Sweden 1948, all through 1960.
Period 4: 1960, all through 1974.

Source: Periods 1-3, E. H. Phelps Brown, 'Levels and Movements of Industrial
Productivity and Real Wages Internationally Compared, 1860-1970', *Economic
Journal* (Mar. 1973), Table II. Period 4, compiled by the author from the UN
Statistics.

[1]Manufacturing sector only.
[2]In periods, 1, 2, 3 including commerce and finance.

In period 1, labour productivity in the UK registered almost no gain,
but it did not matter because European countries were then less advanced,
and the UK's industrial output was comparable in size with their joint

output. However, while the UK's position looked at that time quite comfortable, the underlying trends were not.

The roots of the post-war 'crisis' in the UK appear thus to go back to the turn of the century.

3. Two Growth Equations for the Long Term: The Supply Side

Let Y, K and L stand for, respectively, (gross) value added, fixed (gross) capital and labour (expressed in manhours), all referring to the manufacturing sector, and let $Y = F(K,L;t)$. Assuming constant returns to scale, the standard growth equation is as follows.

$$g_Y = \pi g_K + (1 - \pi)g_L + \lambda \qquad \ldots (1)$$

where g_Y, g_K and g_L are the growth rates of, respectively, value added, capital and labour, π is the elasticity of output with respect to capital (equal to the share of profits under perfect competition) and $\lambda = \frac{1}{Y}\frac{\partial F}{\partial t}$ is the productivity residual. In (1) πg_K and $(1-\pi)g_L$ represent the contributions to output growth of the quantitative changes in K and L, respectively, and λ is the combined contribution of all qualitative factors of growth, such as changes in the quality of labour and capital, changes in the product mix, introduction of new products and new production processes, organisational and institutional changes, etc. Those changes are usually referred to as technical progress, which is clearly an umbrella term for all qualitative changes.

However, it is most important to realise that λ is only the instantaneous contribution of technical progress to growth. If technical progress is maintained at λ for a longer period of time, it raises not only g_Y over that period, but also g_K, producing an additional, indirect contribution to g_Y.

The full total contribution of technical progress to growth in the long run is seen separately if Eq. 1 is rearranged to read:[7]

$$g_Y = \frac{\pi}{1 - \pi}(g_K - g_Y) + g_L + \frac{\pi}{1 - \pi}\lambda \qquad \ldots (1a)$$

---

[7] At a constant share of investment in output, a rise in g_Y by λ increases immediately the growth rate of investment by λ and, over time, it also increases g_K by λ, producing a feedback effect on the growth rate of output of a size $\pi\lambda$. This additional increase in g_Y raises the growth rate of investment, and hence g_K, further by $\pi\lambda$, having an additional feedback effect on g_Y of a size $\pi^2\lambda$. The appearance of technical progress at rate λ is seen to generate what may be called a *growth propagation process*, the contribution of which to g_Y is equal to $\lambda + \pi\lambda + \pi^2\lambda + \ldots = \frac{1}{1-\pi}\lambda$. The long term dependence of g_K on λ has the effect of multiplying the direct contribution λ by the multiplier $\frac{1}{1-\pi}$.

Let v represent the ratio K/Y. Note that $g_K - g_Y = g_v$. Hence (1a) may be written in the form $g_Y - g_L = qg_v + \alpha$, where $q = \frac{\pi}{1-\pi}$ and $\alpha = \frac{\pi}{1-\pi}$. Since investments $I = sY = \dot{K}$, and since from $K = vY$ it follows that $\dot{K} = \dot{v}Y + v\dot{Y}$, the share of investment in output needed to sustain growth g_Y is, then

$$s = vg_Y + \dot{v} \qquad \ldots (2)$$

Eqs. 1a and 2 are correct whatever the change in v over time. But in the long-run the v's actually observed are seen in Table 1 to be fairly constant.[8] Hence, approximately, we have the potential growth of output (as allowed by the supply of labour):

$$g_Y = g_L + \alpha \qquad \ldots (1b)$$

and the necessary investment share,

$$s = v\,g_Y \qquad \ldots (2a)$$

We do not have reliable methods of estimating λ. However, from Eq. (1b) it follows that the long-run rate of technical change α is (approximately) equal to the growth rate of labour productivity, and this we can measure more reliably. Therefore, the wide international diversity recorded in the latter must be approximately equal to, as well as implied by, the difference in the former.

The Factor of Changing (Static) X-inefficiency

In writing $Y = F(K,L;t)$ I assumed, however, the full utilisation both of existing capital and of employed labour. This assumption is likely to be unrealistic not only in the short-run, say during a depression, but also in the long-run. Let u_K and u_L be the utilization rates of K and L, respectively, calculated at some 'standard' intensity of work. Hence $Y = F(u_K K, u_L L; t)$. Now, instead of Eq. (1a) we have $g_Y - g_L = q(g_v + g_{u,K}) + g_{u,L} + \alpha$ and where $g_{u,K}$ and $g_{u,L}$ are the growth rates of u_K and u_L, respectively. Assuming as before qg_v to be a minor term, we have

$$g_Y \cong g_L + \alpha + g_u \qquad \ldots (1c)$$

where $g_u = q \cdot g_{u,K} + g_{u,L}$. (1c) and (2a) are our two basic equations.

---

[8]Compare also Tables 10.1 and 10.3 in A. Maddison's contribution to this volume. It is not clear why should the capital/output ratio be so much more stable than the labour/output ratio. For a discussion of the types of technical progress consistent with this phenomenon see A. Chilosi and S. Gomulka, 'Technological Cordition for Balanced Growth: A criticism and Restatement', *Journal of Economic Theory* (Oct. 1974).

It may be noted that $g_Y - g_L$ in (1c) equals the rate of growth of output per manhour (labour productivity), and so we know the value of the sum $\alpha + g_u$. But we know much less about the value of its components, α and g_u, and this gives room for the two interpretations of the UK's slow productivity we mentioned in the introduction.

4. Increasing Inefficiency versus Slow Innovation: the Evidence

Manufacturing output per manhour is in many countries, both Eastern and Western, so much lower than in the US, while the capital/output ratio is the same or higher, that substantial US technological superiority is believed to exist. In the case of the USSR and Eastern Europe there is in fact a considerable volume of evidence indicating the existence of a technological gap. Also in the case of Western Europe and Japan it is widely assumed that after World War II these areas were technologically less advanced than the US.

In general, in view of her relatively high capital/output ratio, the UK's lower *level* of labour productivity must be discussed in terms of (i) a lower technological level and/or (ii) higher efficiency in using labour and capital. But, as Eq. (1c) shows clearly, the slow *growth* of that productivity must be associated with (iii) low α, that is relatively slow product, process and organisational innovation and/or (iv) increasing relative inefficiency, that is a comparatively faster increase in under-production and overmanning (intensity of work included).

The evidence which we briefly summarize below is inadequate to assess the dynamics in the UK's relative inefficiency. But it does suggest a higher level of inefficiency and slower rate of innovation.
(i)   A research team from the University of Birmingham's Department of Engineering Production made a study of the distribution of time during a working day by operatives and machines in 40 engineering and metal working firms over the years 1968-72 and a series of case studies in 45 firms during the period 1970-74. It shows that, on average, operatives use 16 per cent of their working time for 'waiting' and 48 per cent for 'operating' activities, and machines are idle for about 50 per cent of the working time.[9] These data suggest that relatively small-scale organizational and technical improvements are capable of increasing labour productivity instantly by about 35 per cent and capital productivity by up to 100 per cent.
(ii) Bacon and Eltis made a detailed comparison of the manufacturing tools in Britain and the United States, and found that those in Britain were no older on average than those in the USA.[10] However, nothing specific is known about the technical quality of these

[9] *Midlands Tomorrow*, West Midlands Economic Planning Council, No. 8, 1975: 3-5.
[10] *The Age of US and UK Machinery*, N.E.D.O. Monograph 3 (London, 1974).

machines. But we know that output per machine tool (as well as per man) is in the US about 2 to 3 times greater than in the UK.[11] Thus it would appear that both countries have about the same number of man per machine, but, to take the extreme cases, either the technical efficiency of US machines is much higher or UK machines are run for only one third to one half of the time they are run in the US. Judging from the findings of the Birmingham study, the intermediate cases seem more likely.

(iii) According to another study, in 1970 US manufacturing firms in Britain employed somewhat less than 10 per cent of the work force in this sector, but they accounted for nearly 13 per cent of its output and about 25 per cent of exports to Western Europe—the UK's prime overseas market.[12] Since the capital/output ratios were about the same, the better productivity and export record would indicate that US affiliates are generally more technologically advanced or better managed than the UK firms. However, it is also true that the productivity performance of these UK-based affiliates is much less impressive than that of the manufacturing industry in the US itself.

(iv) UK-based operations of the same multinational firms are also found to have lower labour productivity than the firms' operations in some other countries.[13] Compared with the UK, the average intrafirm differences are 50 per cent for the USA and Canada, 27 per cent for West Germany and 15 per cent for France. The causes of these productivity differentials appear to be mainly larger scale of production in the USA and less efficient use of manpower at the UK factories. However, it is important to note that these intrafirm differentials are not more than about a half of the productivity differences in the whole manufacturing industry between the UK and the other countries. Lower technology or poorer management must account for the remaining half.

(v) While the share of the UK's manufacturing exports in world markets had been falling in almost all commodity groups, the fall was relatively much greater in the commodity groups for which world demand was growing rapidly. This important finding[14] indicates slower product innovation in UK manufacturing, and inability to

[11]R. Bacon and W. Eltis, *Britain's Economic Problem: Too Few Producers* (London, 1976). Table 2 gives the total number of machine tools in the US to be about 2 to 3 times that in the UK. The corresponding ratio of industrial output is about 6.
[12]*US Industry in Britain 1950-1970*, report by the Economic Advisory Group, an independent research organisation (London, 1972).
[13]C. F. Pratten and A. G. Atkinson, 'The Use of Manpower in British Manufacturing Industry', *Department of Employment Gazette* (June, 1976).
[14]M. Panic and A. H. Rajan, *Product Changes in Industrial Countries' Trade: 1955-1968*, N.E.D.O. Monograph 2 (London, 1971).

adjust fast the product mix to the rapidly changing patterns of demand.

(vi) A further evidence of slow product innovation is given by a N.E.D.O. report, according to which the better quality, more modern design and higher technical performance of foreign products, but not their prices, are the factors which have contributed most to the rapid growth of the UK's imports of manufactured goods.[15]

(vii) Recently A. P. Thirlwall reported his findings of income elasticities for imports and exports in 113 UK manufacturing industries 1963-77.[16] His conclusion is that 'the UK income elasticity of demand for imports is not particularly high in relation to our main competitors. The problem is on the export side where the (world income) elasticity is much lower compared with most of our international competitors'.[17] This difference in elasticities, which must be associated with facts (v) and (vi) above, gives rise to the balance-of-payments constraint on the UK's growth of total output and employment.

These pieces of evidence can be interpreted as follows. High inefficiency (in particular, high overmanning and poor use of machines) are certain to exist, and increasing inefficiency cannot be excluded. Slow innovation and (possibly) increasing inefficiency underline slow productivity growth, while lower technological level and slow innovation underline slow export growth. Slow both productivity and export growth give rise to slow output and employment growth.

5. The Structural Imbalance Phenomenon of Bacon and Eltis

Another potential cause of slower output growth is fall in the supply of labour. Bacon and Eltis draw attention to the fact that employment in UK industry was rising until 1966, but has since declined.[18] In the

---

[15] After M. Panic, 'Why the UK's Propensity to Import is High', *Lloyds Bank Review* (Jan. 1975). See also 'International price competitiveness, non-price factors and export performance', N.E.D.O. (London, 1977).

[16] Thirlwall, op. cit.

[17] Thirlwall, op. cit., p. 30.

[18] Bacon and Eltis, op. cit. At the core of the Bacon-Eltis model are two identities, one gives the distribution of marketable goods and the other is the government's budget equation. Let M denote the sector producing marketable goods, the flow of which is Y_M, and N the sector producing non-marketables. The identies are (1) $b_T = 1 - i_M - C_M - C_N - G_O$ and (2) $b_G = t - G_O - (1-t)G_1$. All components of these equations are shares of Y_M. i_M is the investment going to sector M, C_M and C_N are the consumptions of persons employed in M and N, respectively, G_O is the government investment in N and its consumption, and b_T is the trade surplus. The tax rates on profits and wages are assumed to be the same. Therefore, in terms of Y_M, t represents the total taxes in sector M, $(1-t)G_1$ are wages (net of taxes) in

period 1961–74 the ratio of non-industrial to industrial employment increased in the UK by 33.9 per cent, compared with 14.2 per cent in West Germany and 18.6 per cent in France. They argue that this post-1966 outflow of workers has had a considerable destabilizing effect on the whole economy, contributing to the balance-of-payments deficit, stimulating inflation, depressing investment and employment prospects. This is what may be called 'structural imbalance phenomenon'.

In the Bacon-Eltis model the structural imbalance emerges only when the government perceives the public to be permanently unwilling to pay in higher taxes for what it receives in higher 'social wages'. To that extent it is a political phenomenon, although with potentially important economic consequences.

But stability should not be confused with growth, especially with long-term growth. The increase of employment in services sector was of government's making, and it is almost certain that it has, over the recent years, contributed to the balance-of-payments problems. But it can be argued that the outflow of workers from industry was an effect rather than a cause of slow growth. Moreover, even if it were a cause it would have been a relatively minor one.

To see first its relative weight, let us suppose that the level of employment in UK manufacturing after 1966 could have been kept at the 1966 level. Output in 1974 would then have been higher by 8.6 per cent. But if output per man-hour had been increasing at 5.5 per cent per annum from 1950 on, as in France and West Germany, instead of the actual 3.2 per cent, then the 1974 output level would have been 70 per cent

---

sector N, and b_G is the budget surplus. If π is the share of non-wage incomes (profits plus interest on savings) in Y_M, then $C_M = ((1-s_\pi)\pi + (1-s_W)(1-\pi))(1-t)$ and $C_N = (1-s_W)(1-t)G_1$, where s_W and s_π are the (constant) savings propersities. On taking account of these two expressions, (1) can be rearranged to read (1a) $i_M + b_T = (1-t)(s_\pi - s_W)\pi + s_W(1-G_O)$. In order to have the economy in a growth equilibrium in which $b_T = b_G = O$ and $i_M = vg_M^*$, where g_M^* is the desirable (full-employment growth rate of marketable output, π and t must obtain certain values, say π^* and t^*. According to Bacon and Eltis, since 1965 t has increased above t^* and π declined below π^*, forcing the sum $i_M + b_T$ to decline. This does appear to be what has happened, but the causality of the process is far from clear. In contrast to the Bacon-Eltis interpretation, one may argue that b_T has declined because of low non-price competitiveness and, as a result of the ensuing balance-of-trade problems, it has led to the post-1973 arrest of demand, increase in spare capacity and, consequently, to the recent decline of the investment activity. From Eq.(1a) above it follows that π would then fall. Under this interpretation, a fall in π is an effect rather than a cause of the deteriorating macro economic situation.

higher than it was. The difference between 70 per cent and 8.6 per cent speaks for itself. Had that 5.5 per cent annual gain been achieved, moreover, the economy could probably have withstood the post-1966 outflow of manpower from industry. After all, the share of that manpower in the economically active population, at about 38.8 per cent in 1966, was one of the highest in the world. The maximum social wage which the public is prepared to finance by taxes is also likely to be positively associated with the output of marketed goods per person. Had productivity been 70 per cent higher, then the real wage could well have been sufficiently high to be (again politically) consistent with the tax rate that is required to support the present social wage.

More importantly, Bacon and Eltis fail to consider the evidence which suggests that since about 1960 UK industry has been facing the technologically highly advanced Western Europe and Japan. This change in the relative technological/organizational position has had a stimulating effect on the rate of innovational diffusion from the outside world to the UK, and thereby on the UK labour productivity growth. At the same time the German and Japanese revival has made it more difficult for the UK firms to compete in domestic and international markets. Under such circumstances, the UK industry has been unable to increase the growth rates of exports, and therefore output, but was able to reduce employment. The government has been under pressure to keep unemployment down by running a budget deficit and expanding the services sector. The end results of this alternative explanation of the post-1966 deterioration are the same as in their model—an increasing balance of trade deficit and a structural change in favour of services—but the actual cause could have been the advent of more efficient and competitive industrial powers, and not the alleged government's policy of starving industry of manpower. In the absence of government's intervention the workers made redundant in industry would simply remain unemployed.

6. Some Traditional Explanations of Slow Innovation in the UK

If slow innovation is the root of Britain's economic problem, then the next step is to consider why it is slow. Before an answer is attempted, it may be instructive to discuss the general question of the likely causes of international differences in the rate of innovation. I shall begin with a brief review of three hypotheses concerning the main determinants of technical change. It will be argued that these hypotheses are in fact incompatible with the empirical evidence. An alternative view on the determinants of technical change will be presented in the following section.

6.1. The Verndoorn-Kaldor Hypothesis

Formulated first by P. J. Verdoorn (1949) on the basis of Italian industrial data, this hypothesis postulates the existence of a linear relationship between the growth rate of labour productivity and the growth rate of output g_Y, with the coefficient of proportionality being equal to about 0.5. Because $g_Y = \alpha + g_L$, the relationship can be stated also in terms of α, on one hand, and g_L on the other. If $\alpha = .5g_Y +$ constant $= .5 \, (\alpha + g_L) +$ constant, then α should be equal to g_L plus another constant.

In 1966 N. Kaldor, in his inaugural lecture at Cambridge University, accepted the 'Verdoorn Law' for manufacturing industries, on the basis of data for twelve developed countries from the period 1952/52-1963/64. In Kaldor's view, the UK α was low compared to the α for other developed countries because of a difference, to the UK's disadvantage, in the growth rate of labour available for employment in the manufacturing sector.[19]

A detailed analysis of the available empirical evidence shows that the growth rates g_L and α are in fact mutually independent. Gomulka showed this by enlarging Kaldor's sample of 12 countries to the sample of 39 countries, and Rowthorn showed the same by reducing Kaldor's sample to 11 countries by excluding Japan.[20]

6.2. The Rate of Investment and the Rate of the Technical Change

The popular view is that it is the rate of investments $s = I/Y$ which determines α. Thus, α in the UK would be relatively low because the rate of investment tends to be low, either as a result of low propensities to save, out of profits and out of non-profit incomes, or both. I shall argue that the empirical evidence runs counter to this view.

Taking account of (1c) and (2a), the postulated relationship that $\alpha = H(s)$, where $H'(s) > 0$, may be written in the form (assuming capital/output ratio v constant):

$$\alpha = H(v(g_L + \alpha)) \qquad \ldots (3)$$

Now it may be noticed that Eq. (3) represents the same type of relationship, between the rate of technical change and the growth rate of employment, which we discussed above in Section 7.1. The only difference is that (3) is in general a non-linear relationship. On differentiating

---

[19] N. Kaldor, *Causes of the Slow Rate of Economic Growth of the United Kingdom: An Inaugural Lecture* (Cambridge, 1966).

[20] S. Gomulka, *Inventive Activity, Diffusion and the Stages of Economic Growth* (Aarhus (Denmark), 1971). R. E. Rowthorn 'What remains of Kaldor's Law', *Economic Journal* (Mar. 1975). In his reply to Rowthorn (*Economic Journal*, Dec. 1975), Kaldor maintains that the growth rate of output should be regarded as the independent variable which influences both employment and productivity growth. Productivity growth was found to be positively related with output growth (with the UK an exception), but since the share of the former in the latter is so dominant, the relationship may be a spurious one.

(3) with respect to g_L one obtains:

$$\frac{\partial \alpha}{\partial g_L} = v(1 + \frac{\partial \alpha}{\partial g_L}) \frac{\partial H}{\partial s} \qquad \ldots (4)$$

As we know, the empirical evidence strongly suggests that $\frac{\partial \alpha}{\partial g_L} = 0$.
By (4) we also have $\frac{\partial H}{\partial s} = 0$.

The above argument is against the view that causality runs from s to α. One may argue, however, that the direction of causality is from α to s. Note that from $s = v(g_L + \alpha)$ it follows that when an increase in national α is not matched by an increase in s, then, at a given v, the growth rate of employment must decline, causing an increase in the unemployment rate. This in turn forces the labour to accept a higher share of pre-tax profits in the national income or the government to decrease profit tax and/or to increase public investment. Whichever happens, an increase in national s should be the outcome. This adjustment mechanism provides a link between the true agens of techncial change, which are the determinants of α, and the rate of investment. The UK's s was much lower compared with Japan and somewhat lower compared with Europe. It was apparently not too low, however, since the rate of unemployment has been maintained at a relatively low level. In the case of the manufacturing sector, all three post-1962 booms were arrested by the balance of trade constraint, and apparently not by unwillingness to invest or lack of finance. In 1977, the expansion of industrial output is again held up by huge trade deficits with Europe and Japan, and not by lack of capacity.

6.3. The Kaldor Technical Progress Function

Before turning to the Verdoorn Law as a basis to explain poor British economic performance, Kaldor argued that the growth rate of capital per man is the key determinant of the growth rate of labour productivity.[21] Kaldor's 'technical progress function' has the form:

$$g_Y - g_L = f(g_K - g_L) \qquad \ldots (5)$$

where it is assumed that $f(o) > 0$, $f' > 0$ and $f'' < 0$. But since $g_K = g_Y + g_v$, Eq. 5 may be solved with respect to $g_Y - g_L$ to give

$$g_Y - g_L = F(g_v) \qquad \ldots (6)$$

Since $g_v \cong 0$ for all major industrial countries, Eq. 6 fails to explain the observed wide international differences in the labour productivity growth. An assumption of $F(o)$ being specific for each country only

---

[21]N. Kaldor and J. D. Mirrlees, 'A New Model for Economic Growth', *Review of Economic Studies* (1966).

avoids the problem. Moreover, the trend growth rate of labour productivity in individual countries changes considerably over time, despite relatively stable capital/output ratio. In particular, labour productivity in the UK manufacturing sector increased at 0.7 per cent annually in the years 1890–1930, at 2.0 per cent in the years 1931–1960 (the war years excluded), and at 4.0 per cent from 1961 to 1974.

7. Alternative View on the Determinants of Technical Change

7.1. *Five Agents of Technical Change*

Innovations are produced either domestically or acquired from abroad. The home-made innovations may be produced (i) by a specialized sector, called the research and development sector (R and D), or (ii) by workers engaged normally in non-research activities, who may produce innovations either independently of what they do or as a result of what Arrow calls the 'process of learning by doing'. The foreign made innovations may be acquired through three channels. These are (iii) diffusion in the form of imported licences and patents, (iv) almost cost-free 'natural diffusion' in the form of technological espionage, scientific journals, exchange of personnel, etc., and (v) embodied diffusion, in the form of imported capital and intermediate goods which already incorporate new innovations. The k's agent of technical progress, $k = 1, 2, \ldots, 5$, contributes, say, $\dot{T}_k$ to the total change in technological level T. Hence $\dot{T} = \Sigma \dot{T}_k$, and

$$\dot{T}/T = \alpha = \sum_{k=1}^{5} \alpha_k = \sum_{k=1}^{5} \eta_k \, \alpha^*_k \qquad \ldots (7)$$

where $\eta_k = T_k/T$ is the share of the agent's k contribution to the total stock of accumulated technology, and where $\alpha_k^* = \dot{T}_k/T_k$ is the growth rate of technical change which agent k generates and which would be equal to α in the absence of other agents. We shall call α_k^* the characteristic growth rate for agent k. These characteristic rates are, as a rule, different in magnitude. From (12) it follows that α tends to approach the characteristic rate which dominates the other rates, that is

$$\alpha \rightarrow \max_{k} \, (\alpha_k^*) \qquad \qquad \ldots (8)$$

Thus, although all five agents are usually contributing to α, it is the dominant agent which will, in the long run, determine α.

7.2. *Diffusion–the Dominant Agent for Much of the World*

In technologically leading countries only the R and D sector can be the dominant, α–determining agent. The aggregate output of that sector is 'determined' by the sector's aggregate inputs, labour R and capital M.

Applying the production function approach one obtains

$$\alpha_1^* = b_1 g_M + b_2 g_R \qquad \qquad \ldots (9)$$

where the elasticities b_1 and b_2 are positive.[22] The US growth rates g_M and g_R would be thus the principal determinants of both the US growth rate of technical change and (about equal to it) the US growth rate of labour productivity.

Data on g_M and g_R are not fully available nor internationally fully comparable. Nevertheless, on the basis of what is available, it seems correct to say that in the period 1930–1970 the US R and D sector, with g_M about 11 per cent and g_R about 5 per cent, has been expanding more rapidly than the West European R and D sector. In spite of this, in the post-war period Western Europe has experienced a labour productivity growth (in the manufacturing sector) nearly twice as fast as the US growth. This indicates that in post-war Western Europe the characteristic growth rate associated with technological diffusion has *dominated* the growth rate generated by her R and D sector.

The notion that only diffusion of innovations from (technologically) more advanced areas is able to generate rapid productivity growth in (technologically) less developed countries is now increasingly recognised, especially among business and government economists. It is also increasingly mirrored in practical policies adopted by firms and governments.

One of the most impressive examples is of course Japan. Spencer and Woroniak point to the massive transfer of technology as the major dynamic force in her growth.[23] They identify the high educational and technology absorptive capability of the Japanese economy, widespread concensus to acquire new technology, and a suitable institutional framework as the main factors which have made this transfer possible. More details about this framework are given by R. Kosobud.[24] According to him: 'Within the Ministry of International Trade and Industry (MITI), and within its industry councils, business representatives and government officials could discuss in detail the implementation of policies (concerning transfer of technology) . . . . . . MITI had control over scarce foreign exchange and could allocate it for purchase of patents, licences, royalty payments, and the like. A mechanism for validation of technology agreements within MITI provided for apparently extremely detailed reviews of agreements among Japanese and foreign firms, including a

---

[22]E. S. Phelps, 'Models of Technical Progress and the Golden Rule of Research', *Review of Economic Studies* (Apr. 1966). Also S. Gomulka 'Extensions of the "Golden Rule of Research" of Phelps', *Review of Economic Studies* (Jan. 1970).
[23]'The feasibility of developing technology transfer functions', *Kyklos*, XX, 1967.
[24]R. Kosobud, The Role of International Transfer of Technology in Japan's Economic Growth, *Technological Forecasting and Social Change*, No. 5 1973: 395–406.

review of the terms for royalty payments. Another mechanism within MITI provided for the diffusion of new technology to other firms, even rivals in the receiving industry, so that the benefit of new practical knowledge may well have been larger in the case of Japan than if restrictive practices had been more revalent. It also appears that the Federal Trade Commission was used to prevent restrictive practices with respect to the use of technology and also to prevent technology agreements from restricting the markets of Japanese firms.'

7.3. The Hat-Shape Relationship

If diffusion is so important, the question of its determinants becomes crucial. We will need some new concepts to tackle this problem, in particular the concept of 'technological gap'.

Technological level may be defined to be proportional to the labour productivity which would obtain at the same capital/output ratio. To the extent that actually observable capital/output ratios are relatively stable and not very different from one country to another, labour productivity may be used in national as well as international comparisons as a proxy for technological levels. In such cases the labour productivity gap can be used as an approximate measure of the technological gap.

The notion of technological gap can be employed to develop macro-models of diffusion. These modesl suggest that the impact of diffusion upon the growth rate of labour productivity is greatest in the countries which are in the range of medium-sized (relative) technological gaps. Essentially this is so because such countries (a) being *still* surrounded by (significantly) more advanced economies and (b) having *already* developed considerable absorptive capacity, operate in conditions potentially most conducive to large-scale technological diffusion from abroad, and thereby also most conducive to rapid labour productivity growth. On the whole, the empirical evidence supports this theoretical result.[25]

[25]Gomulka, op. cit. (1971) ch. IV. N. Kaldor in "Economic Growth and the Verdoorn Law: A Comment on Mr. Rowthorn's article' notes that 'Gomulka's thesis, favoured by Rowthorn—that the more rapid growth of productivity of latecomers like Japan was to be explained by the diffusion of technical knowledge—could hardly explain how the higher productivity growth rates could have continued after the productivity levels of the diffuses came to surpass those of the diffusants' (*Economic Journal* (Dec. 1975), p. 896). However, neither Japan nor Western Europe have yet surpassed the US level. In the past, a change in technological leadership could and did occur. Partly because different parts of the world were very much isolated each from other and partly because of intercountry differences in the size of the inventive activity. Over the last century, the larger and apparently more competitive US economy was also in a position to exploit the large-scale production technology, which the disintegrated Western Europe could not do to that extent.

The data show, however, that the band of growth paths generated under the impact of diffusion is of considerable width. It is evident that for many countries the technological gap is not the only, or even the most significant, macro-variable influencing the growth rate of imported innovations. There must be a number of other variables which jointly characterise the extent to which the opportunities of (diffusion-induced) technical progress, present at a given relative technological gap, are actually taken advantage of. These variables include the amount of money spent on the import of licences and patents, and the amount and the technological content of machinery imports from the (technologically) more advanced countries. These variables characterise the country's 'degree of openness', which is an umbrella term, covering also a variety of social, cultural, institutional and political factors, which also influence the rate of inflow and the degree of application of the (essentially) cost-free innovations. Examples of these factors are: drive and determination of the managerial staff in locating and adopting the world best practice technology; willingness by workers and by their trade unions to accept technical change and its consequences; psychological readiness to accept foreign-made innovations; degree of exposure of the domestic markets to the pressures of international competition; degree of pressure to adopt the world best products and processes applied by the government agencies; international agreements on technical exchange, trade barriers and embargos.

From Table 9.3, it would appear that Japan is by far the largest net

TABLE 9.3.
Technological Balance of Payments,
Selected Countries, 1971 ($ million)

	Receipts	Payments	Surplus (+) or Deficit (−)	Ratio of receipts to payments
United States	2,465	218	+2,247	11.31
United Kingdom	282.7	264.7	+18.0	1.07
West Germany	148.9	405.2	−256.3	0.37
France	263.8	450.3	−186.5	0.59
Japan	60.0	488.0	−428.0	0.12

Source: Tuvia Blumenthal, 'Japan's Technological Strategy', *Journal of Development Economics* 3 (1976), Table 1. The original source is Japanese Bureau of Science and Technology.

importer of foreign technology, while the US is the only major net exporter. Both France and West Germany run a considerable deficit in the trade in technology. However, the UK imports about as much as it exports. There is evidence which suggests that the large Japanese R and D sector is organised to serve above all as an instrument of channelling and adopting foreign technology rather than of producing new technology. The Western European R and D sector and, especially, the UK sector seem to give more attention to original research.

Embodied technical diffusion, i.e. import of modern equipment and whole plants, has become for many less-advanced countries such as Spain, Brazil, Turkey, Rumania, Iran, Greece, South Korea, Poland and recently some Arab countries, the main agent of their technological modernization and the core of their strategies of rapid growth. This strategy of import-induced growth is clearly more attractive for those low labour productivity countries which cannot count on disembodied diffusion as their main channel of product and process innovation. But the embodied diffusion may play a significant role also in those relatively well-developed countries where labour productivity is in the range between, say, 30 per cent and 60 per cent of the US labour productivity, that is in such countries as the USSR and UK at present, or Japan and Western Europe until recently.[26]

Any quantitative result giving the share of embodied diffusion in the growth rate of labour productivity is bound to be approximate. This low standard of accuracy is caused by lack of proper data, high level of aggregation and some more fundamental measurement problems. Nevertheless, an attempt has been made to estimate that share for the manufacturing sector in five countries, UK included.[27]

While the absolute value of that estimate for any particular year is not very reliable, the share's upward trend is likely to be correct. It indicates that the observed acceleration in the UK productivity growth may be to a considerable extent caused by the increased imports of investment goods from abroad.

The contribution of embodied diffusion has been increasing over time, because increasingly greater proportion of the total UK investments in machinery and transport equipment has been imported from the technologically more advanced countries, and because the technological gaps between these countries were themselves increasing. In the early fifties the UK economy was almost self sufficient in the investment

[26]An attempt to accelerate growth through imports was undertaken recently by Poland. The implications of this policy for industrial growth are discussed by S. Gomulka in 'Growth and the Import of Technology: Poland 1971–1980', *Cambridge Journal of Economics* (Mar. 1978).

[27]S. Gomulka and J. Sylwestrowicz, op. cit.

goods. During the years 1951-1974 the share of exports of machinery and transport equipment in total exports (both in current prices) remained at an almost unchanged level of about 36 per cent. But at the same time the ratio of imports to exports of machinery and equipment increased from 9.1 per cent in 1950 to 64.5 per cent in 1974. The corresponding figures for the category of machinery alone are 13.9 per cent and 70.5 per cent. The increase has been so dramatic that if it continues at the past rate, then by the late 80s the UK will become a net importer of machinery, a state of affairs typical for countries which are technologically significantly less advanced. (In the years 1975-77 the imports of machinery increased by 17 per cent while exports by 2 per cent. The corresponding figures for machinery and transport equipment are 25 per cent and 5 per cent. All these percentages refer to volumes, or trade at constant prices).

8. Possible Causes of the Slow Innovation in the UK

In the previous section it was argued that the more rapid growth of productivity of latecomers like Japan can be explained by the relatively greater diffusion of technical knowledge from the countries which in specific fields form the world's technological frontier area. However, in our search for the factors influencing diffusion it was noted that at a given relative technological gap, which is thought to be an important such factor, there are still considerable variations in the productivity growth. We have stressed that the exact reasons for these variations remain unclear. Or, more precisely, the reasons for greater diffusion appear to be cultural and institutional rather than purely economic: things like more receptive management attitudes; less worker resistance; higher degree of exposure to the competitive pressures; and strong government institutions which assist in the technological transfer, especially the scientific effort and technical education.

Characteristically, commenting on the findings of a large-scale empirical study of technological diffusion in six countries, Ray noted that 'Whether large company or small, the least tangible factor is likely to have the greatest impact on the application of any new technique—the attitude of management'.[28] Inevitably, it is among these less tangible factors that one has to look for possible causes of slow innovation in the UK. The purpose of this section is not to provide their full list, but rather to suggest that no government policy is likely to remove them quickly.

8.1. The Educational Factor; the Argument of Gowing and Allen

Margaret Gowing, a historian of science at Oxford, accepts that

---

[28]'The Diffusion of New Processes', *Intereconomics* (Nov. 1969).

'All the evidence agrees on the technological backwardness of much of British manufacturing industry—on leads lost, opportunities missed, markets relinquished that need not have been.'[29]

She argues that Britain's failure to develop a modern technical education early enough has been an important cause of the above phenomenon:'

'Britain had achieved so much in the early nineteenth century with so little education, that she (that is the governing elite) had felt no need to create the education infrastructure which her potential competitors were building in advance of their industrialization . . . (and so) the infra-structure had not been created in Britain when the century ended.'[30]

In view of the well documented absence of any wide and sustained interest in technical education among the upper and middle classes, the only way to expand this type of education was to open it to the working classes, which in this country as elsewhere saw it as a means to advance the social status for their children. But, as Gowing notes in the same article,

'In 1870 government expenditure (on education) was a much lower percentage of gross national product than in 1850; and in 1890 it was lower still. . . . (Consequently) . . . fees were high and far beyond the reach of humbler classes. Here, too, England differed from foreign countries, where such fees were deliberately kept very low.'

The doctrine that higher education had to be self-supporting made it a powerful factor constraining social mobility. One can therefore argue, as G. C. Allen does, that Britain's educational system was also socially more divisive than elsewhere, and that it has contributed to the continuance of attitudes and social relations between managers and workers hostile to an efficient, modern economy.[31] Moreover, the dislike of technical education by the upper and middle classes, and the consequent lower social status of technicians compared to, say, bankers and civil servants, has reduced the flow of the most success-minded and adventurous people to industry, presumably making the latter less dynamic.

8.2. The Industrial Relations Factor

It is often said, and there is an increasing volume of ad-hoc evidence to support this view, that the industrial practices at the plant level have

---

[29]This statement by David Landes is quoted by M. Gowing in 'Lost Opportunities in an Age of Imperialism', *The Times Higher Education Supplement*, 26 Nov. 1976.
[30]Ibid.
[31]*The British disease: a short essay on the nature and causes of the nation's lagging wealth*, Institute of Economic Affairs, (London, 1976).

been less successful in the UK than in Western Europe and certainly less than in Japan, in making workers and their trade unions an ally of faster innovation.[32]

It is probably true to say that workers usually accept that higher real wages are associated closely with higher labour productivity. Yet they tend to regard the latter as an alien aim, especially if it is perceived to be a threat to their own or their colleagues job security. Since the managers tend to place much greater emphasis on productivity than job security, a real and important conflict of priorities may easily arise. It seems that managers in Western Europe and Japan have been more successful than the UK's managers in reconciling these two priorities by coupling relatively faster labour-saving innovation with faster product innovation and greater marketing effort, so that, in parallel to a high growth in labour productivity and (therefore) real wages, also a high output and (therefore) job security have been achieved.

Clearly a faster product innovation and greater marketing effort is mainly the responsibility of managements and senior technical staffs. Yet a low degree of identification of the ordinary workers with the firm's fortunes may influence adversely the quality and intensity of their work, as well as the attitude to innovation. It is therefore not surprising that the Japanese management doctrine sees firms as fighting units, in which things like dedication to the firm and high internal integration of the total workforce are seen as vital. But the distinctly British tradition of many different trade unions operating in one company might be divisive, as it is likely to stimulate the temptation to gain more through internal redistribution of work and wages rather than through external expansion. This internal divisiveness is possibly also stimulated by the apparent reluctance of many British managements to reduce substantially the traditionally wide social distance between themselves and the workers.[33]

Other possible causes of slow innovation in the UK include:
(i)   low competitive pressures in the export sector;
(ii) government dominant concern with the demand rather than the supply side of the economy;
(iii) too much profit and personal taxation; and the consequent erosion of incentives to invest and to work harder;
(iv) government stop-go policies.

The case for (i) may be based on the fact that in the postwar period the British pound was declining in value more rapidly than the ratio of world prices to British prices for the manufactured goods. One may

[32] An excellent comparative study is R. Dore, *British Factory – Japanese Factory* (London, 1973).
[33] The link between "the will to work" and cultural factors is discussed forcefully by P. Wiles in 'Notes on the Efficiency of Labour', *Oxford Economic Papers* (June 1951).

argue that the better price position of British goods on international markets obtained through successive devaluations was an open invitation for British exporters to lessen their efforts to innovate, and so also to perpetuate the balance of trade problems. Moreover, the former colonies, later the Commonwealth countries, represented 'captive markets' for the UK producers, with the local and non-British competition relatively insignificant. It must be remembered, however, that the French captive markets are also considerable, and yet the French rate of innovation has been possibly highest in Western Europe in the postwar period.

In connection with (ii), it is true that the French and Japanese governments are taking great interest in the supply side of their economies. However, the difference in this respect between the UK and, say, Germany does not seem to be significant.

Some Scandanavian countries, especially Sweden, provide good reasons for not regarding (iii) as a major cause. Moreover, one cannot use (iii) to explain the UK's very slow productivity improvement in the period 1880-1940 when the US had established its present productivity lead.

Finally, the stop-go policies of government may be considered to be the effect of slow innovation, leading to the balance of trade barrier, rather than its cause.

9. Conclusions

With the labour productivity levels in the German, French and Japanese manufacturing sectors already in te range between 60 per cent and 80 per cent of the corresponding US level, we may expect a gradual slow-down in their annual growth rates, from between 5 per cent and 10 per cent in 1951–74, to more or less the US rate of about 3 per cent. The UK industry, however, is at present under the increasing influence of the technologically and organizationally more innovative, and apparently already more advanced, Western Europe and Japan. So, in principle, one may expect a further, though temporary, rise in the UK's productivity growth rate, from about 2.3 per cent in the 1950s, 4 per cent in the years 1961–74, to 5 per cent or so characteristic now for Western Europe and Japan, followed by a decline to the US rate of about 3 per cent per annum. Towards the end of this century, the differences in productivity growth rates among major advanced industrial nations will, according to this scenario, all but disappear. In such a growth equilibrium, the cultural and institutional differences will remain to be reflected in different productivity levels, with the Japanese level possibily higher than the US level.

The prospects for output and employment growth will continue to depend mainly on the ability to compete with foreign producers in home and international markets. If the non-price characteristics of the UK products continue to be somewhat poorer than those of the UK's major competitors (as I would expect them to be), then lower export prices (implying low exchange rate or high subsidies), and/or import restrictions (implying lower pressure for static x-efficiency and innovation) will increase in importance, and possibly become the chief instruments of defending a reasonably high level of employment. The government may also have to curtail the relative wages, and/or the employment, in the activities (of the service or of the industrial type) which, after taking full account of their direct and indirect impact on exports and imports, are found to contribute to net imports.

The desire to catch up with the UK in the 19th century and with the USA in the 20th century has, in Japan and Western Europe, contributed to a specific brand of the 'growth culture'. This brand is distinguished by its strong emphasis on a high degree of openness to foreign expertise and, generally, by its promotion of values and attitudes which help to stimulate the process of pursuit of the world's technological leaders. For example, it has an exceptionally high regard for science and technology, it gives a very high social status to engineers and industrial managers, and it cultivates hard work and expansionist and competitive spirits. In some of the catching-up countries, notably in those under state socialism, the state ideology and the mass media are the main agents of these values and attitudes.[34] They are supported further by the state's active economic role, especially in the areas of education, industrial investment, exports, and the expansion of infrastructure.

Once the UK has been overtaken by several other countries, one may expect her more 'relaxed' brand of the 'growth culture' to undergo a gradual change. Such a 'natural' process of change has been taking place in the post-war period, especially over the last ten years or so, when the facts about the relative economic position of this country had been noted and disseminated by the mass media. The role of the state in this process of national 'reeducation' and restructuring of the traditional values and attitudes, should not be overestimated. Nevertheless, the government may try to assist the 'natural' process of change. Its specific policies may include, for example, lowering personal taxation to stimulate effort and attract talent; making available more risk capital at a low interest rate, or as outright gifts, to stimulate product innovation and more rapid expansion of proven products, giving greater incentives to attract foreign management expertise, especially from Japan, in order to assist in the diffusion of attitudes stimulating innovation and effort.

One may also take the view that, at this stage of the world's develop-

---

[34] I discuss these matters at a somewhat greater length in 'Economic Factors in the Democratization of Socialism and the Socialization of Capitalism', *Journal of Comparative Economics*, (Dec. 1977).

ment, there is really no need, in the UK, to form an environment of attitudes and incentives which would be more suitable for economic/material growth than is the present environment. On the contrary, what is actually needed is the adoption, by the more competitive and growth-minded nations, of the UK's growth-restraining values and attitudes. According to this view, the UK is leading the world again, this time towards the post-industrial and 'zero growth' society.

10

LONG RUN DYNAMICS
OF PRODUCTIVITY GROWTH*

by Angus Maddison
University of Groningen

This paper analyses developments in labour productivity over the past century. It examines the major factors which explain variations in the pace of growth. I distinguish three main phases 1870–1913, 1913–50 and 1950 onwards, and break down postwar experience into three subphases – the fifties, the sixties and the seventies. The major concern is to explain why the postwar record has been so brilliant by historical standards, and why performance has slackened in the 1970s.

1. The Record Since 1870

It is clear from Table 10.1 that since 1950 output per man hour has risen at unprecedented rates. Average growth was 4.3 per cent a year—two and a half times the pace achieved in the previous eighty years. This postwar acceleration was sharpest in cases (e.g. France, Germany, Italy, Japan) where productivity stagnated or fell during and after the war. But the acceleration affected all the countries in some degree except the USA.

Productivity levels are highest in the United States. 1976 US productivity was 32 per cent higher than the average for the group. But in several cases the gap between US and European productivity levels is now small and the lowest level— in Japan—is over half of that in the USA. There has been a considerable convergence in productivity levels. The spread between these countries is now less than 2:1 whereas in 1870 it was 8:1 and in 1950 7:1.

Although the US productivity lead has been challenged and greatly reduced, it has lasted a long time. The USA has had a lead over 11 of the countries as far back as we have carried the record, it overtook the Netherlands in the 1870s, Belgium in the 1880s, the UK in the 1890s and Australia (a rather special case) during the first world war. This phenomenon of US leadership, and the fact that the USA is such a huge

*I am greatly indebted to Rita Varley for help with the statistics and graphs.

TABLE 10.1.

Phases of Producitivity Growth (GDP per Man Hour) 1870-1976

	annual average compound growth rates					
	1870–1913	1913–50	1950–76	1950–60	1960–70	1970–76
Australia	0.9	1.4	2.8	2.8	2.4	3.3
Austria	2.1	0.8	5.7	5.9	5.9	5.0
Belgium	1.2	1.5	4.5	3.1	5.0	6.1
Canada	2.0	2.3	2.8	3.1	2.8	2.3
Denmark	1.9	1.7	4.0	3.0	5.1	3.1
Finland	1.8	1.9	5.0	4.1	6.8	3.6
France	1.8	1.7	4.9	4.4	5.3	5.0
Germany	1.9	1.2	5.8	6.8	5.4	4.7
Italy	1.2	1.8	5.3	4.3	6.5	5.0
Japan	1.8	1.4	7.5	5.8	10.1	6.1
Netherlands	1.2	1.5	4.1	3.5	4.7	4.1
Norway	1.6	2.5	4.4	4.1	5.2	3.6
Sweden	2.4	2.9	3.8	3.5	4.8	2.7
Switzerland	1.5	1.9	3.4	3.5	4.0	2.3
UK	1.1	1.5	2.8	2.3	3.3	2.8
USA	2.1	2.5	2.3	2.4	2.5	1.8
Average	1.7	1.8	4.3	3.9	5.0	3.8

Source: For output, see A. Maddison, 'Phases of Capitalist Development', *Banca Nazionale del Lavoro Quarterly Review* (June 1977).

economy compared with the others, is a fundamental element in my explanation of why the other economies have been able to do so well since the war.

Productivity growth slowed down in the 1970s. In all except two countries performance was worse than in the 1960s. But the average growth for the 16 countries was practically the same in the seventies as in the fifties, with half the countries doing better and half doing worse.

Figure 10.1 summarizes the productivity record as a series of binary comparisons of each of 15 countries with the USA. The graph shows comparative levels and trends over time. The productivity curves up to 1950 appear rather smooth because they refer only to 8 benchmark years in the 80 year period. Thereafter the graph is based on annual data. However, productivity growth has tended to be genuinely smoother than other macro-economic indicators such as GDP and GDP per head. It has shown less cyclical sensitivity and has also varied less from one phase to another. Average productivity growth for the 16 countries was similiar in the 1870-1913 and 1913-50 periods (which were clearly differentiated phases in terms of output and output per head). Similarly the slackening

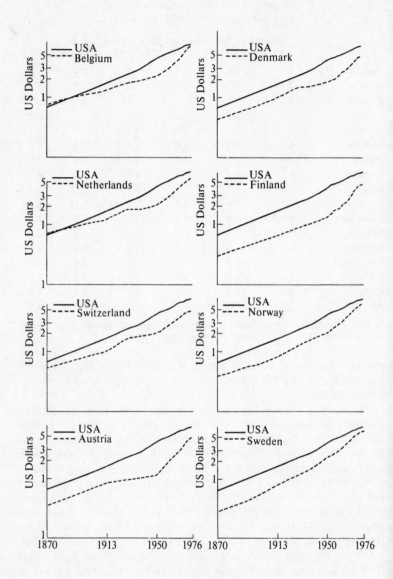

Fig. 10.1. Binary Comparisons of the Level and Growth of GDP
Per Man Hour 1870–1976 ($ of 1970 U.S. purchasing power)

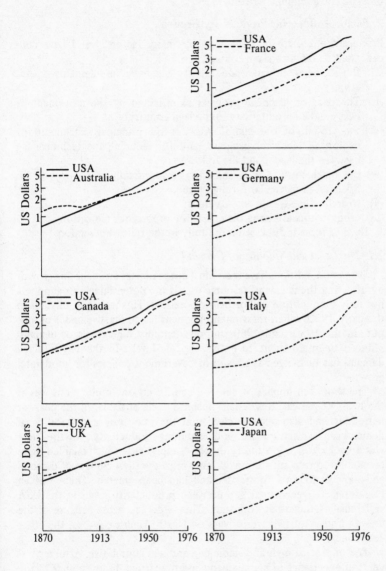

Fig. 10.1. *Continued*

in the 1970s has been less marked than for the other two main indicators of aggregate economic performance.

2. Factors Influencing Productivity Growth

Productivity growth is influenced by many factors, but I have concentrated on 6 which seem strategic, i.e.:

(i) the degree of buoyancy and stability in *demand* and demand expectations;

(ii) The pace of *technical progress* as reflected by the movement of best-practice productivity in the lead country;

(iii) the growth of the *capital stock*, as the principal instrument for exploiting technical progress, and for reducing the technical lag between the leader and the followers;

(iv) the mechanisms for *intercountry transmission* of pro-growth influences, in particular through trade;

(v) *structural changes in employment*;

(vi) other factors affecting the *efficiency* of resource allocation.

Each of these is discussed more fully in the following sections:

2.1. The Level and Stability of Demand

Demand conditions have their most direct impact on economic growth by affecting the degree of resource use. If the potential labour supply is not fully used, output will be below potential. This was most obvious in the early 1930s when mass unemployment led to massive losses of output. In the 1950s and 1960s unprecedentedly high levels of demand reduced unemployment to extremely low levels. In the 1970s, slack demand has reemerged as a result of government policies for 'moderate' growth.

The short run impact of demand conditions on employment was at the heart of prewar 'Keynesian' business cycle analysis. In the postwar period, it had also become clear that the buoyancy and stability of demand can be a major factor in determining productivity growth. There was a backlog of opportunity on the 'supply' side which enabled these economies to respond very favourably once the right climate of demand and expectations of future demand had been created. There was an unnaturally large postwar gap between productivity levels in the USA and most of the other countries. This wide gap arose because of the uneven impact of two world wars on North America and on the other economies.

The impact of high and stable demand was cumulative. After several years of experience of high demand and the virtual disappearance of the business cycle, entrepreneurial expectations became euphoric and the aggregate rate of investment in these countries rose steadily. The 1950s were already a period of unprecedentedly high investment by historical

TABLE 10.2.
Productivity Levels
(GDP per Man Hour) in 1870 and 1976

	1870 $ per man hour	1976 $ per man hour	Coefficient of multiplication 1870-1976	Annual Average Compound Growth Rate 1870-1976
Australia	1.218	5.864	5	1.49
Austria	0.355	4.945	14	2.52
Belgium	0.735	6.884	9	2.13
Canada	0.594	6.571	11	2.29
Denmark	0.433	5.050	12	2.34
Finland	0.297	4.686	16	2.64
France	0.413	5.716	14	2.51
Germany	0.419	6.110	15	2.56
Italy	0.397	4.924	12	2.40
Japan	0.161	3.824	24	3.03
Netherlands	0.713	5.745	8	1.99
Norway	0.398	6.253	16	2.63
Sweden	0.298	6.190	20	2.90
Switzerland	0.532	4.750	9	2.09
UK	0.814	4.617	6	1.65
USA	0.669	7.414	11	2.30
Arithmetic Average	0.518	5.596	11	2.25

Source: 1970 GDP level derived from I. B. Kravis, A. Heston and R. Summers, *International Comparisons of Real Product and Purchasing Power*, John Hopkins (1978) for Belgium, France, Germany, Italy, Japan, Netherlands, UK and USA. Other countries, as described in A. Maddison, op. cit. For a discussion of the statistical problems fo such comparisons, See A. Maddison, 'Productivity Trends and Prospects in Continental Western Europe, 1950-1990, *The Future of Productivity*, National Center for Productivity and Quality of Working Life, Washington D. C. (Winter 1977).

standards, but the 1960s were even better. Profit expectations of entrepreneurs, investment decisions, wage expectations of labour were interrelated and self reinforcing.

The main instrument by which high demand created high productivity growth was by raising the rate of investment and the growth of the capital stock. There were other transmission mechanisms which also favoured growth in this virtuous circle situation, which were of lesser importance but significant in their contribution to growth. High demand flushed surplus labour out of low productivity occupations, improved efficiency, helped promote economies of scale, promoted migration, etc.

The 1970s have seen a partial reversal of this happy context. It is not easy to quantify and compare demand situations at different periods but it is clear that the situation in the seventies has been less favourable than in the earlier postwar decades, though still a good deal better than the longer run historical experience of prewar years. There was a generalised recession in 1974-5 induced by the oil shock, and the subsequent economic recovery has not been sufficient to restore full employment. This conjuncture is not a business cycle in the classical sense but the fruit of concerted governmental policies to restrict demand in the hope of mitigating price increases and balance of payments disequilibria.

The change in the climate of demand and expectations, and the experimentation with new policy weapons have affected both labour input and productivity.

The average unemployment rate for these countries as a whole has risen steadily since 1973. By 1978 unemployment reached 15 millions. However, this is only a partial indication of the labour market situation, because governmental policy has diverted a good deal of the labour slack into channels other than overt unemployment. Curbs on migration absorbed part of the slack in France, Germany and Switzerland. Italy and Japan have emphasised work sharing schemes which cut hours worked rather than employment. Normal labour supply has been curtailed in a number of cases by encouraging people to enter training schemes, to take premature retirement or even sickness benefits rather than register as unemployed.

Given the complexity of these policies, it is difficult to assess how much slack there is. Policies on migration might well have been modified somewhat without a recession. Working hours would have fallen somewhat in any case and it is difficult to assess what part of the recent fall is involuntary. Some would argue that the full employment rate of unemployment has been on the rise for 'structural' reasons, the ratio of unemployment benefits to wages has increased, the proportion of marginal workers such as married women has risen. Both factors tend to prolong job search. It is also argued in the USA that minimum wage legislation increases unemployment.

One can get some clues on the size of labour slack by comparing growth rates of the labour force and of labour input. It is normal that labour force growth continued at the same pace, but labour input declined by 0.5 points a year. This suggests that labour slack in the 70s developed at about 1 per cent a year and that the cumulative labour slack in 1976 was about 6 per cent for these countries as a whole.
0.5 points a year. This suggests that labour slack in the 70s developed at about 1 per cent a year and that the cumulative labour slack in 1976 was about 6 per cent for these countries as a whole.

It is difficult to judge the degree to which demand conditions affected productivity in the 1970s. Governments have subsidised employment and penalised lay-offs. This has encouraged labour hoarding and curtailed

productivity growth somewhat. Firms have also hoarded labour voluntarily to some degree and the efficiency of their operations has been
handicapped because markets are smaller than they had expected. Long
run growth potential has been more fundamentally damaged to the
degree that investment has been cut back, though this has not
happened on the scale that might have been expected.

My own feeling is that although the recession and the 'moderate
growth' strategy have had an adverse 'cyclical' impact on productivity
growth, the longer run productivity potential has not yet been seriously
weakened by the demand situation. However, there are some more
fundamental reasons for thinking that the long run productivity growth
potential of these economies could not have been sustained at the
extraordinary pace maintained in the 1960s. These forces making for
deceleration could normally have been expected to take effect rather
gradually as explained in the sections below, but they would already
have had some effect in slowing productivity growth in the 1970s.

2.2 Technical Progress

The most elusive problem in productivity analysis is the role of
technical progress. It is sometimes asserted that the postwar acceleration
of productivity growth is due in large part to a faster pace of technical
advance. This argument often comes from those who measure technical
progress as a residual in production functions in which the growth in
capital stock is given only a third the weight of labour input.

My own view is quite different. I would measure the pace of technical
progress by the rate of advance of best practice productivity. This is not
measurable directly, but as a rough proxy, I would use the rate of growth
of the average productivity level in the lead country—the USA. In fact,
US productivity growth has been much steadier than that in the other
countries. Most importantly, the USA has not had the postwar acceleration in productivity growth which has occurred in all the other countries.

Over most of the range of production processes and product innovation, the other countries have not had to break new ground. They
have had to imitate rather than innovate. One should not exaggerate the
ease of this process. They have had to adapt known technology to their
particular needs in terms of product-mix, factor prices, resource endowments, labour relations, consumer tastes, export ambitions, size of plant,
etc. All this requires 'improvement engineering', technical and managerial
skills, and an ability to remain familiar with a range of technical practice
which is constantly changing in the lead country. Nevertheless the
followers have not faced the same risks and problems as the leader except
in those small sectors of their economy—Japan with TV sets, the UK
and France with Concorde—where they have surpassed or tried to surpass
US performance.

As other countries draw nearer to US productivity levels, their pace of development will be much more dependent on the pace of advance of the technical frontier and to that extent can be expected to be slower. The USA, however, will no longer have to bear the pioneering burden alone, and its potential pace of development should quicken. In this context it is interesting to note that the combined size of the 3 big economies likely to draw level with US productivity in the 1980s (France, Germany, Japan) is the same as that of the United States, so that in this coming period, technical leadership will be collective in a really significant sense.

US productivity growth has slowed down in a rather striking way in the 1970s and this tends to contradict my conclusion in the preceding paragraph. However, there are some special temporary factors (apart from the severity of the 1974-5 recession in the USA) which help explain this.

More than 70 per cent of the US employment increase from 1970 to 1976 consisted of females (who generally have lower skills and productivity than males). Canada is the only other country to approach the US pattern with 57 per cent of the 1970s increase in employment being accounted for by women. Elsewhere the situation was quite different. In Germany females represented only 20 per cent of the change in employment; in Japan, female employment fell by a quarter million in the 1970s, and male employment rose by 2 million.

Another temporary factor slowing productivity growth has been the growth in regulations regarding the environment, pollution, public safety, work safety, and health all of which require diversion of workers and capital to activities which are not reflected in the measure of output. Denison has estimated that these regulatory measures and the cost of crime reduced growth of US output per unit of input by 0.3 per cent a year in the 1970s.[1] Similiar problems have also curtailed productivity growth in other countries but probably to a much smaller extent.

2.3. *Growth and Level of the Capital Stock*

In my view, the fundamental instrument (on the supply side) for faster postwar productivity growth has been the acceleration in growth of the capital stock per hour worked.

Table 10.3 shows the historical record for the seven biggest countries. The figures refer to the fixed non-residential tangible capital stock (excluding land). They show:
(i)   that, on average, postwar growth of capital stock per hour worked has been three times as fast as in the previous 80 years. This postwar

[1]See E. F. Denison, 'Effects of Selected Changes in the Institutional and Human Environment Upon Output Per Unit of Input', *Survey of Current Business* (Jan. 1978).

acceleration has been most modest in the USA. There is thus a rather striking degree of parallelism in the productivity and the capital stock records in the long run;

(ii) faster growth of capital in the 1960s than in the 50s (which is also true of productivity growth). However, the deceleration in the pace of growth of capital stock per man hour from the 1960s to the 1970s has been modest or non existent except for the USA and Japan. Hence recent developments in the capital stock do not do much to explain the slow-down in productivity growth in the 1970s.

TABLE 10.3.
Rate of Growth of
Non Residential Fixed Capital Stock Per Man Hour

annual average compound growth rate (average of gross and net stocks)

	1870–1913	1913–50	1950–76	1950–60	1960–70	1970–76
Canada	n.a.	1.8[d]	4.9	4.5	2.6	2.5
France[e]	n.a.	(1.8)	5.7	3.9	6.5	7.5
Germany	(2.1)	(0.9)	6.4	4.7	7.2	7.2
Italy	2.3[a]	[2.6]	[5.6]	[2.8]	[7.0]	[7.3]
Japan	2.0[b]	[2.9]	8.7[f]	2.7[f]	11.2[f]	8.9[f]
UK	0.6	0.9	4.2	2.8	5.3	4.9
USA	2.7[c]	1.8	3.4	2.6	2.9	2.0
Average	1.9	1.8	5.6	3.4	6.1	5.8

Notes: All figures are adjusted to eliminate the impact of geographic change. Figures in round brackets refer to net stock only, figures in square brackets to gross stock only.

[a] 1882–1913; [b] 1879–13; [c] 1869/78–1913; [d] 1926–50
[e] refers to private stock
[f] net stock refers only to the private sector.

Figure 10.2 makes binary comparisons of the level of capital stock per man hour in the USA and 6 other countries back to 1870.[2] The estimates are necessarily crude, but they are robust enough to conclude that the US capital stock per hour worked is still higher than that elsewhere (markedly so for the UK, Italy, and Japan, but only marginally in the case of Germany and Canada). There is also a striking resemblance between the level and growth of capital stock per man hour and changes in the level and growth of labour productivity shown in Figure 10.1.

[2] The 1976 estimate of capital stock in Figure 10.2 was made by cumulating non-residential fixed capital investment at constant prices from mid 1946 to mid 1976. Stocks were converted into US dollars using purchasing power parities derived from *et al.*, Kravis op. cit. The backward extrapolation was made from the movement in capital stock as derived from national estimates.

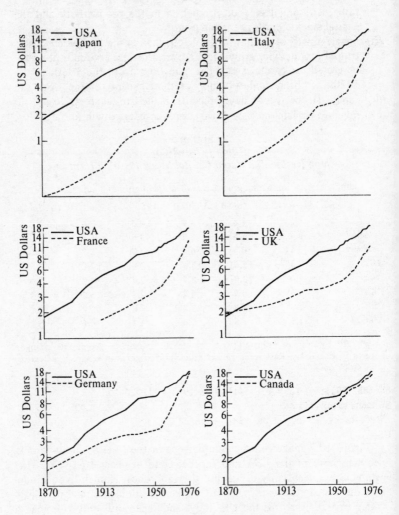

Fig. 10.2. Gross Non Residential Fixed Capital Stock
Per Man Hour at 1970 US prices 1870–1976

US technical leadership over eight decades has been reflected by its continuously higher capital stock. One can see the US takeover of leadership from the UK in the nineteenth century. The sharp narrowing in the capital stock gaps in the postwar period is also very obvious and parallels the narrowing of the productivity gap.

2.4. International Diffusion Mechanisms

There are a number of dimensions in which growth influences can be diffused between countries, of which the most important is probably trade. Trade affects growth by its impact on both supply and demand.

The influence of trade on growth is rather complex and I do not have space to analyse the type of influence it has had in any detail. However, there is a reason to suppose that when trade grows faster than GDP it is likely to exert a positive influence on productivity growth, particularly if the expansion is induced by removal of trade barriers.

TABLE 10.4.
Volume of Exports 1870-76[a]

annual average compound growth rates

	1870-1913	1913-50	1950-76	1950-60	1960-70	1970-76
Australia	4.3	1.3	5.6	4.2	7.6	4.6
Austria	3.5	−3.0	10.3	12.5	9.9	7.6
Belgium	4.2	0.3	8.6	7.2	10.8	7.2
Canada	4.1	3.1	6.2	4.0	9.6	4.2
Denmark	3.3	2.4	6.4	7.0	7.0	4.3
Finland	3.9	1.9	6.3	8.0	6.8	2.7
France	2.8	1.1	7.9	7.2	8.6	7.9
Germany	4.1	−2.8	11.5	16.1	9.6	7.2
Italy	2.2	0.6	11.0	11.2	13.2	7.2
Japan	8.5	2.0	15.1	16.0	16.3	11.8
Netherlands	3.3	1.5	9.5	10.0	9.9	7.9
Norway	3.2	2.7	7.2	5.6	8.8	7.1
Sweden	3.1	2.8	5.9	5.7	7.8	3.1
Switzerland	3.9	0.3	7.4	8.1	8.6	4.5
UK	2.8	0.0	3.8	1.8	4.8	5.6
USA	4.9	2.2	5.9	5.6	5.8	6.6
Arithmetic Average	3.9	1.0	8.0	8.1	9.1	6.2

[a]The figures are not adjusted for changes in geographic boundaries

It is clear from Table 10.4 that the expansion of trade volume from 1950 to 1976 (at 8 per cent a year on average for these countries) was much greater than in the preceding 80 years. Furthermore the relative pace of postwar expansion has tended to be related to the ranking of countries in terms of productivity growth, Japan being the best performer with exports growing at 15.1 per cent a year and the UK the laggard with export growth of only 3.8 per cent. On the other hand it should be noted that the average productivity growth of these countries was similar in the 1870-1913 and the 1913-50 periods even though the trade experience was very much worse in the second than in the first period.

It is difficult therefore to say what precise contribution trade has made to the postwar acceleration of productivity growth, or the influence which the slackening of trade expansion in the 1970s has had. My own view is that the relatively liberal trade policies of the postwar period and the reasonably cooperative attitudes of the countries in international payments matters (by interwar standards) have been a major influence in creating favourable growth expectations. They were the international component of the favourable demand climate in domestic markets which nurtured high rates of investment and economic activity.

This positive influence of trade on the demand and investment climate made a more fundamental contribution to faster postwar growth than the beneficial impact which removal of trade barriers made to the efficiency of resource allocation. However, it seems clear that in the 1970s both types of growth stimulus deriving from trade were weakened. The pace of trade liberalisation was at its greatest in the 50s and 60s, and cannot be expected to make the same contribution in future.

In the 1970s, there was a drastic change in the payments system of these countries with the move from pegged to floating exchange rates. The old system collapsed under the strain of widely different rates of inflation between countries, the openness of capital markets to large speculative movements, the desire of the reserve currency country to change its parity relative to other major traders, and the reluctance of the latter to revalue. The new system has worked reasonably well considering the nature of the disturbances involved, trade has continued to expand, and the vast size of the international capital market which was a nuisance in a fixed rate world helped considerably in launching the new system—where flexibility, diversity, and anonymity were needed by the new OPEC creditors. In principle the new system reduces efficiency slightly by raising transaction costs for traders, but it gives more leeway to independent national policies for promoting full employment and economic growth. The latter possibilities have not yet been fully exploited, and the operation of the new system has been complicated to some degree by continued pursuit of policies more appropriate to a fixed rate system, and by efforts to modify and 'manage' the extent of the float.

2.5. Impact of Structural Change

Changes in the pattern of demand, output and employment have been very considerable in the past century, and must be taken into account in interpreting the nature of productivity growth.

Since 1870, there has been a massive reduction in the share of agricultural employment, a big increase in the share of services and moderate growth in industry. The first two phenomena have operated more or less continuously in the same direction in all the countries. By contrast, the industrial share rose and fell, peaking somewhat below 50 per cent of the employed population. In 1870 agriculture occupied half of the population of these countries, in 1976 only a twelfth. Service employment now predominates, representing well over half of total employment.

TABLE 10.5.
Structure of Employment 1870–1976

(average of country shares)

	Agriculture[a]	Industry[b]	Services
1870	48.8	27.5	23.7
1950	(24.9)	(36.4)	38.7
1976	8.3	36.1	55.6

[a] includes forestry and fisheries; [b] includes construction.

The timing of 'deindustrialisation' has varied. In 1976, the industrial share was below its 1950 level in Australia, Belgium, Canada, the Netherlands, Sweden, the UK and the USA; it did not change much in Denmark, France, Germany, Norway and Switzerland; it rose substantially in Austria, Finland, Italy and Japan. However, even in the latter group it seems to have peaked in the 1970s, as real income and productivity levels in these countries converged with those elsewhere. In one or two countries, the past few years have seen an absolute drop in industrial employment—a tendency most marked in the UK.

Table 10.6 shows growth of output per man (*not* man hour) by sector for the postwar period for the countries where rough estimates are feasible. It also shows the pattern of employment change by sector. Productivity performance in the service sector has been a good deal slower in every case than in commodity production, and productivity in agriculture has grown faster than in industry in most countries.

At first sight it would appear that the structural shifts in employment have been unfavourable to productivity growth as employment has fallen in agriculture, risen only moderately in industry and generally faster in services, i.e. the employment movements are inversely related to the pace of productivity growth. However, the productivity effects of structural change do not derive simply from movements of employment between sectors with different growth rates. They also depend on the absolute level of productivity in different sectors. In most countries the productivity level in agriculture was about half of that in the rest of the economy in 1950. Hence the outflow of labour from low-level

TABLE 10.6.

Growth of Output Per Person and Employment by Sector 1950–76

annual average compound growth rates

	Output Per Person Employed 1950–76				Rate of Growth of Employment 1950–76			
	Agriculture	Industry	Services	GDP	Agriculture	Industry	Services	Total
Austria	(6.1)	(5.1)	(2.9)	5.1	−3.8	0.5	1.7	0.0
Denmark	3.7	3.6	1.6	2.8	−3.0	0.5	2.2	0.8
Finland	5.6	4.1	1.9	4.3	−4.2	1.2	3.1	0.4
France	(5.1)	(4.8)	(2.8)	4.4	−3.3	0.7	1.8	0.5
Germany	5.8	5.4	2.9	4.7	−3.8	0.8	2.0	0.7
Italy	5.6	4.3	1.8	4.2	−3.4	2.3	2.6	0.7
Japan	(6.8)	(8.1)	(3.9)	7.2	−3.7	3.3	3.8	1.5
Netherlands	4.8	5.3	2.0	3.4	−1.8	0.4	2.2	1.2
Norway	4.3	3.7	2.3	3.4	−3.5	0.9	2.6	0.9
Sweden	4.6	3.9	1.6	2.8	−3.8	0.2	2.3	0.7
UK	4.0	2.6	1.3	2.3	−2.1	−0.3	1.0	0.3
USA	5.1	2.8	1.4	1.8	−3.3	0.9	2.4	1.5
Average	5.1	4.5	2.2	3.9	−3.3	1.0	2.3	0.8

productivity jobs in agriculture has generally been favourable to total productivity growth. Indeed high productivity growth in agriculture in the postwar period was due in large degree to the 'pull' effect of high demand elsewhere in the economy which provided an outlet for under-employed labour in agriculture—particularly in Austria, Finland, Italy and Japan where the proportion of labour in agriculture was very large in 1950.

In 1950, the productivity *level* in services was higher than elsewhere in the economy in all cases except the USA, for this sector, though very heterogeneous, contains the most capital—intensive industries and the bulk of the most highly educated people.

Structural changes in employment reflect two basic forces which have operated on all the countries as they have reached successively higher levels of real income and productivity. The first of these is the elasticity of consumer demand for particular products which has been rather similar at given levels of real income (particularly as relative price structures have moved in similar directions). These demand forces have reduced the share of agricultrual products in consumption and raised demand for the products of industry and services. The second basic factor has been the differential pace of technological advance between sectors. Productivity growth has been slower in services than in com-modity production, partly because of the intrinsic character of many of personal services. partly because of measurement conventions which exclude the possibility of productivity growth in some services.

The pattern of employment is also affected by international trade.

Trade proportions vary because of size, climate, natural endowment and competivity of the different economies, and this is a major reason for variations in employment structure between countries at the same level of income, though there are some constraints on the range of variation because a fair part of consumer demand is for items which are difficult to trade internationally. Institutional arrangements, past economic history and policy can also affect structures differentially. Hence, countries which entered the postwar period with a large amount of underemployed labour in agriculture—particularly Austria, Finland, Italy and Japan—were able to enjoy structural changes particularly favourable to growth, because for a given growth in total labour supply they were able to switch more labour into the high productivity

The significance of structural shifts can easily be exaggerated. The in-sector productivity movements are not independent of the sectoral shifts (as we have already noted for agriculture) and the division of the economy into three sectors is arbitrary. The apparent impact of structural shifts can be changed by disaggregating the economy in a different way, and the service sector is a very heterogeneous category which includes branches with very rapid as well as very slow productivity growth.

The acceleration in postwar growth is not due to any major degree to structural change. In the 1870-1950 period, lower overall productivity growth was reflected in lower productivity growth within each sector. The pattern of structural change in employment was in the same direction as in the postwar period. The major difference was in the pace of sectoral change, i.e. the switch out of agriculture was slower. Similarly, intercountry variations in overall productivity growth between countries in the postwar period are not attributable to a very significant degree to structural change. They mainly reflect divergences in productivity growth in individual sectors of the economy. This is clear from Table 10.6.

2.6. Increases in Efficiency

Finally there are a number of influences on productivity growth which arise from changes in the efficiency of resource allocation. As technology is constantly changing it is natural to assume as Arrow and Lundberg have done, that the process of 'learning by doing' is continuous. Methods of using equipment may well continue to be improved until the machines are scrapped, and then the process starts all over again with new machinery. The optimum use of resources as sumed by neoclassical growth theorists may never be achieved in practice. It is not the case that the 'entrepreneur instantly perceives and adopts the best line of action in any given situation. Instead he is seen as perpetually groping in a mist of uncertainty, gradually and imperfectly learning his way on the basis of experience accruing to him.'[3] Given the accelerated pace of investment in the postwar period, it seems likely that the amount of learning by doing has increased.

The learning process is difficult to dissociate from economies of a scale which have been given particular emphasis by Kaldor as a source of growth in manufacturing.[4] I feel that Kaldor exaggerates the importance of this source of growth, which may have been more important in the time of Adam Smith than in the postwar priod.

Finally some authors stress the importance of changes in managerial and labour efficiency in the growth process. Personally I doubt whether these have been a major source of growth in the long term, but they probably vary cyclically as do the other aspects of efficiency mentioned above. Hence some of the slackening in productivity growth during the 1970s may well be due to inefficiency in resource allocation induced the recession and subsequent inadequate recovery, but it is not possible to quantify their impact.

4. Summary and Conclusions

Productivity growth accelerated greatly in the postwar period, growing more than 2.5 times as fast on average as in the 8 decades 1870-1950. This acceleration affected all countries except the USA.

The US productivity lead which has existed since the 1890s has been greatly reduced but is still a third higher than the average for the other countries.

The major forces for the postwar acceleration have been high and steady levels of demand, both nationally and internationally which induced a major acceleration in investment and in the growth of capital stock—which has matched the acceleration in productivity improvements in resource allocation because of the elimination of underemployed labour in agricultrure and elimination of international trade barriers gave an extra once-for-all boost to productivity growth. These two special factors have now waned in importance.

There is no evidence that the postwar acceleration was due to a faster pace of technical innovation. The frontier of technology lies predominantly in the US economy and its pace of productivity growth did not increase. On the technical level, the acceleration of growth outside the USA is basically explicable in terms of a reduction in the technical lag. This raises interesting questions for the future when the other countries

---

[3]See F. H. Hahn and R. C. O. Matthews, 'The Theory of Economic Growth: A Survey', *Economic Journal* (Dec. 1964).
[4]See N. Kaldor, *Causes of the Slow Rate of Economic Growth of the United Kingdom* (Cambridge, 1966), whose main point was the correlation between employment and productivity growth in manufacturing known as Verdoorn's Law and 'The Irrelevance of Equilibrium Economics', *Economic Journal* (Dec. 1972), where he adds a new argument about the 3 dimensional character of space.

and particularly the big economies (France, Germany and Japan) are likely to catch up to US productivity levels. Will their investment pace slacken as the burden of pioneering new techniques and products falls more heavily on them? I feel that it probably will, because risks will be higher and profit expectations lower. However, the pace at which the technical frontier is expanded may be faster than in the past because the USA will no longer be alone at the frontier, and the momentum of these economies and rate of capital formation when they hit the frontier may well be higher than has historically been the case in the USA. Hence some slow-down in productivity growth in most of the countries can be expected in future on these grounds, though their pace of growth may well be better than the USA has experienced in the past. This retarding effect on the approach to the frontier probably started to take effect in the 1970s.

In the 1970s, productivity growth slackened, but not nearly so much as did GDP growth. GDP growth slackened in the 70s because of the 1974-5 recession and the cautious demand policies followed by most governments since then which have prevented the full production potential of these economies from being exploited. The impact of these 'moderate growth' policies is reasonably clear in labour markets. If one takes a broad view of the degree of labour slack, rather than the more conventional indicators of unemployment, which understate the impact of the 'moderate growth' policies, it would appear that growth in the 1970s lagged about 1 per cent a year below its potential, with cumulative slack in 1976 of about 6 per cent.

It is not possible to estimate the degree of productivity slack in the 1970s due to these policy-cyclical factors. Average productivity growth for this group of countries in the 1970s was remarkably high by historical standards—twice the prewar average and about the same in the 1950s. It can only be construed as disappointing if the comparison is made with the 1960s in which several factors were particularly favourable to growth as mentioned above—particularly in countries with a big technical backlog and large reserves of underemployed labour in agriculture, i.e. Austria, Finland, Italy and Japan.

My conclusion therefore is that the policy-cyclical factors have generally had a rather modest impact in slowing down productivity growth so far in the 1970s (and that some of the slowdown in the USA has been due to rather special factors). However, the outlook for the future is rather clouded. The basic 'supply' factors seem to warrant future rates of productivity growth a good deal higher than prewar experience, but if the climate of demand and expectations are weakened enough to lower investment incentives at a stage when the challenge of technical pioneering and risk taking has to be faced on a much wider front, then the momentum of these economies could be considerably weakened. The experience of 1913–50 demonstrates clearly enough that the 'technical' possibilities of growth offered by technical backlogs can be squandered by inadequate demand policy. The postwar situation which favoured high and relatively steady expansion of demand has been interrupted by policy challenges which have also brought new rules of behaviour. Governments have not yet adjusted their policy mix very satisfactorily to these new challenges, though they have not yet done anything really disastrous. The effective adaption of policy to new circumstances is likely to be slow, and in the meantime investment may be depressed below potential to a greater degree than has already occurred. Some of the cyclical slack in the economies will be a once-for-all loss, but the existence of slack does of course mean that the short run capacity for expansion is rather large if policy is reversed.

11

WILL A SHORTAGE OF ENERGY BRAKE ECONOMIC GROWTH?

by Michael V. Posner*

Pembroke College, Cambridge

1. Introduction

In the aftermath of the OPEC price rises of 1973, the public were bombarded with a number of predictions of ultimate gloom. One version of these stories—to be called loosely the Club of Rome story—asked us to visualise a sort of 'space ship earth' whose ultimate resources were necessarily limited, and was therefore constrained in the rate of energy conversion that it could ultimately accommodate. (The scientific or more properly thermodynamic basis of this story was not always properly spelt out in popular accounts, and the law of the conservation of energy was sometimes forgotten. But if it is assumed that in the process of energy conservation a lot of heat is dissipated outside our world for the benefit of the rest of the universe, then the story becomes a little more plausible.) The pot was stirred a little more fearsomely by adding moral and economic flavours; one economist of my acquaintance offered the analogy of the white man who had waxed rich by living on the benefits of the black man's back gardens, and would now have to tighten his belt as the less developed nations found it necessary to draw on the raw materials from their own allotments.

The counter-attack against the Club of Rome has in fact been led by the Editor of this volume, who has delighted and enlightened us all with his ironic account of a world running short of the scarce element Beckermonium—indeed, under his influence and that of several other writers, in my view the pendulum of argument has swung rather too far in an anti-Club of Rome direction. I do think there is a sense in which we, or our great grandchildren, risk running out of pleasant places to live, empty spaces to walk in, country lanes along which to

*I am indebted to comments by Richard Kahn, Tom Kennedy, Robin Matthews and Richard Ormerod. Errors of fact and analysis which remain are my own.

drive to work, unpolluted air to breath, and cheap petrol to put into our tanks. But it is only the last of these—cheap petrol—which is the proper subject matter of this paper.

It is indeed the assertion that energy (or rather, bearing in mind the thermodynamic problem, 'fuel') will in future be expensive, which forms the second and far more important version of the gloom story. This doctrine, that 1973 marks a watershed in the price of fuel, and that from that time onwards the trend is inexorably and sharply upwards, forms the main theme of this paper, and the main argument to be investigated. This doctrine is believed in by what I have called elsewhere the 'two energy establishments'. It is believed both by the oil companies, the atomic energy authorities, President Carter, the International Energy Agency, and most official spokesmen on this sort of topic in most rich countries. And it is believed by the alternative establishment of energy conservationists, lovers of windmills and tidal power, and those who would have us abandon as rapidly as possible the energy intensive way of life that has been built up in most rich countries, particularly North America, over the last half-century: anybody who tells me that I must walk to work, cease to fly off by charter flight on cheap winter holidays and wear wool close to the skin is surely telling me that he believes fuel to be an extremely expensive commodity!

The way these two energy establishments co-exist, like wolves and lambs lying down together, is sometimes amusing. I have sat in more than one conference with Middle East potentates; long haired conservationists with bicycle clips rather than driving licences; and Fellows of the Royal Society determined to surround our coasts with either nuclear power stations or enormous and ugly windmills: they have all gloried in telling us that the days of cheap fuel are gone.

I assume in this paper that these twin establishments are correct. From personal experience, I would warn my audience to approach this characteristic unanimity of professional opinion with deep caution and suspicion. When I first came into the energy business, in the mid 1960s, it was generally received opinion that oil would be available for ever and ever at $2.0 per barrel. The OPEC countries, we were told, would never unite, and proved reserves were a produceable commodity, to be manufactured at a predictable rate by additional dollops of exploration. Well, the flip-flop in the circuit has turned over, and we now have a new unanimity of opinion pointing in the opposite direction. Economists are accustomed to this sort of reversal of view— the five year cycle of fashion about the movements of the terms of trade betwen manufactured goods and primary material is wellknown, and every time a new doctrine appears the law which it enunciates is always inexorable, inelectuable, and to be questioned only by the ignorant or obstinate. It is very likely, in my view, that fuel is going to go up in price over the next thirty years by quite large amounts, but this is not *certain*: and we must therefore at some stage in this paper ask how the possibility that the assumptions are wrong changes the policy conclusions.

2. How Does the Prospect of Expensive Fuel Affect Economic Growth?

The Club of Rome doctrine had very clear implications for economic performance. Growth, we were told, would come to an end. If the process of growth were measured by some physical test—the number of tons of steel per year—then there could be continuing economies in labour input, both direct and indirect (through the supply of capital equipment in increasing quantities), but it would certainly be necessary to envisage more iron ore being processed, and more coal or oil being burnt. If there is a finite limit on the amount of raw materials available, growth can continue only to the extent that *material productivity* increases by the same amount. (I would say in passing that my own experience in productivity measurement in manufacturing industry in the early 1950s suggests that a main source *both* of changes in overall productivity *and* of changes in measured labour productivity is in fact the economising of raw materials—electric motors now weigh much less than their pre-war equivalents, and both semi-conductors and micro-circuits use a tiny fraction of the copper or steel required for their technological precursors. Bearing this in mind, even the Club of Rome constraint on growth is far from absolute.)

The constraint upon growth caused by certain materials—in the case we are investigating, fuels—beginning to cost very much more, is rather different. In its most abstract form, it becomes that favourite of economists, the index number problem. We are all now familiar with the point that UK economic growth in the late 1970s looks much better with 1975 price weights than with 1970 price weights, because of the greatly increased weight given to North Sea Oil in the later set of prices. In a rather similar way, we could anticipate that the reaction to higher relative fuel prices in the next century would generate a statistical series which, when expressed as quantity indices with the weights of 1970, would show very much lower rates of increase than they would do if weighted by the price relatives of the twenty first century.

In more concrete terms, the job of economising in fuel might appropriate so much of our resources of capital and labour that there would be less available for increasing the volume of final goods and services in the hands of the consumer.

Still another way of putting the same point is to suggest that, for the production of a given shopping basket of final goods and services we might have to spend far more on intermediate goods, because the generosity of nature is becoming more limited, and we have to climb higher up the valley and pasture our sheep on the more barren uplands instead of the rich valleys of the past.

In formal terms, resource costs have risen. If 7 per cent of the total cost of our standard of living in 1975 were energy costs,[1] and energy were to cost in the year 2000 something like four times its 1975 cost in real terms, then this would use up resources equal to an extra 20 per cent of the 1975 national income. If growth were otherwise occurring at 3 per cent a year, this means that we would have permanently lost 7 years growth, which in turn would have meant being in the year 2000 only as rich as we would otherwise have been in the year 1993. Yet another way of putting it is that high price energy might conceivably knock half a percentage point off the UK growth rate.

That is the crude and simple minded measure of the energy problem, and in the next section we subject it to various refinements.

3. Some Complications

A number of amendments must immediately be made to this way of looking at things. I will deal with them seriatim.
(i) A four fold increase in *final* energy prices is far in excess of anything we have yet experienced. At its peak, the price of crude oil free-on-board the Persian Gulf, all taxes and other costs paid, rose about four times in real terms after 1972—that increase has now fallen back to something like a threefold increase, because world prices of other goods have risen faster than the crude oil price since 1975. But the maximum real increase of final energy prices in the UK market has been of the order of magnitude of only 30 per cent, one tenth of the 300 per cent increase in the crude oil price! And indeed the average final energy price in the UK, relative to all other prices, is now probably not much more than 20 per cent above its level of 1972/3, while some energy prices—notably that of petrol pump gasoline—have actually *fallen* in real terms since 1972. Admittedly, other sources of final energy—notably coal and indigenous natural gas—have not risen nearly so fast in *this* energy crisis, as has crude oil, and thus, in so far as we are expecting *all* energy to rise in price over the next 25 years, the damper operating between primary energy prices and final energy prices will be diminished in power, and the simple minded figuring at the end of the previous section remains adequate. But at least a part of the feared energy price increases of the future will, most observers believe, take the form of a differentially sharp rise in the price of liquid hydro-carbons, particularly crude oil.

---

[1]The relevant statistic here is valued added in the primary and the secondary industries within the UK, plus the value of net imports, all before indirect taxation. Expressed as a percentage of GDP in 1975, this was nearer 9 than 7 per cent: but my understanding, in advance of the later figures, is that the proportion had fallen to nearer 7 by the date this paper was written.

So, on balance, I do advise readers to be very chary indeed of assuming that 'a fourfold increase in crude oil prices means a fourfold increase in the final fuel bill facing the individual householder'.

So even if we expected, as most of the energy establishment does, another 1 or 2 '1973' type oil price increases between now and the first quartile of the next century, it is very hard indeed to envisage real relative energy prices in the final consumer market being as much as 5 times higher in the year 2000 than they were in 1970. The reason for this is quite straightforward—as everybody knows who has ever paid a gas or electricity bill, the primary fuel input into the fuel conversion industries is only a small part of total costs — the cost of piping, meter reading, power station construction, etc. loom very large indeed, as, above all, do consumer government taxes: if the tax at the petrol pump had been a proportional tax rather than an excise duty, gasoline prices would be twice their present level.

It follows that, as far as we can see at this stage in the argument the order of magnitude of the problem suggested at the end of Section 2 is certainly excessive.

(ii) In any case we must note that this energy establishment view about the crude oil price is not a number derived by arithmetic or 'modelling'. None of the really sophisticated experts, in either of the twin establishments, are foolish enough to go nap on a single number for the end of the century. The usual approach is that exemplified by my friends in the Workshop for Alternative Energy Strategies—they ask themselves what sort of price increase might conceivably be large enough to choke off demand through conservation measures, or stimulate extra supply from new sources of fuel, of a size sufficient to wipe out projected imbalances between demand and supply. No one knows how big a price increase might be necessary to do this trick, and a lot depends on the dynamics of the system (when the price increase occurs, and how stable the new higher price turns out ot be), but most observers believe that a three or fourfold increase in primary energy prices will do the trick. More might be expected from the elasticity of supply—the production of alternative forms of energy at the very much higher prices assumed to be available in the market place—than from the elasticity of demand. The guess at a three or fourfold increase is based on careful study of what is at present known about these elasticities. It is not just a shot in the dark. But it is meant to be a symbol of a large problem, a flag waved to attract attention, rather than a scientific projection.

(iii) However, for our purposes, it is important to note that not *all* primary energy will cost this much—if a free market system, or something like it survives, then the *marginal* cost of energy may reach this level, and may be therefore many other prices will approximate to it: but this means that there will be substantial economic rents to be earned by some suppliers of some energy elsewhere, and it is far from obvious that these rents represent real cost to the the rest of the community. I interpret this paragraph as suggesting that the sorts of figures used at the end of Section 2 may be an outside upper estimate of the sort of resource problem that we ought to be considering.

This question of the division of the economic rent from the energy price increase is an important one, as was recognised by, for instance, the OECD experts as early as 1973. In particular, the international division between energy producers and energy consumers is most important—by that test the UK's position throughout the 80s and early 90s might be one of 'neutrality'. But unless we take a far more active stance in developments of indigenous onshore energy sources in the next decade or two we may end up as very large importers in the first quartile of the next century.

On the whole net importers suffer more than the 'world as a whole' from high energy prices, because they pay a rent, being the excess of selling price over resource costs, to the net exporters. But even those countries who are not net importers—for instance the UK in the next two decades—will suffer tangentially, in so far as there is a deflationary effect on world trade and economic activity generally because of the transfer problem which is imposed on net importers by the necessity to pay tribute to the exporters. I argue below that this malign tangential effect is likely to be larger than the losses imposed by OPEC rent collectors.

There are similar problems of rent in the domestic economy itself. The wages of miners in relatively productive pits are already showing tendencies to rise in such a way as to push the index of miners pay well up above its habitual position in the traditional pecking order of wage differentials. This process is likely to continue, to such an extent that some observers claim that the resource costs of coal will rise—the higher wages will become a necessary part of the remuneration of underground workers, and will not compose a rent at all. This raises questions of analysis and policy outside the scope of the present paper.

(iv) An additional burden might however be imposed if the elasticities of supply are less favourable than assumed in the preceding argument. In this context alone it is appropriate to remind ourselves that, because change in energy use is closely related in change in GDP, the quantum of energy employed in the year 2000 may be double that of 1975; this fact itself is not sufficient to change the burden of our arithmetic, because it merely represents a factor of scale. But it is relevant that supply will 'have' to double over the next quarter of a century, and therefore the search for alternatives to cheap Middle Eastern crude oil may already have pushed the margin of production into very unfavourable areas of geology and technology.

This argument suggests that the price elasticity of supply may be less favourable than is assumed in the paragraph (i) of this section; and it would follow that, taking the arguments of the two paragraphs together, it is appropriate to stick to the figure of 20 per cent of the GDP as an effective outside limit of the damage high price energy might do to our prosperity.

(v) The argument as we have cast it so far is in the terms of the annual renewable resource costs of energy utilized by, say, the British economy at some future date. Another way of looking at this is to consider the disposition of total investment between energy and other economic purposes over the next 25 years. Since a very large element in energy costs—particularly in incremental energy costs—it is likely to be capital expenditure, these two ways of looking at things can readily be made consistent. It is very hard to arrive, however, at plausible figures for investment needs. But combining some rather out of date estimates from the OECD with more up to date figures covering the oil industry only,[2] we might think of energy investment rising from 7 per cent of gross OECD investment to perhaps as much as 25 per cent over the next 2 decades. I suppose that change on its own might conceivably (if the Editor will allow some limited use of the ICOR concept) mean a reduction in the annual rate of economic growth of around one-seventh, which is nicely consistent with the figuring I attempted in Section 3.

4. Smooth Adjustments or a Bumpy Ride?

So far we have been assuming that the process of adjustment to even higher energy prices in the future would be smooth. If we were considering a text book perfect market, that might be quite a sensible assumption. For instance, small annual increases in the demand for superior French wines, caused by, say, the introduction of the Japanese consumer to this market and the gradual rise of living standards elsewhere, might well lead to a fairly slow discernible trend of increases, perhaps with small leaps at times of particularly good vintages, but nothing to suggest a 'wine crisis'! The energy market, by common agreement, is not much like that and it is bound to be influenced for the next 20 years at least by the looming importance of 3 or 4 governments in the Middle East who together dominate the market for traded oil. I am not one of those who suggest that the O.P.E.C. can be best modelled as a 'cartel', but there are a sufficiently small number of oligopolists (and at least one oligopsonist—the United States) for developments to be dominated by the estimates of quite few decision makers. I have described elsewhere, and there is now a large economic literature on, the nature of the 'depletion decision' that faces an owner of a resource which might be used today or instead kept until tomorrow. At any point of time, if the market is in equilibrium, the expected rate of increase in the price will not be far off the real rate of return on holding Wall Street assets. But in an oligopolistic market, adjustments in both the future expected level of prices and the path towards those prices are unlikely to be smooth.

Indeed, those with a gloomy frame of mind have often reflected aloud that the owner of a large energy resource would be best advised to allow the price to increase through ups and downs rather than along any steady path. A steady increase will stimulate a host of measures of economy—'conservation'—and will provide the conditions in which alternative sources can be confidently developed. But a period in which prices are very soft or falling, like those of 1978 when this paper was delivered, discourages conservation, enables politicians to put off unpleasant decisions about nuclear energy or whatever, and tends to reinforce the market strength of existing energy sources.

However I do not really believe that anybody with power is very moved by these maximisation calculations, and while I welcome employment for my ingenious colleagues in simulating the sundry variants of the games that might be played, I myself belong to the 'one damn thing after another' school of energy history. Nobody quite knows what the future will bring, and this type of uncertainty brings about periods of stagnation in prices followed by periods of lemming-like movement in either direction. This model has I believe worked pretty well over the last few years as an explanation of stock exchange behaviour, and I regret that it now seems to work also fairly well in the energy field.

If there is anything in this fear, or indeed anything in the more sophisticated belief that owners of energy resources are out to exploit the rest of us in the most clever way offered by economic science, we have have to consider an additional dimension to the problem— that presented by potential 'crunches' or discontinuities in the movements of energy prices over the next quarter of a century. Now in a sensible, moderate and skillful world—by which of course I mean a world run by Section F of The British Association—we could ride out this sort of bump quite easily. But anybody reflecting on the lamentable record of Western finance ministries and central banks in face of the oil price rise of 1973 can have no confidence whatsoever that such paths of reason will be followed. The OPEC financial surplus has not been accommodated adequately and now (1979) is once more rapidly increasing; indeed it has been magnified by the indefensible surpluses rung up by Japan and West Germany. The only country which has behaved with reason and decency in this matter — the United States — has been rewarded by the unanimous admonitions of the world central bankers. (I wish I could say equally nice things about United States energy policies, but the truth of the matter is that United States policies in most fields are policies of 'neglect' and this neglect turns out to be sometimes benign and sometimes malign!). Sharp rises in energy prices need not always have this sort of effect on international trade and payments, but will do so while trade in energy remains as important as it seems likely to for the next two decades.

The importance of this sort of consideration cannot in my view be over estimated. If I were asked to point to the one reason why I feared the impact of rising energy prices on world economic performance, it would be the fear of energy crunches, OPEC surpluses, and bad financial reactions from OECD central banks which would be first in my mind.

5. Suppose the Story is Wrong

If I were writing about energy policy rather than the implications of events in the energy sector for economic growth generally, I would give very great emphasis to the way one should balance the various risks arising from our imperfect knowledge of the future. We have long passed the simple minded days of single valued guesses about the future, and now attempt the analysis of uncertainty by discussion of the principles of insurance, of the degree of risk aversion we should practice, and of such principles as 'minimising the maximum loss that society might incur'. Great sophistication can be used in this type of work, but my own experience of it suggests that there is an irreducible element of judgement and individual preference in the choice of objective function, and governments have not yet shown themselves willing to discuss this sort of matter in the manner necessary for scientific choice between alternative strategies.

Be that as it may, my present main expositional purposes do not require me to put together either an objective function or a strategy to maximise it. What, ideally, the analysis does require is an enumeration of a range of possible combinations of possible states of nature, paired with the strategies which these emerging facts of life might induce governments to adopt. This also I have not attempted in any formal sense. But I guess that the single most likely outcome will be a rather inadequate upward pressure on the prices of primary energy during the next 10 or 15 years, and therefore a quantum of investment in alternative energy sources or in energy conservation which will be less than the high figures I have quoted above, and less than necessary to get us to the best possible position, on my guess about the state of the world by the year 2000.

I believe this to be a pretty robust prediction for the next 10 or 15 years. Certainly, within the United Kingdom, the additional expenditure on energy supply or energy conservation is running in hundreds of millions of pounds per year rather than the thousands of millions which would be necessary for it to become statistically significant as a call on resources. And I know of no other OECD country where the reverse is true.

A possible qualification to this comment is the very high investment in the North Sea and in fairly conventional oil exploration in many other parts of the world. There is no doubt that, if the real price of crude oil were stuck at its 1972 level, a half or more of the North Sea would not at present be exploited, and a lot of the offshore exploration in South Asia and North America would not now be in train. The sums involved here are very large—in the case of the North Sea of an order of magnitude of perhaps one third of onshore gross capital expenditure, and a larger proportion of industrial investment. But my proposition is this: Energy investment, once it has been jacked up to this relatively high level, will not increase further as a proportion of GDP unless real energy prices are thought to be rapidly increasing over the next 2 or 3 decades, and there is little sign that this is happening.

Certainly the nuclear energy programme, all over the world, is going more slowly than seemed likely before the events of 1973, and this is to be explained not only by the environmental objections, but also by the lack of sharp economic pressures of physical shortages of other fuels.

6. Too Little Investment in Energy

I regard therefore my figure of half a percentage point a year off the UK growth potential as somewhat of an over estimate of what might be true over the next 10 or 15 years. But equally, I believe that a result of this relative slowness in energy investment must be the increased likelihood of sharper price rises and apparent physical shortages appearing later in the century. Looking back on events from the standpoint of, say, the year 2010, our children may well feel that it would have been better for the world if we had taken further measures of energy investment in the 1980s and 1990s, because the cumulative net results on resource availability by the year 2010 would thereby have been minimised.

I do not mean by this remark to suggest that there is something intrinsically wicked about our generation taking the bounty of nature— the readily available liquid hydro-carbons—and leaving it to our successors to exploit more expensive sources of fuel. There is something inherently sensible, as well as very natural, about picking the most readily available apples from the tree first, and leaving it till later in the season to engage in the dangerous and tiresome process of climbing the ladder. Admittedly, there are awkward questions all raised by the thought that it is the wealthy white citizens who are enjoying the easily available fruits today, while the poorer peoples of the developing world will have to pay the higher costs tomorrow: but this is just part of the general problem of the relationship between the rich and the poor, and I do not think it has particular implications for the way we exploit our energy sources.

My reason for believing that it would be better to do more energy investment in the next 10 years is because I fear the 'crunch' which I considered in the previous section of this paper and believe that crunch will hurt 'us' quite as much as it will hurt the grandchildren of our neighbours.

Of course it may not work out in this way. Slow economic growth may in fact not only postpone the expected shortages of energy—it may abolish them altogether. If economic growth over the next 30 years in the OECD world were half its rate in the 1960s, and if the developing world failed to raise their standard of living at all, it is conceivable that we would be able to play out time on the energy from until the fast breeders and fusion technology were available on a scale sufficient to bale us out. But that is rather like hoping that the growth of our children will be so stunted that we will not have to buy them new shoes next winter. And I would warn that even if we went flat out with breeder reactors from now onwards, and even if fusion technology developed as fast as other people are hoping, it would not be until the second quartile of the next century that these sources of energy would be contributing more than 10 per cent of the world's needs. The time lags of construction and the development of technology are very long indeed.

7. Is the Energy Effect Additional to Other Threats to Growth?

The whole of the preceding argument has been based on the assumption that the costs imposed on the economy by an incipient energy shortage need to be added to other possible charges against growth potential. Essentially, we have been following those economists who argue that a potent cause of deceleration in growth over the next two decades will be the failure of investors to mobilise sufficient resources for productive investment. If the pool of investment is exogenously determined, and an increasing share of that pool were to be taken by the needs of the energy sector, the outcome would be that men working in factories would be deprived of the new machinery which they needed to increase output because the investible resources were being diverted elsewhere— e.g. in digging for inaccessible oil or building highly capital intensive nuclear power stations.

Of course, slower economic growth would reduce the demand for energy (a point to which I return below), but eventually the higher cost of providing even a one-for-one replacement of the present low cost fuel sources might eat into the investment we need for growth in manufacturing industry.

But to regard the quantum of investment as fixed in this way is neither realistic nor analytically respectable. The trade off between present consumption and future consumption implicit in the rate of saving by all sectors of the economy could change; if that were true, then even in the face of the sort of costs which we have been considering above, the *rate of growth* of output may not be diminished in the way I have suggested; instead, consumption out of the initial level of GDP will be lower, investment will be higher, GDP in the year 2000 could be the same level which it would have been in the absence of an increase in energy costs, but the capital-output ratio of that year would be higher. To economists familiar with the game of playing with growth models, this appears an outcome quite as plausible as the one which I have been discussing above.

Nevertheless, the picture of a 'constraint on investment and savings' has a certain vogue, and I would concede that, for those who believe that such a constraint exists, the increased cost of energy will reduce the growth rate of GDP: that is the message of the preceding analysis, although I have suggested that it is the 'bumpiness' of the path of energy costs rather than its steepness which is the real threat to the future.

As regards other causes of a possible slow down in growth, it is I suppose possible that other raw materials will be harder to get and more expensive to use, for environmental reasons, as the decades go on. I do believe that there is something rather special about 'energy' or fuel, because the price elasticity of demand for this particular category of material is less than that for any other single resource—if we are short of copper, we can switch to aluminium, for many electrical purposes, or indeed to electronic devices which greatly reduce the mass of metal that we need for say, the transmission of telecommunications messages. But this is in part a problem of definition: one of the reasons why a shortage of liquid hydro-carbons is not so tragic a possibility as some observers have suggested is that coal, or uranium, or the biomass are to some extent reasonable substitutes, and this goes to increase the elasticity of demand for oil. The more widely one defines the materials which might become scarce, the greater the fear that the scarcity may bring severe economic penalties; but the wider the definition the less plausible is the generalised fear of shortage.

However, if experts from other fields put their hands on their hearts and say that shortages of this that or the other raw material are very likely, I would be prepared in principle to accept that these fears, and the costs that they threaten, are additive to the threats to economic growth imposed by the risks of energy shortages which I have been discussing.

But many of the reasons advanced by those who believe that it will be impossible for the OECD countries to grow in the way which they did in the postwar decades have nothing to do with the supply factors—a shortage of labour for instance, or a slow down of technical progress generally; other economists fear some prolonged secular stagnation through a deficiency of effective demand; perhaps the most generalised fear is that inflationary pressures, or the incompetence of governments, will lead to monetary constraints on the growth of demand. My contention is that all these causes of slower growth are *alternative* to, rather than *additive* to energy shortage as factors which might brake economic growth.

The reasoning here is I believe extremely simple. It is difficult and probably very expensive to reduce the energy co-efficient, or the income elasticity of the demand for energy; if GDP in this country were to double by the end of the century, it is hard to see our consumption of energy increasing by less than say 60 or 70 per cent. So if my colleagues tell me that for this that or the other reason it will be impossible for GDP to increase at that pace, I will retort that energy demand will therefore grow more slowly, and the upwards pressure on energy prices will be less. Less resources will need to be put into new methods of energy supply, and less money will have to be spent on conservation. If I may attempt an aphorism: the risk of energy shortage is a curse of growth, and to the extent to which we cannot attain any desired growth path, the energy shortage will not materialise.

8. Conclusion

This paper has examined one particular aspect of the energy shortage which many observers claim to exist. I have investigated the suggestion that a shortage of energy will slow down economic growth in the OECD world in the next 2 or 3 decades. I find some relatively small reason to support the suggestion that energy shortages will brake growth—perhaps in the UK's case, by as much as a half a percentage point a year. I regard however this figure as somewhat of an outside estimate, and believe that a more serious fear is that our failure (in the rich world as a whole) to do anything about the energy shortage risks the stimulation of crises in the future rather like that of 1973, with resulting financial and monetary imbalances which will cause far more trouble than the energy shortage itself. This fear apart, the effects of the energy shortage are for the most part, alternative to, rather than additional to, other threats to growth. The policy implication is that it would be wise to err, if at all, by *overinvesting* in energy supply and energy conservation measures in the next two decades.

12

BRITAIN'S CHRONIC RECESSION—
CAN ANYTHING BE DONE?

by Wynne Godley

Department of Applied Economics, Cambridge

When I was asked to give this talk it was put to me as an opportunity to air whatever seemed urgently important in the area of economic policy in an essentially non professional forum. I propose to take this prospectus *au pied de la lettre*. That is, I am not going to read out a paper which is written for posterity; I am speaking words to this group of people in this room today and hoping to communicate something to them and also to learn something.

I would like to start by making a personal statement about my professional position, even at the risk of indiscretion. This will reveal the motivation for structuring this short talk in the way that I have.

I am disconcerted and distressed to find myself, together with the group of people with whom I work in Cambridge, in such an isolated position. For we seem to be the only professional group of economists who entertain the possibility that control of international trade *may* be the only way of recovering and maintaining the prosperity of this country; that free trade *may* be an enemy for the relatively weak, impoverished and, yes, for the inefficient.

More generally, I seem to see, on the one hand, quite manifest processes at work making for progressive depression: on the other hand what seems to be the absolute refusal of anyone other than ourselves to consider dispassionately, or at all, what should be done.

It is this lack of intelligent feedback when we try to analyse the problem in public which really has me worried at a personal level. For if someone sees something very clearly which other people do not see at all this person is normally classified as insane.

I just recently received a clipping from a foreign newspaper. The author of the article had read our stuff and then gone to talk to 'a top official' in the DTI. The top official was quoted as saying 'the Cambridge group are barmy', when I read that I had a spasm of genuine fear. Then followed the following 3 paragraphs:

'They're barmy, for much of what they say, of course, is right. We are second best in almost everything—not everything, mind you; we're best in food processing and in some services like entertainment.

Most of our manufacturers are indeed beyond the point of recovery. But we can't go protectionist publicly. We'd break all our treaties. What we have to do instead is to do much of what those Cambridge fellows say we should, without talking about it.

Like the way we have already quietly told the Japanese to stop sending us any more cars, and not to send us any trucks, which they can easily sell here'.

At this point I calmly decided that this top official was not barmy but intellectually dishonest; and dangerously mistaken as to how international trade should be controlled if it should ever come to that. For the method of control, I shall argue, is crucial to the argument; if operated as the top official had in mind, piecemeal, by default and under the influence of interest pressure groups, then all the standard arguments against protection come into their own.

Coming back to the British economy, I do believe, in common with many of my colleagues in Cambridge, that the process about which we have reason to be alarmed is the trend towards the destruction of our manufacturing industry on which the present and future prosperity of our country in the form we know it essentially depends.

I shall begin by rehearsing the characteristics of this process, even though the main features are well known; and the fact that this *is* happening is not even controversial.

First let me cast my mind back to the mid-50s when I first joined the Treasury. This was the period of 'you've never had it so good' when the economy could be—and was—run at full stretch for years at a time; there was in effect no unemployment at that time—it hovered around the 1½ per cent mark for a prolonged period.

But we had periodic checks to growth when the inability to export enough to pay for our imports produced a balance of payments crisis and the growth of aggregate demand had to be cut back.

It amuses me, incidentally, to recall that the fashionable way to knock the Treasury in those days was to criticize it for being insufficiently expansionary in its fiscal policy and that some of the very same people who indulged in this sport as late as 1962, have moved round 180 per cent to the currently fashionable method.

But the complaint about 'stop go' was essentially a complaint that *fluctuations* were taking place—and indeed the problem of the British economy, apart from slow growth, always appeared as essentially a cyclical one. But there lies in the figures for the 50s and 60s, when looked at *ex post facto,* a clear long term trend for the worse. Each crisis produced a recession deeper than each previous one; each expansionary period came to an end with a higher level of unemployment than each previous one.

Now those people who tried to consider medium term problems and think out a medium term strategy, despite the observed trend which now seems so clear, generally tended to come up with optimistic forecasts; things would soon come right.

The reasons why they obtained these results was simple and very plausible. The medium term optimism stemmed from the following simple propositions:

(i)   trade in manufacture expands much faster than trade in food and raw materials

(ii) we are large importers of food and raw materials and very large net exporters of manufactures. True, imports of finished manufactures have been doubling every 5 years or so, but that is something to do with the immediate post-war period and also with the fact that in absolute terms imports of manufactures are very low. In due course (the story went) the fact that we have this huge surplus in our balance of trade in manufactures must lead us to prosperity just because trade in manufactures is expanding so fast.

This general view proved entirely mistaken. It was continuously held and continuously proved wrong. For, on the contrary, imports of manufactures have continued their underlying trend exponentially. For a large number of years the full implications of the process were concealed by the fact that, although there was a big difference in growth rates of exports and imports, the absolute difference between them only changed very slowly; this arose from the *accident* of the absolute size initially of exports relative to imports.

But at the beginning of the 70s a change in kind took place; the absolute gap betwen exports and imports of manufactures started to narrow rapidly. The external constraint began to grip us by the throat: the depression accelerated.

Last year—1977—I think I am right in saying that everyone's econometric equations went wrong about imports of manufactures (ours certainly did) in the direction that these were much too high given the state of domestic activity. For whereas manufacturing output in the UK had risen 1.6 per cent compared with 1975, imports of finished manufactures were up by 24 per cent over the same period. A common and very tricky problem of interpretation arose: would this residual get larger, smaller, or remain the same.

The most recent returns suggest the most pessimistic conclusions. Manufacturing output has recently been about 2 per cent above the 1977 level, but imports of finished manufactures have been up by about 14 per cent.

In contrast to the early 60s, all people who operate models capable of simulating the medium term futures and who do not fiddle their results get, so far as I know, a picture of deepening recession, if it is assumed that the future conduct of policy is the same as the past. The prospect tends to get represented by people, including ourselves, as a high level of unemployment—3 or 4 million in 5 or 6 years time; and much worse if the oil starts to fall or even level off. These figures are reached as conditional projections of unemployment from output, using standard econometric relationships. Actually it is very unlikely that registered unemployment will be so high. To say 3 or 4 million is a way of representing simply a condition of growing chronic depression, the precise manifestations of which it is idle to try and characterise in detail.

In practice, there would be job sharing, job creation, early retirement and emigration. And we would have increasing numbers of derelict industrial regions (i.e. the incidence of recession would be highly uneven) and generally there would be low income and deteriorating public services, the whole process provocative of social and political tensions the precise nature of which I cannot at the moment imagine.

I have devoted a large amount of energy to trying to get people to take seriously this strategic problem. They do not do so. The focus of attention is entirely in a different position. In the process I have unfortunately become identified in peoples' minds with one solution only—viz import controls—to an extent which does not correctly represent my views. What I encounter is a refusal to discuss the issues calmly and rationally which has, I'm sorry to use the expression, a hysterical or delusional aspect. *I do not understand this.*

There seem to be three possibilities worth mentioning.

(i) The first I mention only to reject. This is the view that by cutting public expenditure and taxation the Government can somehow release vital energies which will of themselves generate a recovery. Quite apart from the fact that the processes by which this is supposed to happen are wholly obscure, international comparisons do not support the argument: other countries which are as heavily taxed as ourselves still manage to grow satisfactorily.

(ii) The second view is that things will be all right without any real change of policy; the trends may not continue adverse, the argument runs, and the present position is just about bearable. This view is, I suppose, worthy of respect. Maybe things *will* be all right and the present position *is* bearable. It would not have been thought so a few years ago and personally I don't think it is now. But people who hold this view should nevertheless be thinking very hard about how much worse things would have to get before they become *un*bearable and what they would then do. And they should bear in mind that the further we go down the harder it may be to come up.

(iii) For anyone who wants to remove the external constraint if they consider it intolerable now, or who will wish to remove it should it deteriorate to a degree which they will think intolerable, there appear to be 2 broad possibilities. They are both ways of removing the balance of payments constraint—of ensuring that exports net of imports contribute adequately. These are, of course, policies of devaluation on the one hand and import control on the other.

I have always entertained the possibility that devaluation could be used as a strategic weapon for recovery as the closest to being a market solution for removing the external constraint.

Some of the problems with devaluation are as follows. There is no reason to suppose that unimpeded market forces will fix a value for sterling such as would generate a balanced external position at full employment. It is a sufficient proof of this that it has not done so. But the reason why it has not is pretty obvious. The exchange rate is determined not only by our competitiveness in world markets but also by our fiscal and monetary policy at home. If, as has broadly been the case, we maintain balance of payments equilibrium by fiscal and monetary policy (albeit at the cost of recession) then the exchange rate obviously won't go down at all, let alone enough.

It would in fact require intervention of a very complicated kind to get the exchange rate down. It now appears to be well established that the responses of trade to real exchange rate movements are rather small and slow acting. As the processes we are fighting are strong—i.e. the rate of increase in import penetration is very high — devaluation would have to be large and preemptive. It is very difficult to set out a realistic 'scenario' for such a policy. The devaluation would have to be engineered by a seemingly imprudent and expansionary fiscal and monetary policy; the growth of net export demand would have to be preluded by a consumption led expansion. I find this story most implausible and think it most likely that such an experiment would end up exactly like every other major expansion of domestic demand (1954, 1959, 1963 or 1973).

Furthermore as the trade responses to devaluation are slow, there must be a long interim period when real wage income is *lower* than it otherwise would have been. Unless a successful incomes policy is implemented the devaluation will simply turn up as inflation and may fail to get the virtuous process going. Many people now think it most unlikely that any outcome other than inflation would result, and although I don't myself take such a pessimistic view, I do think it would result in much *more* inflation than would otherwise have occurred.

So let me finally come to import controls.

I am concerned here not so much to argue a case in *favour* as to suggest that, subject to precisely defined conditions, all the standard objections are insubstantial or irrelevant or downright wrong.

First distinguish a form of protection to which the standard objections apply in full force. This is what may be called *creeping protectionism*. I define it as a policy of protection which is selectively directed towards those industries which are *relative failures*; a policy of waiting for a big firm or industry to nearly go bust and then rescue it in this particular way. By *creeping protectionism* I also mean a policy conceived in isolation from other policies which could make the economy as a whole grow. I think it is this aspect of creeping protectionsim that I most fear; the failures would be hospitalised and given some form of help, but the average industry, even the relatively successful industries and indeed the economy as a whole, would still be committed to ever deepening depression.

It is, I think, creeping protection, and creeping protection by the back door that the 'top official' had in mind.

Let me then postulate an alternative syndrome of policies, without committing myself to advocating them in precisely this form.

(i) I postulate first a form of import control which is *wholly non discriminatory*. It would consist of a high tariff applied uniformly on all imports. Alternatively one might postulate some form of auction quota scheme which shall be completely indiscriminate as between different categories of imports. The Government would sell some given quantity of foreign exchange for importing in some close correspondence to the foreign exchange earned by exports. It would sell this to whoever paid the highest price for it.

(ii) The Government would simultaneously cut general taxation by enough to stimulate the economy so much *that the total volume of imports is as high as it otherwise would have been*. In other words the control of imports would not be used to make our balance of payments any better than it otherwise would have been: the whole of the adjustment would be to make domestic output higher than it otherwise would have been.

Note an important feature of this story. The total level of imports being as high as it otherwise would have been, if we could postulate that the composition of our imports were also the same, then all our trading partners would be in exactly the same position as they otherwise would have been.

Suppose, however, more plausibily, that the composition of imports were changed in favour of complementary as compared with competitive imports, i.e. in favour of raw materials and away from manufactures, then the imports from LDCs would be higher than otherwise. And since these countries (with the important exception of OPEC) are usuallly balance-of-payments constrained, they will import correspondingly more manufactures than otherwise. So countries which lose trade to us can make it up elsewhere. Therefore the net effect is to increase, not to diminish, world trade and output.

So let me end by running through the standard list of objections.

(i) *It would restrict world trade and output*: it would be a beggar my neighbour policy preserving our jobs at the expense of those in other countries. I have just shown that on the *contrary* it would, on my assumptions, increase trade and output in the rest of the world. Indeed, if we could assume, not too implausibly, that the LDCs increased imports by the full amount of the addition to their exports there need be no losers in this game.

(ii) *It would require government intervention in industry.* It would not so long as a market mechanism determines the allocation of quotas.

(iii) *It would cause inflation.* As compared with devaluation this is pretty obviously wrong. Since by assumption the same level of real output is reached in each case there can be nothing to choose, with regard to the inflationary implications, on the grounds of *demand* pressure. On the other hand the initial stages of an expansionary period generated by devaluation is certain to be more inflationary than import controls because prices rise relative to wages and some spiralling response is in practice inevitable. Under import control, given our macroeconomic assumptions, *more than all* the tariff is given back in general tax relief so the initial impetus, in sharp contrast to devaluation, is to *reduce* prices.

It could more reasonably be held that the import control strategy is inflationary compared with *deflation*—(defining deflation as acceptance of the balance of payments constraint and allowing the recession to proceed). This is of course very controversial ground. In my view the British post war data is inconsistent with any strong view about the pressure of demand and prices; sufficient evidence is provided by the experience of the fifties when the rate of change in the retail price index fell from 13 per cent in 1951 to *minus* ½ per cent in 1959 despite an average unemployment level of about 1½ per cent. If anything the post war British experience supports the view that high pressure of demand and the associated high level of real income is favourable to cost and price inflation.

(iv) *It 'distorts' consumer choice.* Well it does, but only in ways similar to that in which indirect taxation already operates. The far more important point is that real income and output would be 10-20 per cent higher than otherwise in a few years time; unemployment would be much lower; the place not going down the drain. The arguments about consumer choice incredibly enough are normally built explicitly on the assumption that aggregate output is given under all circumstances.[1]

[1]H. Corbet, *et. al.*, On How to Cope with Britain's Trade Position, Thames Essays, 1977.

Such studies are question begging and irrelevant.

(v) *It would featherbed inefficiency*. It would not do so so long as the non selective principle is adhered to, for the *relatively* inefficient firm or industry will still be destroyed unless it pulls its socks up. In a sense the British economy *as a whole* is being featherbedded. But this is just what I want to achieve, because I believe that a long period of un-interrupted expansion is a necessary condition for *increasing* investment and productivity. Individual industries may go bust under my assumption, British industry as a whole cannot do so.

(vi) *It would provoke retaliation*. Here my imaginary adversary is begin-ning to use the weapons of defeat. If operated under the postulated conditions no one need lose; some would be better off. There would therefore be no valid motive for retaliation.

(vii) *It is contrary to International Agreements*. Here the argument has shifted away from the merits of the case and if it turned on this alone I would regard the intellectual (my prime concern as an academic) case as conceded. In any case these agreements were made to improve our prosperity not to force us to commit suicide. And the EEC at least is very good at changing its rules when these are operating to everyone's disadvantage. And there is a very good example to hand. One of the main features of the original association was to have free trade in agricultural products. Yet when currencies—determined largely by performance in trade for manufactures—started to diverge it was found to be disadvantageous particularly because the revaluing countries' farmers were threatened with extinction. So free trade in agricultural products was quickly abandoned although introduction of the green currency system preserved a fiction of common prices—but it was a fiction indeed.

INDEX